WORKERS' COMPENSATION LAW

Second Edition

by

Margaret C. Jasper

Oceana's Legal Almanac Series:
Law for the Layperson

Oceana®
NEW YORK

OXFORD

UNIVERSITY PRESS

Oxford University Press, Inc., publishes works that further Oxford University's objective of excellence in research, scholarship, and education.

Copyright © 2008 by Oxford University Press, Inc.
Published by Oxford University Press, Inc.
198 Madison Avenue, New York, New York 10016

Library of Congress Cataloging-in-Publication Data

Jasper, Margaret C.
    Workers' compensation law / by Margaret C. Jasper.-- 2nd ed.
      p. cm. -- (Oceana's legal almanac series: law for the layperson)
    Summary: "Discusses common elements of a workers' compensation program, including filing of a claim; receipt of benefits. Provides overview of the Federal program for disabled non-military federal employees; Longshore & Harbor Workers' Compensation Program; Black Lung Benefits Program; Energy Employees' Occupational Illness Compensation Program; Federal Employment Liability Act; Merchant Marine Act; Veterans Disability programs; Social Security Disability Insurance program"--Provided by publisher.
    Includes bibliographical references.
    ISBN 978-0-19-536907-6 ((clothbound) : alk. paper)   1. Workers' compensation--Law and legislation--United States--Popular works.   I. Title.
    KF3615.Z9J37 2008
    344.7302'1--dc22   2007046104

Note to Readers:

This publication is designed to provide accurate and authoritative information in regard to the subject matter covered. It is based upon sources believed to be accurate and reliable and is intended to be current as of the time it was written. It is sold with the understanding that the publisher is not engaged in rendering legal, accounting, or other professional services. If legal advice or other expert assistance is required, the services of a competent professional person should be sought. Also, to confirm that the information has not been affected or changed by recent developments, traditional legal research techniques should be used, including checking primary sources where appropriate.

(Based on the Declaration of Principles jointly adopted by a Committee of the American Bar Association and a Committee of Publishers and Associations.)

You may order this or any other Oxford University Press publication by visiting the Oxford University Press website at www.oup.com

To My Husband Chris

Your love and support

are my motivation and inspiration

To My Sons, Michael, Nick and Chris

-and-

In memory of my son, Jimmy

Table of Contents

CHAPTER 3:
WORKERS' COMPENSATION BENEFITS

CHAPTER 4:
THE FEDERAL EMPLOYEES' COMPENSATION PROGRAM

APPENDICES

ABOUT THE AUTHOR

MARGARET C. JASPER is an attorney engaged in the general practice of law in South Salem, New York, concentrating in the areas of personal injury and entertainment law. Ms. Jasper holds a Juris Doctor degree from Pace University School of Law, White Plains, New York, is a member of the New York and Connecticut bars, and is certified to practice before the United States District Courts for the Southern and Eastern Districts of New York, the United States Court of Appeals for the Second Circuit, and the United States Supreme Court.

Ms. Jasper has been appointed to the law guardian panel for the Family Court of the State of New York, is a member of a number of professional organizations and associations, and is a New York State licensed real estate broker operating as Jasper Real Estate, in South Salem, New York.

Margaret Jasper maintains a website at http://www.JasperLawOffice.com.

In 2004, Ms. Jasper successfully argued a case before the New York Court of Appeals, which gives mothers of babies who are stillborn due to medical negligence the right to bring a legal action and recover emotional distress damages. This successful appeal overturned a 26-year old New York case precedent, which previously prevented mothers of stillborn babies from suing their negligent medical providers.

Ms. Jasper is the author and general editor of the following legal almanacs:

Adoption Law

AIDS Law

The Americans with Disabilities Act

Animal Rights Law

Auto Leasing

Bankruptcy Law for the Individual Debtor

Banks and their Customers

Becoming a Citizen

Buying and Selling Your Home

Commercial Law

Consumer Rights and the Law

Co-ops and Condominiums: Your Rights and Obligations As Owner

Copyright Law

Credit Cards and the Law

Custodial Rights

Dealing with Debt

Dictionary of Selected Legal Terms

Drunk Driving Law

DWI, DUI and the Law

Education Law

Elder Law

Employee Rights in the Workplace

Employment Discrimination Under Title VII

Environmental Law

Estate Planning

Everyday Legal Forms

Executors and Personal Representatives: Rights and Responsibilities

Guardianship and the Law

Harassment in the Workplace

Health Care and Your Rights

Health Care Directives

Hiring Household Help and Contractors: Your Rights and Obligations Under the Law

Home Mortgage Law Primer

Hospital Liability Law

How To Change Your Name

How To Form an LLC

How To Protect Your Challenged Child

How To Start Your Own Business

Identity Theft and How To Protect Yourself

Individual Bankruptcy and Restructuring

Injured on the Job: Employee Rights, Worker's Compensation and Disability Insurance Law

International Adoption

Juvenile Justice and Children's Law

Labor Law

Landlord-Tenant Law

Law for the Small Business Owner

The Law of Attachment and Garnishment

The Law of Buying and Selling

The Law of Capital Punishment

The Law of Child Custody

The Law of Contracts

The Law of Debt Collection

The Law of Dispute Resolution

The Law of Immigration

The Law of Libel and Slander

The Law of Medical Malpractice

The Law of No-Fault Insurance

The Law of Obscenity and Pornography

The Law of Personal Injury

The Law of Premises Liability

The Law of Product Liability

The Law of Speech and the First Amendment

Lemon Laws

Living Together: Practical Legal Issues

Marriage and Divorce

Missing and Exploited Children: How to Protect Your Child

Motor Vehicle Law

Nursing Home Negligence

Patent Law

Pet Law

Prescription Drugs

Privacy and the Internet: Your Rights and Expectations Under the Law

Probate Law

Protecting Your Business: Disaster Preparation and the Law

Real Estate Law for the Homeowner and Broker

Religion and the Law

Retirement Planning

The Right to Die

Rights of Single Parents

Small Claims Court

Social Security Law

Special Education Law

Teenagers and Substance Abuse

Trademark Law

Trouble Next Door: What to do With Your Neighbor

Victim's Rights Law

Violence Against Women

Welfare: Your Rights and the Law

What if It Happened to You: Violent Crimes and Victims' Rights

What if the Product Doesn't Work: Warranties & Guarantees

Workers' Compensation Law

Your Child's Legal Rights: An Overview

Your Rights in a Class Action Suit

Your Rights as a Tenant

Your Rights Under the Family and Medical Leave Act

You've Been Fired: Your Rights and Remedies

INTRODUCTION

Workers' Compensation laws were enacted to protect employees who suffer work-related disability resulting from injury or disease, by providing monetary compensation and other benefits. This helps the employee avoid the financial disaster associated with loss of income and mounting medical bills, and eliminates the need for litigation with the employer. In addition, workers compensation laws provide benefits to the dependents of an employee who dies as a result of work-related injury or illness.

Workers' compensation laws are based on Federal and state statutes. State workers' compensation laws cover most workers who are not federal employees. The Federal statutes apply to federal workers. In addition, because Congress is constitutionally required to regulate interstate commerce pursuant to Article 1, Section 8 of the U.S. Constitution, certain workers employed in interstate commerce related activities are also covered under Federal law.

Although state workers' compensation laws may vary, this Almanac sets forth a general discussion of the common characteristics of a workers' compensation system. The reader is advised to check his or her own jurisdiction concerning issues that are state-specific, such as procedural rules or available benefits.

This Almanac also sets forth an overview of the Federal workers' compensation programs administered by the U.S. Department of Labor's Office of Workers' Compensation Programs ("OWCP"). The primary federal statute governing compensation for disabled non-military federal employees is the Federal Employment Compensation Act ("FECA").

In addition, this Almanac discusses the three other major federal disability programs administered by the OWCP: The Longshore and Harbor Workers' Compensation Program, which provides compensation and benefits to maritime employees and other related groups; The Black Lung Benefits Program, which provides compensation and benefits to coal miners suffering from an occupational illness known as "black lung" disease; and The Energy Employees' Occupational Illness Compensation Program, which provides compensation and benefits to employees of the Department of Energy.

An overview of additional federal disability programs is also presented, including the Federal Employment Liability Act; the Merchant Marine Act; Veterans' Disability programs; and the Social Security Disability Insurance program.

The Appendix provides sample forms, applicable statutes, and other pertinent information and data. The Glossary contains definitions of many of the terms used throughout the Almanac.

CHAPTER 1:
OVERVIEW OF WORKERS'
COMPENSATION

IN GENERAL

When an employee suffers a work-related injury or illness, and as a result becomes disabled and unable to work, he or she may be entitled to receive certain benefits under a system known as workers' compensation. Workers' compensation is insurance that provides cash benefits and/or medical care for workers who are injured or become ill as a direct result of their job.

Employers pay for workers' compensation insurance, and may not require the employee to contribute to the cost of compensation. In addition, no one party is determined to be at fault. The amount that a claimant receives is not decreased by his or her carelessness, nor increased by an employer's fault.

Weekly cash benefits and medical care are paid by the employer's insurance carrier, as directed by a Workers' Compensation Board. The Workers' Compensation Board is a state agency that processes the claims and determines, through a judicial proceeding, whether a worker will receive benefits and/or medical care, and how much he or she will receive.

A claim is paid if the employer or insurance carrier agrees that the injury or illness is work-related. If the employer or insurance carrier disputes the claim, no cash benefits are paid until a workers' compensation court decides who is right.

As more fully set forth in this Almanac, the Federal government and every state administers some type of workers' compensation program according to its own statutory scheme. Because statutory provisions vary depending on the particular jurisdiction, the reader is advised to check the law of his or her own jurisdiction concerning specific questions. This Almanac sets forth a general discussion of workers' compensation law applicable to most jurisdictions.

HISTORICAL BACKGROUND

Workers' compensation was the first social insurance to develop widely in the United States to try and address the growing problem of work-related injuries and illnesses that accompanied the era of the Industrial Revolution.

Before workers' compensation laws were enacted, a disabled worker's only recourse was to prove that his or her injuries were caused by the negligent acts of the employer. Recovery for work-related injuries was dependent upon a successful lawsuit brought against the employer and other liable parties. Maintaining a lawsuit was a complex, costly and time-consuming process that often produced unfair results. This was due, in large part, to the availability of common law defenses, such as assumption of risk and contributory negligence.

Workers and their families suffered financial disaster because there was no interim means of support while waiting for their cases to slowly progress through the adversarial litigation system. Largely due to public dissatisfaction and the increasing demand for changes in this burdensome and inadequate process, workers' compensation laws began to be enacted in the early 20th century.

ADVENT OF WORKERS' COMPENSATION

In 1908, the first workers' compensation program covering certain Federal civilian employees in hazardous work was enacted. Similar laws were passed in 1911 in some states for workers in private industry, but it was not until late 1949 that all states had established programs to furnish income-maintenance protection to workers disabled by work-related illness or injury.

Workers' compensation laws basically dispensed with common-law actions based on employer liability, and replaced them with a type of no-fault system. Under the new system, disabled workers no longer had to prove that the employer was negligent. In return, employers who maintain workers' compensation insurance for its employees were granted immunity from common-law negligence actions brought by their employees for work-related injuries or illnesses. There are some exceptions to this general immunity. For example, an employer who intentionally causes injury to an employee is generally not immune from a lawsuit.

Presently, workers' compensation laws are in effect in all 50 states, the District of Columbia, Guam, Puerto Rico, and the U.S. Virgin Islands. In addition, three separate programs cover longshore, harbor, and other maritime workers; Federal employees; and coalminers.

PURPOSE

As set forth by the U.S. Chamber of Commerce in its 1995 Analysis of Workers' Compensation Laws, the following six basic objectives underlie workers' compensation laws:

1. To provide sure, prompt and reasonable income and medical benefits to work-accident victims, or income benefits to their dependents, regardless of fault;

2. To provide a single remedy and reduce court delays, costs and workloads arising out of personal injury litigation;

3. To relieve public and private charities of financial drains incident to uncompensated industrial accidents;

4. To eliminate payment of fees to lawyers and witnesses as well as time-consuming trials and appeals;

5. To encourage maximum employer interest in safety and rehabilitation through appropriate experience-rating mechanisms; and

6. To promote frank study of causes of accidents—rather than concealment of fault—reducing preventable accidents and human suffering.

Further, the workers' compensation system was established so that disabled employees would not risk financial ruin and the uncertainty of a lawsuit. Employers benefit by avoiding the time and expense of litigation by making sure their workers receive benefits for work-related disabilities.

Most workers are covered by their own state's workers' compensation program unless they fall under those categories entitled to Federal coverage. Federal statutes have been enacted to provide coverage for certain classes of employees.

FEDERAL WORKERS' COMPENSATION PROGRAMS

As set forth below, there are four federal workers' compensation programs, all of which are administered by The Office of Workers'

Compensation Programs ("OWCP") under the jurisdiction of the U.S. Department of Labor:

1. The Federal Employees' Compensation Program—The Federal Employees' Compensation Program protects U.S. Government civilian employees;

2. The Longshore and Harbor Workers' Compensation Program—The Longshore and Harbor Workers' Compensation Program protects maritime workers and certain other classes of workers;

3. The Black Lung Benefits Program—The Black Lung Benefits Program protects coal miners; and

4. The Energy Employees' Occupational Illness Compensation Program— the Energy Employees' Occupational Illness Compensation Program protects employees of the Department of Energy.

In administering these programs, OWCP's goal is to protect the interests of workers, employers and the Federal Government by ensuring timely and accurate claims adjudication and provision of benefits, by responsibly administering the funds authorized for this purpose, and by helping injured workers return to the workforce when their injury or illness permits. There are 12 OWCP district offices located throughout the United States.

A directory of the OWCP District Offices is set forth in Appendix 1.

In addition to the four federal workers' compensation programs, there are additional federal disability programs that provide disability benefits to certain workers, including railroad employees, merchant marines, and veterans of the armed forces.

The Federal Employees' Compensation Program

The Federal Employees' Compensation Act (FECA) [5 U.S.C. §§8101-8193] established a workers' compensation program that provides compensation for non-military, federal employees who are injured on the job. Awards are limited to "disability or death" sustained while in the performance of the employee's duties, which are not caused wilfully by the employee, or by the employee's intoxication.

Because many of the provisions of the Federal Employees' Compensation Act are typical of state workers' compensation laws, the selected provisions of the Act are set forth in Appendix 2 as an example of a model workers' compensation statute.

Under the FECA, a disabled employee receives two-thirds of his or her normal monthly salary during their period of disability, and may receive more for permanent physical injuries, or if he or she has dependents. Medical expenses due to the disability are also covered, and the employee may be required to undergo job retraining. The FECA also provides compensation for survivors of employees who are killed on the job.

The Federal Employees' Compensation Program is discussed more fully in Chapter 4 of this Almanac.

The Longshore and Harbor Workers' Compensation Program

The Longshore and Harbor Workers' Compensation Act (LHWCA) [33 U.S.C. §§901-950] established a program that provides workers' compensation to approximately one-half million maritime workers injured or killed upon the navigable waters of the United States, as well as employees working on piers, docks and terminals.

Selected provisions of the Longshore and Harbor Workers' Compensation Act are set forth in Appendix 3.

The LHWCA also covers overseas employees of defense contractors; employees at military post exchanges; workers engaged in the extraction of natural resources on the outer continental shelf; and certain other classes of private industry workers. The LHWCA provides lost wages compensation, medical benefits, and rehabilitation services, to employees who suffer work-related injuries or illness.

The Longshore and Harbor Workers' Compensation Program is discussed more fully in Chapter 5 of this Almanac.

The Black Lung Benefits Program

The Black Lung Benefits Act [30 U.S.C.§§901-945] established a program that requires liable mine operators to pay workers' compensation payments to coal miners who are totally disabled as a result of work-related black lung disease known as pneumoconiosis.

Selected provisions of the Black Lung Benefits Act are set forth in Appendix 4.

In addition to compensation benefits, if the worker dies, his or her surviving dependents are eligible to receive benefits. The Black Lung Benefits Act also established a fund administered by the Secretary of Labor providing disability payments to miners where the mine operator is unknown or unable to pay.

The Black Lung Benefits Program is discussed more fully in Chapter 6 of this Almanac.

The Energy Employees' Occupational Illness Compensation Program

The Energy Employees Occupational Illness Compensation Program (EEOICP) provides benefits authorized by the Energy Employees' Occupational Illness Compensation Program Act (EEOICPA). The mission of the program is to provide lump-sum compensation and health benefits to eligible Department of Energy nuclear weapons workers, including employees, former employees, contractors and subcontractors, and lump-sum compensation to certain survivors if the worker is deceased.

The Energy Employees' Occupational Illness Compensation Program is discussed more fully in Chapter 7 of this Almanac.

ADDITIONAL FEDERAL DISABILITY PROGRAMS

The Federal Employment Liability Act

The Federal Employment Liability Act (FELA) [45 U.S.C. §§51-60], while not a workers' compensation statute, provides that railroad workers injured in a railroad-related accident have the right to recover compensation. However, in order to recover, the worker must demonstrate that his or her injuries are the result of the railroad's negligence

Under the FELA, the injured worker may recover lost wages, medical expenses and treatments, pain and suffering, and compensation for partial or permanent disability. If a worker is killed on the job, his or her survivors are entitled to recover damages that they have suffered as a result of the worker's death.

The Federal Employment Liability Act is discussed more fully in Chapter 8, "Additional Federal Disability Programs," of this Almanac.

The Merchant Marine Act

The Merchant Marine Act [46 U.S.C. §688]—also known as "The Jones Act"—provides seamen with the same protection from employer negligence as FELA provides railroad workers.

Under the Act, an injured seaman is entitled to transportation, lost wages, and medical expenses and treatments. If the seaman can prove that his or her injuries were the result of negligence, a seaman may also recover damages for pain and suffering from the employer and ship owner.

The Merchant Marine Act is discussed more fully in Chapter 8, "Additional Federal Disability Programs," of this Almanac.

Veterans' Disability Programs

The United States Department of Veterans Affairs (VA) administers disability programs for service members who are disabled as a result of their military service.

Veterans' Disability Compensation is discussed more fully in Chapter 8, "Additional Federal Disability Programs," of this Almanac.

Social Security Disability Insurance

Under the Social Security Amendments of 1954, a disability insurance program was implemented which provides workers with additional benefits if they have to stop working at any time before age 65 due to health reasons.

Social Security Disability Insurance is discussed more fully in Chapter 8, "Additional Federal Disability Programs," of this Almanac.

STATE WORKERS' COMPENSATION PROGRAMS

Each state has a workers' compensation law designed to ensure that employees who are injured or disabled on the job are provided with fixed monetary awards, eliminating the need for litigation.

These laws also provide benefits for dependents of those workers who are killed because of work-related accidents or illnesses. Some laws also protect employers and fellow workers by limiting the amount an injured employee can recover from an employer and by eliminating the liability of co-workers in most accidents.

A directory of State Workers' Compensation Boards is set forth in Appendix 5.

Type of Insurance Coverage Required

In general, most states require employers to maintain workers' compensation insurance for their employees, unless there is a statutory exception. Depending on the jurisdiction, workers' compensation laws may be either compulsory or elective.

Compulsory Laws

The majority of states have enacted compulsory workers' compensation laws. This means that employers are required to maintain workers' compensation coverage for their employees. Employers who fail to maintain the required insurance may be sued by the employee, and are liable for damages. Depending on the jurisdiction, non-complying employers may be further penalized.

Elective Laws

A minority of jurisdictions, including New Jersey, South Carolina and Texas, have elective workers' compensation laws. Under an elective law, the employer may choose to accept or reject coverage under the law. However, if the employer rejects such coverage, they lose the customary common law defenses, thus if a lawsuit for damages is brought by an injured employee, the employer cannot assert the three common law defenses of contributory negligence, assumption of risk, or fellow servant negligence.

A table setting forth the type of insurance requirements under state workers' compensation laws is set forth in Appendix 6.

Purchasing Workers' Compensation Insurance

Employers may purchase workers' compensation insurance from a State Insurance Fund or an authorized private insurance carrier. In addition, an employer may elect to insure itself.

State Insurance Funds

In a minority of jurisdictions, employers are required to obtain insurance through a state insurance fund. Privately obtained workers' compensation insurance is not permitted, although some of these jurisdictions do permit employer self-insurance. Although state insurance funds are generally adequately funded, they are criticized for their inefficiency, such as the timeliness in making compensation payments.

Private Insurance Carriers

The majority of states permit employers to obtain private workers' compensation coverage. Employers are free to choose from any number of private insurance companies that offer this coverage.

Self-Insured Employers

Approximately 48 states permit self-insurance. A self-insured employer assumes liability for workers' compensation, and generally sets up a reserve fund to pay benefits to disabled employees. Self-insurance usually requires authorization by the appropriate State Workers' Compensation Board officials. The employer seeking to be self-insured must demonstrate that it has the financial ability to carry the associated risks.

Eligibility for Workers' Compensation Benefits

In general, state and Federal workers' compensation laws cover most of the nation's labor force. However, there are exemptions. Many programs exempt employees of nonprofit, charitable, or religious institutions, and some limit coverage to workers in hazardous occupations. Common coverage exemptions are domestic service, agricultural employment, and casual labor, although some programs cover agricultural and domestic workers.

A table setting forth coverage requirements for agricultural; and domestic workers under state workers' compensation laws is set forth in Appendix 7.

The coverage of state and local public employees differs widely among state programs. States may provide full coverage, specifying no exclusions. Some have broad coverage, excluding only such groups as elected or appointed officials. Other programs limit coverage to public employees of specified political subdivisions or to employees engaged in hazardous occupations. In some states, coverage of government employees is optional with the state, city, or other political subdivision.

Financing

Workers' compensation programs are almost exclusively financed by employers, based on the principle that the cost of work-related accidents is a business expense. The employer's cost of protecting workers varies with the risk involved and is influenced primarily by such factors as the employer's industrial classification and the hazards of that industry.

The premium rate an employer pays in a given state, compared with the premium rate for the same industrial classification in another state, also reflects the level of benefits provided in a given jurisdiction. Costs are also influenced by the method used to insure for compensation liability—e.g., through a commercial carrier, through an exclusive or competitive state fund, or through a self-insured program.

In three-fourths of the states, state costs of administering the workers' compensation laws and supervising the operations of the insurance medium—private carriers, the self-insured, or state funds—may be provided through assessments on insurance carriers and self-insurers, including premium receipts in states with exclusive state funds. In the remaining states, administrative costs are derived from either general revenues or a combination of general revenues and assessments.

Program Administration

State workers' compensation programs are generally administered by commissions or boards created by law. Court administration exists in three states with limited administrative activities performed by an administrative unit. The Federal workers' compensation programs are administered by the Office of Workers' Compensation Programs (OWCP) of the Department of Labor, except for part of the Black Lung program that is administered by the Social Security Administration (SSA).

Generally, state administrative agencies supervise, adjudicate, and enforce payment of obligations and compliance with the laws. These tasks are often carried out by boards or commissions. However, in states that maintain exclusive state funds, tasks of administration are merged with those of providing the insurance protection—that is, setting rates, collecting premiums, and paying benefits.

Reporting Requirements

The workers' compensation programs may require reports by employers of all work-related accidents or injuries; or they may require such reports only under the following circumstances:

1. Medical care beyond first aid is required;

2. Time is lost after the day of the accident; or

3. Compensation is to be paid.

Time Limits

The time limits for an employee to provide notice of their injury to their employer are set, as well as the time limits for filing claims for compensation. The deadline is commonly no longer than 1 or 2 years after the injury, onset of disability, or death. These deadlines may be extended under certain conditions, particularly with regard to occupational diseases.

Payment of Compensation

Under most programs, the employer or the carrier, when notified of the injury, is required to begin the payment of compensation to the worker or his or her dependents. The injured worker does not have to enter into an agreement and need not sign any papers before compensation starts. The law specifies the amount a worker should get. If the worker fails to receive that amount, the administrative agency can step in, investigate the matter, and correct any error. In many cases, however, these provisions have not been actively enforced.

Under some programs, uncontested cases are settled by agreement among the employing firm, its insurance carrier, and the worker before payments start. Further, the agreement must be approved by the administrative agency under a few of the laws. In contested cases, most workers' compensation laws are adjudicated through hearings before an administrative body that usually has exclusive jurisdiction over the determination of facts. Appeals to the courts usually are limited to questions of law.

Employer Immunity

If you are receiving workers' compensation benefits due to a work-related injury or illness, you cannot file a lawsuit against your employer or a co-worker for negligence. Workers' compensation is the exclusive remedy for an employee to obtain wage replacement for work-related injuries or illnesses, and your employer is generally immune from liability.

Exceptions to Employer Immunity

If your employer does not have workers' compensation insurance, you are generally entitled to sue your employer and recover damages if you can prove that your employer's negligence caused your injuries.

In addition, your employer would not be entitled to immunity if they intentionally caused your injuries. An intentional tort differs from an act of negligence in that it requires the element of intent. Common intentional tort claims include assault and battery and defamation.

Retaliation

An employer may not fire or otherwise retaliate against an employee or applicant who has claimed or attempted to claim workers' compensation. An employee who has testified or is about to testify in a workers' compensation proceeding is also protected. Violators of the law are subject to a monetary penalty.

A worker who believes that he or she has been retaliated against must file a complaint with their local workers' compensation board. If the workers' compensation board finds that an employee was improperly discharged, it will order that the employee be restored to their previous position or privilege. The employee will also be paid by the employer for any loss of compensation arising out of the retaliation.

Disability Discrimination

The Americans with Disabilities Act of 1990 (ADA) prohibits discrimination against people with disabilities in employment, and ensures them equal access to government services, public accommodations, transportation, and telecommunications. This law can help injured employees who want to return to work.

Additional information explaining the Americans with Disabilities Act can be found in this author's legal Almanac entitled The Americans with Disabilities Act, published by Oxford University Press.

DISABILITY BENEFITS FOR WORKERS WHO SUFFER NON-EMPLOYMENT RELATED INJURIES OR ILLNESSES

If you are injured or become ill and unable to work, and your injury or illness is not causally related to your employment, you will not be covered under your employer's workers' compensation program. Thus, it is important to have some type of disability insurance policy in place in case you are injured or become ill and unable to work.

Disability insurance is designed to provide financial benefits to an injured or disabled worker. However, unlike the other workers' compensation programs discussed in this Almanac, disability insurance applies to injuries that are sustained outside of the workplace.

This is particularly important if you are the breadwinner of your family, and your income is crucial to keep up with your financial obligations. Any savings you have could quickly disappear if you are disabled for a lengthy period of time without any income.

Disability insurance is similar to a state workers' compensation programs in that it provides "wage-replacement" during the period of time you are unable to work due to an injury or illness. The benefits payable are generally a percentage of your regular income while you are disabled. However, unlike a state workers' compensation program that covers employees who suffer a work-related injury or illness, private disability insurance covers you for injuries and illnesses that are not job-related.

You should check with your employer to find out whether you are covered under a group disability insurance policy. If your employer does not provide group disability insurance, you should consider purchasing an individual policy in order to protect yourself from a financial catastrophe.

Types of Disability Policies

Disability insurance policies fall into two general categories: (1) private insurance and (2) government insurance.

Private Insurance

A private disability insurance policy is one that is purchased from a private insurance carrier. A private policy may be an individual policy or a group policy. An employer may purchase a group policy as an employee benefit. Private disability policies generally offer more comprehensive benefits than government insurance. As set forth below, in five states, employers are required to provide disability insurance to their employees.

Government Insurance

Government disability insurance is provided through state or federal government. As discussed in this Almanac, Workers' Compensation is an example of state government disability insurance. Social Security Disability Insurance (SSDI) is an example of federal government disability insurance. SSDI is discussed more fully in Chapter 8, "Additional Federal Disability Programs," of this Almanac.

Coverage

Disability policies may offer either (1) short-term coverage; or (2) long-term coverage, as discussed below.

Short-Term Disability Insurance

Short-term disability insurance covers employees who will be out of work due to a non-work-related disability, e.g., a short-term illness or injury, pregnancy, or childbirth. Short-term coverage usually begins after you have been out of work for a certain number of days, e.g., eight days. Employees do not receive 100% of their regular earnings during this time period. This serves as an incentive for workers to return to work as soon as they are able.

Long-Term Disability Insurance

Long-term disability generally begins after the short-term disability coverage period ends. Statistics show that one out of seven workers will suffer a long-term disability—e.g., one that lasts five years or longer—before the age of 65. Therefore, long-term disability provides important financial protection if you are out of work for an extended period of time.

Employer-Provided Group Disability Insurance

In the majority of states, employers are not required to provide disability insurance for employees, however, many choose to do so. Employers may purchase a group disability insurance policy from a commercial insurance carrier, or may self-insure a private disability plan. The cost of coverage is usually funded by contributions deducted from the employee's regular salary. Your employer may also contribute to the cost of coverage. The actual insurance policy or plan agreement determines the extent of coverage under the plan.

Mandatory State Disability Programs

Five states—California, Hawaii, New Jersey, New York, and Rhode Island—have mandatory laws that require employers to provide short-term disability coverage to disabled workers through state-run programs, or by private or self-insurance coverage that mirror the state-run program. Rhode Island, however, requires employers to obtain coverage solely through the state-run program. The state-run programs do not provide long-term coverage, and generally provide only minimal benefits.

THIRD PARTY LIABILITY

As set forth above, if you are receiving workers' compensation benefits for an employment-related injury, you cannot sue your employer under the employer immunity provision, however, you still retain your right to sue any negligent third parties who may be responsible for causing or contributing to your injury.

For example, an employee who is injured while using a defective piece of machinery is still permitted to bring a product liability lawsuit against the manufacturer of the defective product, in addition to receiving benefits under their state's workers' compensation program.

Statute of Limitations

If it appears that a third party is responsible for your injuries, you must start your lawsuit before the statute of limitations expires. A statute of limitations is a law that sets forth a time period within which you must initiate a lawsuit. If you do not start the lawsuit before the statute of limitations runs out, you will be forever barred from bringing the lawsuit. The time period varies according to the state and the type of claim being made.

The reader is advised to check the law of his or her jurisdiction to determine the applicable statute of limitations.

Proving Negligence

Negligence encompasses unintentionally caused harms. The basis of liability is the creation of an unreasonable risk of harm to another. A third party cannot be held liable for your injuries unless those injuries were negligently caused. You bear the burden of proving that a third party was responsible for negligently causing your injuries in order to recover damages in a lawsuit.

The elements of a negligence claim that must be proved include: (1) a duty; (2) a breach of that duty; (3) foreseeability; (4) proximate cause, i.e., the breach caused the harm; and (5) resulting damages.

Duty

Duty is defined as that degree of ordinary care owed to another under the circumstances. Ordinary care is the care a prudent and cautious person would take in the same situation. It is your responsibility to prove that a third party acted without ordinary care. The third party has the burden of proving contributory negligence on your part in order to reduce your damage award.

For example, if an independent contractor is hired to wax the floors where you work, he or she has a duty to make sure that the employees who work in the area are not injured. Thus, a prudent person would place signs indicating where the floors are wet and potentially dangerous. You may be able to prove that the contractor acted without ordinary care if he or she did not put up any signs, and you slip and fall on the wet and slippery surface. On the other hand, if you observe the danger sign, and decide to walk across the wet surface, you may be deemed to have contributed to your own injuries because you negligently ignored the warning sign.

Breach of Duty

Once it has been established that there is a relationship between the parties in which a duty has arisen, it must be shown that the third party breached that duty in some manner. Using the above example, the contractor's failure to place appropriate warnings signs would indicate a breach of duty.

Foreseeability

In order for the third party to be deemed negligent, there is a common law requirement that it is foreseeable that his or her conduct created the danger. If a reasonably prudent person could not have foreseen the probability that injury would occur as a result of his or her conduct, there is no negligence and no liability.

Using the above example, it is arguably foreseeable that the contractor's failure to warn employees about the wet and slippery floor created a potentially dangerous situation that could result in serious injuries.

Proximate Cause

In order to prevail in your negligence claim, you must further prove that the injury sustained as a result of the breach of duty was proximately caused by the negligent act or omission of the third party. The act is a proximate cause of the injury if it was a substantial factor in bringing about the injury, and without which the result would not have occurred.

Again, using the above example, the contractor's failure to place warning signs around the wet and slippery floor was a substantial factor in bringing about your injuries, and was thus the proximate cause of your injuries.

Damages

Once you have established that a third party was liable for your injuries, you are entitled to recover damages. Damages are usually measured in terms of monetary compensation. The damage award represents an attempt to compensate you for the injuries you suffered by awarding you an amount of money that will restore you to your pre-injury condition. If complete restoration is not possible, damages may include the monetary value of the difference between your pre-injury and post-injury conditions. Typical items include: (1) medical expenses; (2) lost earnings and impairment of earning capacity; and (3) a monetary award for your pain and suffering.

Document the Accident

As soon as practicable following your accident, you should document the facts and gather evidence in case you decide in the future that you are entitled to pursue a third party claim. You should file a written incident report with your employer. Make sure the facts are accurate and request a copy of the incident report at the time it is made.

You should also obtain the names, addresses and telephone numbers of any witnesses to the accident, as well as any individuals who saw you immediately after the accident occurred. Even if these witnesses did not see the actual accident, they can still testify to your physical condition following the accident, and the circumstances surrounding the accident.

If there is any physical evidence that contributed to your accident, or which demonstrates your injuries—e.g., a defective machine—you should try to preserve that evidence. If the evidence is not within your control, you should take photographs of the area, e.g., a dangerous floor condition. Make sure that you clearly label the photographs with the date and time they were taken

In addition, you should write down all of the circumstances surrounding the accident while the facts are still fresh in your mind, including the manner in which you were injured. Small but important facts can fade in your memory over time, such as comments made by a witness or the responsible party.

Keep a journal of the progression of your pain, your symptoms and injuries. Keep track of how much time you lost at work, and any other physical limitations caused by the accident, e.g., the amount of time spent in the hospital, and confined to your home and/or bed.

Retain an Attorney

If your injuries are serious and/or have caused you any significant damages, you should contact an attorney who will investigate the facts surrounding the incident, and will evaluate whether you have a viable third party claim.

At your first meeting with your prospective attorney, bring the documentation and evidence you previously gathered. This will assist the attorney in investigating your case, and make it more likely that the attorney will take the case and be able to obtain a favorable settlement or verdict on your behalf.

Prior to taking any action on a case, an attorney will typically require you to sign a retainer agreement. A retainer agreement is a contract between you and the lawyer, which sets forth the responsibilities the lawyer is agreeing to undertake, and the compensation the lawyer expects to receive if there is a recovery, by verdict or settlement.

Most personal injury retainer agreements are contingency fee agreements. This means that you do not have to pay any money towards legal fees up front to the lawyer in order for the lawyer to take your case. In return, the lawyer receives a percentage—typically one-third—of the recovery, if there is one. If there is no recovery, the lawyer basically forgoes the legal fee. A personal injury lawyer may also advance some or all of the costs of the case, which are then deducted from the verdict or settlement amount.

Your attorney will contact the appropriate insurance carrier for the responsible third party, and place them on notice that your claim exists. The date, place and manner in which the claim arose will be provided to the insurance carrier, as well as a copy of any police, ambulance, hospital, and/or medical reports, to the extent available at that time.

A claims representative from the owner's insurance company may call to take a statement over the phone concerning the facts surrounding your accident. You should not provide a statement without first speaking with your attorney. The claims representative represents the responsible party, and does not represent your interests. The claims representative may attempt to get you to admit full or partial responsibility for the incident, or try to obtain a quick settlement at an amount well below the value of your claim.

In the months following your accident, your attorney will exchange correspondence and engage in settlement negotiations with the claims representative. During that time, all of your medical records will be provided to the insurance carrier, as well as documentation of lost wages, medical expenses and any other economic damages you may have suffered as a result of the accident. If a mutually agreeable settlement cannot be reached within a reasonable time period, formal legal action will likely be initiated.

MAINTAINING A SAFE WORKPLACE

Over the past 35 years, there has been a concerted effort by America's workers to have effective legislation passed which would protect their health and safety in the workplace. Through this effort, they have been successful in getting some major legislation enacted which addresses health and safety concerns on the job. Thus, all businesses are now required by law to provide a safe and healthy workplace for their employees.

Statistics

Statistics demonstrate that these efforts to reduce workplace injuries have had positive results. Since 1970, there has been a 50% reduction in workplace fatalities, and occupational injury and illness rates have been steadily declining. Nevertheless, nearly 50 American workers are still injured every minute of the 40-hour workweek, and approximately 19 workers die each day. According to the Bureau of Labor Statistics (BLS), the number of fatal injuries in 2006 totaled 5,703.

BLS statistics also demonstrate that the fatality rate for workers in certain occupations is significantly higher. Although the construction sector had the highest number of fatal injuries in 2006 (1,226), the industry sectors with the highest fatality rates were agriculture, forestry, fishing, hunting, and mining.

For example, in an average year, 110 American farm workers are crushed to death by tractor rollovers, and every day, about 228 agricultural workers suffer injuries that result in lost time at work. Approximately 5% of those injuries result in permanent impairment. In addition, an average of 103 children are killed annually on farms, and approximately 40 percent of these deaths are work-related.

The Occupational Safety and Health Administration

The Occupational Safety and Health Administration (OSHA) is a division of the U.S. Department of Labor. Along with its state government counterparts, OSHA employs a combined staff that includes inspectors, complaint discrimination investigators, engineers, physicians, educators, standards writers, and other technical and support personnel. The OSHA staff establishes and enforces protective standards to be used in the workplace, and sponsors workplace safety and health programs for employers and employees.

OSHA administers the Occupational Safety and Health Act of 1970 (The OSH Act). The OSH Act is the main statute protecting the health and safety of workers in the workplace. The OSH Act is designed to provide job safety and health protection for workers by promoting safe and healthy working conditions throughout the nation.

Under the OSH Act, employers are required to maintain their facilities free from any recognized hazards that are causing, or are likely to cause, death or serious harm to an employee. The OSH Act protects just about every working individual with the exception of miners, transportation workers, certain public employees and self-employed persons. Under the OSH Act, employees are also required to comply with all applicable sections of the occupational safety and health standards issued by OSHA.

Employee Rights Under the Occupational Safety and Health Act

Under the OSH Act, an employee has the following rights:

1. The right to obtain training from your employer about the health effects of chemicals you are exposed to at work, including information on how to protect yourself from harm, and the right to get trained on a variety of other health and safety hazards.

2. The right to request information from your employer about OSHA standards, worker injuries and illnesses, job hazards and workers' rights.

3. The right to ask your employer to correct hazards even if they are not violations of specific OSHA standards. You should make your requests in writing and keep copies of all requests you make to your employer to correct hazards in the workplace.

4. The right to file a confidential complaint with OSHA if you believe there are either violations of OSHA standards or serious workplace hazards.

5. The right to have an authorized employee representative accompany the OSHA compliance officer during his or her inspection of your workplace.

6. The right to know the results of the OSHA Inspection, and request a review if OSHA doesn't take action.

7. The right to file an appeal with OSHA concerning the deadlines given to your employer to correct any violations if you believe that the employer has been given too long to improve the conditions.

8. The right to file a discrimination complaint if you believe you have been punished or discriminated against because you filed a complaint, or refused to work under conditions that pose an immediate health and/or safety threat.

9. The right to request the National Institute for Occupational Safety and Health (NIOSH) to conduct a health hazard evaluation if you are concerned about toxic effects of a substance in the workplace.

10. The right to provide comments and testify before OSHA concerning rulemaking on any new standards.

In addition, if you live in a state that has an OSHA-approved state plan, you are entitled to at least the same rights and protections afforded under the OSH Act and, in some cases, you may have additional rights under your state's law.

Filing a Complaint with OSHA

As set forth above, if you believe your working conditions are unsafe or unhealthy, you have the right to file a complaint with OSHA. However, before you file a complaint, you should first try and bring the condition to your employer's attention.

If your employer wants to improve the working conditions, they can contact OSHA for information and guidance on rectifying any unsafe or unhealthy conditions that may exist. OSHA offers free assistance to employers in identifying and correcting workplace safety and health hazards without risking a citation or penalty.

If the workplace conditions are so bad that they present a risk of death or serious physical injury, and your employer has not responded to your request to improve conditions, you may have a legal right to refuse to work under hazardous conditions.

If the situation does not present an immediate threat to your health, but you believe there may be a violation of an OSHA standard or a serious safety or health hazard at work that your employer has not remedied, you should file your complaint with OSHA and request the agency to conduct an inspection of your workplace.

Your complaint can be filed by telephone, mail, fax, or electronically on the internet. The OSHA 24-hour hotline for reporting workplace safety and health emergencies is 1-800-321-OSHA.

A directory of regional OSHA offices is set forth in Appendix 8.

Whistle Blower Protection

As set forth above, if you believe your workplace is unsafe or unhealthy, you can file a confidential complaint with OSHA and request an inspection. In fact, most workplace safety laws, to be effective, rely on employees to report employment hazards. These employees are generally known as "whistle blowers." You can request OSHA to keep your name confidential if you don't want your employer to know you filed the complaint.

To prevent retaliation and encourage compliance, it is illegal for employers to fire or otherwise discriminate against employees who report unsafe conditions to the proper authorities. If an employee who "blew the whistle" believes that they have suffered discrimination as a result, the employee can file a discrimination complaint with OSHA within 30 days of the alleged incident.

Safety Initiatives

Some safety initiatives your employer can take to make sure the workplace is safe for the employees include:

1. Performing regular in-house safety inspections;

2. Establishing a comprehensive safety plan for all employees;

3. Maintaining an adequately stocked first-aid kit readily available;

4. Keeping telephone numbers for emergency medical assistance on display for quick reference if the need arises;

5. Maintaining adequate protective clothing and equipment where the nature of business operations requires such precautions.

If an employer wants to make sure they are in compliance with the law, they may engage the services of a workplace safety consultant, who specializes in bringing companies into compliance with the law.

CHAPTER 2:
FILING THE WORKERS'
COMPENSATION CLAIM

TYPES OF WORKERS' COMPENSATION CLAIMS

As set forth below, workers' compensation claims generally fall into three categories:

1. Injury Claims, including disfigurement claims;

2. Occupational Disease Claims, including occupational hearing loss; and

3. Death Claims.

In order to prevail on a workers' compensation claim, the employee is generally required to prove that the injury or illness is causally related to their employment—i.e., the injury or illness must be one that "arises out of and in the course of the employment."

INJURY CLAIMS

The injury or accident claim is the most common type of workers' compensation claim. It is generally called a "traumatic" injury claim in that it is a sudden and unexpected occurrence caused by a particular event. For example, a back injury caused by lifting a heavy object, or a laceration caused by a meat-slicing machine, would be considered traumatic injuries.

Some statutes specifically define an injury or accident claim so as to differentiate it from an occupational disease claim. In other jurisdictions, the two types of claims overlap with a focus on whether the employee's disability is work-related, regardless of whether the disability is caused by injury or illness.

Under certain circumstances, an employee may not be covered under workers' compensation. For example, injuries or illnesses that are caused by an employee's intoxication—e.g., by drugs or alcohol—are not eligible for compensation. Coverage may also be denied in situations involving:

1. Self-inflicted injuries, or injuries sustained while attempting to injure another;

2. Injuries sustained while committing a crime;

3. Injuries sustained when the employee was not on the job; and

4. Injuries sustained when the employee's conduct violated company policy.

Causal Relationship

In general, to demonstrate that an injury is work-related requires a showing that the time and place of the injury was so closely connected to the employment that it is justly covered by workers' compensation law.

At the Place of Employment

In most cases, when an injury occurs at the place of employment, the work-relatedness of the injury is rarely in dispute. In addition, an employee whose business is primarily conducted away from the office, such as a salesperson, would be entitled to compensation provided the injury occurred while the employee was performing his or her work-related duties.

Off-Site Injuries

Injuries that occur away from the employee's place of employment may or may not be compensable. Case law varies from state to state, depending on the specific fact pattern.

For example, compensability is less clearly defined in circumstances when the employee is away from his or her place of business, although there may be some indirect connection, such as a business luncheon. If the luncheon was clearly for the benefit of the employer, most courts would allow the compensation claim.

An employee who is injured while attending an off-site function held by the employer, such as a convention or party, is generally entitled to compensation since it can be assumed that the employee's attendance at the function was expected.

Personal Activities

Questions of work-relatedness also arise in situations where an employee is injured while attending to personal matters on company time. An important factor to consider would be whether the employer permitted employees to engage in personal activities while on the job.

Lunch and Coffee Breaks

An employee on his or her lunch or coffee break on company premises is generally held to be covered. However, jurisdictions differ on whether an employee is covered for injuries sustained while on lunch or coffee break off-premises.

Travel Time

An employee en route to and from his or her place of employment is generally not covered, however, exceptions have been made in certain cases, e.g., where the employee is paid for their travel time; the employee engages in a work-related task during the trip to or from work; or the employer provides for the employee's transportation, etc.

Thus, the reader is advised to check the workers' compensation case law of his or her own jurisdiction when researching coverage in a specific fact pattern.

DISFIGUREMENT CLAIMS

Disfigurement is a one-time award of compensation to an injured worker who experiences a work-related disfigurement. The majority of jurisdictions provide disfigurement benefits. Disfigurement is generally defined as a serious and permanent scar or other disfigurement to an area normally exposed to public view. Some jurisdictions consider this to mean scars or disfigurement that are visible when the person is wearing a swimsuit, while other jurisdictions only compensate workers who have suffered facial or head disfigurement.

A disfigurement or scar is deemed to be permanent if it exists at least six months after the date of injury, or if a physician has determined that the worker has reached maximum medical improvement. Generally, there is also a requirement that the scar or disfigurement impairs, or may in the future impair, the worker's opportunities to see or retain employment.

A table of jurisdictions that provide disfigurement benefits is set forth in Appendix 9.

OCCUPATIONAL DISEASE CLAIMS

Although workers' compensation programs were at first primarily limited to injuries or diseases traceable to industrial "accidents," the scope of the programs have broadened to cover occupational diseases as well.

The occupational disease claim generally applies when an employee suffers a work-related illness. Occupational disease is primarily distinguishable from an injury because it is not characterized by the suddenness or unexpectedness that usually accompanies a work-related injury or accident.

Causal Relationship

An illness that is characteristic of an employee's occupation is generally held to be one that "arises out of and in the course of the employment." For example, the specific disease must be one that is characteristic of the employee's occupation. An obvious case would be an illness that is presumed to be caused by a certain type of employment.

For example, coal miners are specifically covered under the Black Lung Act for respiratory illness associated with the occupation of coal mining. Employees who are engaged in employment that requires heavy lifting may develop back problems. Employees whose duties involve repetitive movements may develop arthritis. These conditions would likely be considered work-related for the purpose of claiming compensation.

However, illnesses that are self-inflicted, such as alcoholism or drug addiction, are generally ineligible for compensation.

Continuous Trauma

An occupational disease may also be attributed to "continuous trauma." Continuous trauma refers to a gradual deterioration of the employee's physical condition as a result of repetitive work. For example, "carpal tunnel syndrome,"—a condition known to be caused by repetitive hand or wrist movements such as those made in the operation of a computer—would also likely fall under the category of occupational disease.

Of course, the focus would again be on whether the specific illness is work-related, rather than a disease that is ordinarily encountered in one's life, or which is not characteristic of the employee's occupation.

Schedule of Diseases

Many jurisdictions maintain a schedule of diseases that are known to occur in specific occupations or trades. If an employee contracts such a disease during the course of his or her employment in that specific occupation or trade, a presumption may be drawn that it was causally related to the employment.

For example, pneumoconiosis—commonly referred to as "black lung disease"—is a respiratory illness that is specifically covered under the Black Lung Act, because it is known to be caused by working in coal mines.

A coal miner who contracts black lung disease is covered and is entitled to a statutory presumption that the disease is work-related.

If a statutory presumption exists, it is the employer's duty to rebut the presumption. If there is no statutory presumption—i.e., the disease is not scheduled, not characteristic of the employee's occupation, or is one normally encountered in society—the employee would have the burden of proving that he or she contracted the illness as a result of the employment. Thus, if an employee who is not engaged in the particular occupation or trade contracts the same disease, he or she must prove that the illness is work-related.

Medical Documentation

Medical documentation is usually submitted on the employee's behalf to demonstrate the causal relationship. Therefore, it is important that the employee fully detail all of his or her symptoms and complaints to the treating physician. The medical report is crucial in substantiating the employee's disability claim.

The employee cannot depend on the insurance carrier's physician to make his or her disability case. The insurance carrier's physicians are more likely to minimize the seriousness of the disability, or determine that a pre-existing condition is, in fact, the cause of the disability.

If an employee's compensation claim is denied based upon a doctor's report that no injury exists, the employee is generally entitled to get a second opinion from a doctor of his or her choice, at the expense of the insurance carrier.

Aggravation of Pre-Existing Condition

If the employee's disability is caused by aggravation of an employee's pre-existing condition, he or she is entitled to compensation provided the "aggravation" is causally related to the employment. However, if the disability is due to a natural progression of a pre-existing condition that is unrelated to the employment, it would not be compensable.

If the claim is deemed compensable, the employee will be fully covered for the entire disability. There is no apportionment between the pre-existing condition and the aggravation of the condition.

Jurisdictions are split on whether aggravation of a pre-existing condition is compensable as an occupational disease. This is because an occupational disease is one that is caused by the employment. By definition, a pre-existing illness could not have been caused by the employment.

Because of concerns that employers would not hire persons with disabilities due to the financial risk, a "second injury" fund was instituted. A second injury fund distributes the costs of claims that are caused by pre-existing conditions, among the entire workers' compensation system.

In order to qualify for participation in the second injury fund, an employer must demonstrate that it had knowledge of the employee's pre-existing condition. There may be other statutory requirements, therefore, the reader is advised to check the law of his or her own jurisdiction.

Eligibility Restrictions

Protection against occupational disease is somewhat restricted because of time limitations, prevalent in many states, on the filing of claims. Thus, benefits for diseases with long latency periods are not payable in many cases because most state laws pay benefits only if the disability or death occurs within a relatively short period after the last exposure to the occupational disease, e.g., 1–3 years, or if the claim is filed within a similar time frame after manifestation of the disease, or after disability begins. Some programs restrict the scope of benefits in cases of dust-related diseases such as silicosis and asbestosis.

These eligibility restrictions reflect the problems associated with determining the cause of disease. Work-related ailments such as heart disease, respiratory disorders, and other common ailments may be brought on by a variety of traumatic agents in the individual's environment. The role of the workplace in causing such disease is often very difficult to establish for any individual.

OCCUPATIONAL HEARING LOSS

Work-related hearing loss continues to be a critical workplace safety and health issue. Noise-induced hearing loss is 100% preventable but once acquired, hearing loss is permanent and irreversible. Therefore, prevention measures must be taken by employers and workers to ensure the protection of workers' hearing.

Approximately 30 million workers are exposed to hazardous noise on the job and an additional nine million are at risk for hearing loss from other agents such as solvents and metals. Noise-induced hearing loss is one of the most common occupational diseases and the second most self-reported occupational illness or injury.

While any worker can be at risk for noise-induced hearing loss in the workplace, workers in many industries have higher exposures to dangerous levels of noise. Industries with high numbers of exposed workers include: agriculture; mining; construction; manufacturing and utilities; transportation; and military. Nationally, based on workers' compensation statistics, occupational hearing loss costs an estimated $242.4 million per year in disability payments alone, not including medical costs.

A table setting forth the availability of benefits for occupational hearing loss under state workers' compensation laws is set forth in Appendix 10.

DEATH CLAIMS

A death claim is one that is made by the survivors of an employee who died as a result of a work-related injury or illness. Death benefits generally include compensation to the employee's dependents, and payment of funeral expenses.

Even if the employee settled a compensation claim, or never even brought such a claim in their lifetime, the survivors are still permitted to make the claim following his or her death. Of course, the survivors must prove that the death was caused by an injury or disease that was causally related to their decedent's employment.

Survivors who are entitled to compensation on a death claim generally include certain classes of dependents. Depending on the jurisdiction, eligible dependents may include:

1. The surviving spouse;

2. Surviving minor children, including adopted children;

3. Children who, while not minors, are full-time students and were dependent on the decedent;

4. Other family members who were living with the decedent at the time of his or her death and can prove their dependency on the decedent, such as parents, grandparents, grandchildren, and siblings of the decedent.

In general, if an individual is not within one of the classes of persons set forth in the statute, he or she cannot claim survivor benefits even if he or she can establish their dependency upon the decedent.

In addition, all state workers' compensation programs provide for payment of burial expenses subject to a specified maximum amount.

A table setting forth the death benefits payable to surviving spouses and children, and maximum burial allowances, under state workers' compensation laws is set forth in Appendix 11 and 12, respectively.

FILING THE WORKERS' COMPENSATION CLAIM

A claim for workers' compensation benefits is not a lawsuit. It is an application for benefits under an insurance policy for which a premium has been paid by the employer. In some jurisdictions, the employer is entitled to deduct a small contribution from the employee's salary to help defray the cost of the insurance.

Because the success of a workers' compensation system largely depends on expediency, the prompt delivery of benefits and services is essential. The goal is to ensure that the disabled employee and his or her family is not forced into financial crisis caused by the loss of income and mounting medical bills.

In that connection, most workers' compensation statutes set forth specific procedural requirements designed to move claims expeditiously through the various administrative stages.

Thus, it is important that the disabled employee follow the procedural steps set forth under their state workers' compensation law in a timely manner in order to preserve their claim. Initiating a workers' compensation claim generally includes the following steps.

Notice to the Employer

It is extremely important to report all injuries at work to the employer as soon as possible. An untimely or post-termination reporting of the injury will result in a loss of entitlement to benefits. The employer will generally provide the employee with a statement of rights that sets forth the employee's entitlement to workers' compensation benefits and instructions on filing a claim.

A sample Employee's Statement of Rights Under the New York State Workers' Compensation Program is set forth in Appendix 13.

In general, a work-related accidental injury is required to be reported within a certain number of days of its occurrence. Nevertheless, if it is determined that the injured employee could not give timely notice of the claim due to mental incompetence, or because the employee was a minor, the untimely claim will generally not be barred.

Filing the Claim Form

The claim for workers' compensation benefits must be filed with the insurance carrier. The employer is required to provide the employee with the necessary forms to be filed. However, if the disability occurs over a prolonged period of time, such as a gradually developing occupational illness, it must be reported as soon as the employee discovers that he or she is suffering from the illness. If a worker fails to file a claim for workers' compensation, he or she may lose his or her right to benefits and medical care.

Making a false or fraudulent workers' compensation claim is a felony which, depending on the state, may subject the offender to imprisonment and/or a fine. It is also a felony for an employee to make a false statement for the purposes of obtaining compensation benefits, or for an employer to make a false statement for the purposes of denying compensation benefits.

A sample claim form for state workers' compensation disability benefits is set forth in Appendix 14.

Denial of Coverage

Under certain circumstances, an employee's claim may be denied as not covered under workers' compensation. For example, injuries or illnesses that are caused by an employee's intoxication—e.g., by drugs or alcohol—are not eligible for compensation.

Coverage may also be denied in situations involving:

1. Self-inflicted injuries, or injuries sustained while attempting to injure another;

2. Injuries sustained while committing a crime;

3. Injuries sustained when the employee was not on the job; and

4. Injuries sustained when the employee's conduct violated company policy.

THE WORKERS' COMPENSATION HEARING

Workers' compensation matters are generally held before some type of administrative agency, such as a workers' compensation board. The first appearance is usually a conference at which time the parties attempt to settle the claim. Many states have initiated alternative dispute resolution measures to assist in resolving claims.

If a settlement cannot be reached, a trial date is set. Trial dates are frequently adjourned in an attempt to settle cases, in large part due to the limited resources of the workers' compensation boards. If the case goes to trial, it is held before a workers' compensation judge, also known as a "referee" in some jurisdictions. Generally, there are no jury trials held in the workers' compensation system.

The workers' compensation hearings are designed to be informal. Although the employee has the burden of proving that he or she is entitled to compensation, formal rules of evidence are not generally applicable. The degree of proof necessary to prevail on a workers' compensation case is generally "a preponderance of the evidence."

Legal Representation

It is not necessary to retain an attorney to represent you at a workers' compensation hearing because the workers' compensation judge may generally assist the worker in presenting his or her case. Although it is not necessary to be represented by an attorney in workers' compensation proceedings, it may be advisable in certain circumstances. This is so if one's claim is particularly complex, or if the claim is denied in whole or in part and the decision will be appealed.

Attorneys' fees in workers' compensation cases are limited by statute. Fees typically range from about 15% to 25%, and are subject to approval by the judge. The attorney is not permitted to accept any payment directly from the worker. Thus, many workers' compensation attorneys work on a volume basis. They are usually quite familiar with the workers' compensation system, and can assist a claimant with the procedural steps.

A table setting forth the allowable attorney fees under state workers' compensation laws is set forth in Appendix 15.

Findings and Award

Following the trial, the workers' compensation judge will issue what is known as a Finding—a decision setting forth his or her conclusions—and Award. The Award states the total percentage of disability; the number of weeks payable for the disability; and the amount to be paid per week. There will also usually be a finding as to whether future medical treatment is needed.

Settlement

If your injury is permanent, you will likely be able to settle your claim for a lump sum. If you are pursuing settlement of your claim, you should contact an experienced workers' compensation attorney to make sure the terms of the settlement are in your best interests. It is advisable, for example, to make sure that you will be entitled to receive future medical benefits even though you are settling your claim. Settlements are generally reviewed by the workers' compensation judge to make sure the settlement is fair and the claimant's rights are protected.

Right to Appeal

If an employee does not prevail at the hearing, most states permit appeal of the decision to a separate appeals board for review. If an employee is unsuccessful at the administrative level, most states permit judicial review of a final administrative decision. However, most courts are only permitted to review questions of law. Some states do permit limited review of factual issues. All parties, including the administrative agency, are bound by the court's decision.

CHAPTER 3:
WORKERS' COMPENSATION BENEFITS

IN GENERAL

The benefits provided under most workers' compensation programs include periodic cash payments for lost wages; medical benefits; and rehabilitation benefits to the worker during a period of disablement, as well as death and funeral benefits to the worker's survivors.

Lump-sum settlements are permitted under most programs; however, a lump-sum settlement may, in some cases, provide inadequate protection to disabled workers. This is particularly so where a lump-sum payment agreement precludes the payment of future benefits, such as medical care, when the same disabling condition recurs.

WAGE LOSS COMPENSATION

Workers' compensation laws very widely among the states with regard to the number of weeks for which benefits may be paid, and the amount of benefits payable.

Percentage Based on Weekly Earnings

The cash benefits for temporary total disability, permanent total disability, permanent partial disability, and death of a worker are usually calculated as a percentage of weekly earnings at the time of the worker's accident or death—most commonly 66-2/3%. In some states, the percentage varies according to the worker's marital status and number of dependent children, especially in case of death.

All workers' compensation programs, however, place dollar maximums on the weekly amounts payable to a disabled worker or to survivors with the result that some beneficiaries receive less than the amount indicated by these percentages. Five out of six programs have adopted flexible provisions for setting the maximum weekly benefit amounts, basing them on automatic adjustments in relation to the average weekly wage in the jurisdiction.

Length of Time Compensation is Payable

Other provisions in most workers' compensation programs limit the number of weeks for which compensation may be paid or the aggregate amount that may be paid in a given case, and establish waiting-period requirements. These provisions also operate to reduce the specified percentage. Compensation is payable after a waiting period ranging from 3 to 7 days, with 3 days the most common, except in the Virgin Islands, which pays after the first full day of disability.

A table setting forth the waiting periods for benefits under state workers' compensation laws is set forth in Appendix 16.

For workers whose disabilities continue from 4 days to 6 weeks, the payment of benefits is retroactive to the date of injury. If an employee's disability continues for a specific number of days or weeks, lost wages compensation begins, and is usually retroactive back to the date of injury.

A table setting forth retroactivity of benefits under state workers' compensation laws is set forth in Appendix 17.

EXTENT OF DISABILITY

Wage loss compensation is generally paid according to whether the disability is deemed temporary, permanent, partial or total, as further set forth below.

Temporary Total Disability

An employee who suffers a temporary total disability is one who is totally disabled during the period when compensation is paid, but is expected to return to employment once recovered. A large majority of compensation cases involve temporary total injury.

An employee in this category is generally entitled to a weekly benefit that is paid during the period of time the employee cannot work because of the employment-related injury. The weekly benefit is set forth as a percentage of the employee's gross salary—typically 66-2/3% of weekly wages up to the statutory maximum—and continues until the employee is able to return to work.

Most programs provide for temporary disability benefits for the duration of the disability if the possibility exists for further improvement with medical treatment. But sixteen state programs specifically provide that benefits are payable only up to a maximum number of weeks, a maximum monetary total, or both.

A table setting forth the percentage of wages payable for temporary total disability under state workers' compensation laws is set forth in Appendix 18.

Permanent Total Disability

An employee who suffers a permanent total disability is one who is deemed totally disabled and unable to return to any type of gainful employment. An employee who suffers a permanent total disability is generally entitled to a weekly benefit based on his or her diminished ability to compete in the job market.

The weekly benefit is set forth as a percentage of the employee's gross salary, payable for a stated number of weeks, calculated according to the extent of the permanent disability. This compensation continues until either:

1. The employee returns to gainful employment;

2. The employee dies; or

3. In a minority of jurisdictions, the employee reaches the maximum allowable benefit, either in duration or amount. Among those programs where permanent total disability benefits are limited in duration, amount, or both, the periods range from 312 weeks to 500 weeks

Employees who have suffered a severe injury such that he or she is presumed to be permanently and totally disabled, generally receives compensation checks throughout his or her entire life.

A table setting forth the percentage of wages payable for permanent total disability under state workers' compensation laws is set forth in Appendix 19.

Temporary Partial Disability

An employee who suffers a temporary partial disability is usually entitled to wage loss replacement. This is because a partial disability generally affects the employee's current earnings or wage earning ability.

The compensation amount is expressed as a percentage of the employee's wages, and is calculated as the difference between earnings before the injury and earnings after the injury. Because the disability is temporary, the compensation ends when the employee returns to his or her pre-injury status.

Permanent Partial Disability

If the permanent disability of a worker is only partial and may or may not lessen work ability, permanent partial disability benefits are payable—in part as compensation for the injury and ensuing suffering and handicap, and in part as compensation for a potential reduction in earning capacity. Again, the compensation amount is expressed as a percentage of the employee's wages, and is calculated as the difference between earnings before the injury and earnings after the injury.

The typical law recognizes two types of permanent partial disabilities: Specific or "schedule" injuries, as discussed below, and general or "nonscheduled" injuries, such as a disability caused by injury to the head, back, or nervous system.

A table setting forth the percentage of wages payable for permanent partial disability under state workers' compensation laws is set forth in Appendix 20.

SCHEDULED DISABILITIES

Certain disabilities are statutorily listed, depending on the jurisdiction, as "scheduled" injuries. A scheduled injury is one that involves the loss—or loss of use of—a specific body part, such as the loss of an arm, leg, eye, or other part of the body. In such a case, wage loss is presumed based on the type of injury suffered.

Depending on the particular statute, compensation for a scheduled disability is calculated by attributing a specific number of weeks of benefits to the particular body part involved, e.g., loss of an eye = 300 weeks. This number of weeks is then multiplied by a weekly benefit amount, which is based on the employee's earnings at the time of the injury, in order to arrive at a compensation sum.

MEDICAL BENEFITS

An extremely important benefit of the workers' compensation program is the right to receive good medical care. Although most workers' compensation programs require a waiting period before lost wages are payable, this does not apply to medical benefits. Medical benefits, including hospitalization, are effective immediately. In addition, an employee is generally entitled to receive these medical benefits without limitation on duration or cost. In addition, if medical care is necessary, it will be provided even if there has been no lost time from work, and no cash benefits paid.

The employee is usually permitted to choose his or her treating physician for workers' compensation purposes, provided the employer is notified of the employee's choice before the injury occurs. This is known as "predesignating" a physician for workers' compensation purposes. Employers are generally required to advise the employees of their right to predesignate a physician. In some cases, the physician must be chosen from a list prepared by the state agency or the employer.

A table setting forth choice of physician rules under state workers' compensation laws is set forth in Appendix 21.

Depending on the jurisdiction, if an employee has not predesignated his or her treating physician, he or she may be forced into treatment with a physician who is selected by the employer for a certain time period, e.g., 30 days. However, once the specified time period ends, the employee is then usually permitted to choose his or her own treating physician.

Because medical care is generally provided by physicians in private practice on a fee-for-service basis, the programs commonly contain provisions restricting the responsibility of the employer to such charges as generally prevail in the community for treating persons who are of the same general economic status as the employee, and who pay for their own treatment. State programs may also provide for use of medical fee schedules and managed medical care plans.

REHABILITATION BENEFITS

A disabled employee is generally entitled to both medical and vocational rehabilitation. In addition, most workers' compensation laws contain special provisions for retraining, education, and job placement and guidance to help injured workers find suitable work. It is to the mutual benefit of both employer and employee that rehabilitation begins as soon as possible.

Rehabilitation is a program offering special services designed to: eliminate the disability, if that is possible, or to reduce or alleviate the disability to the greatest degree possible; help an injured worker to return to work when possible; or to aid the person with a residual disability to live and work at his/her maximum capability.

Rehabilitation staff generally includes counselors, social workers, a consultant physiatrist and claims examiners to coordinate and follow-up on medical and vocational rehabilitation services. Rehabilitation is voluntary except in limited circumstances.

There are four general types of rehabilitation services offered:

1. Vocational Rehabilitation—Programs for those who, because of their disability, cannot return to their former jobs. These services may provide guidance to help the claimant determine the best way to return to work.

2. Selective Placement—Programs for those claimants who are left with a permanent disability, and who need a job that will fit their abilities.

3. Medical Rehabilitation—Programs include exercise and muscle conditioning, under the supervision of a physician, to restore a person to maximum usefulness. Only a physician may recommend a medical rehabilitation program.

4. Social Services—A staff of social workers available to assist an injured worker with a family or financial problem that is interfering with their rehabilitation.

Workers who are participating in one of the rehabilitation programs continue to receive cash benefits based on the extent of their disability. Workers who return to work but cannot earn the same wages because of an injury may be entitled to compensation benefits at a reduced rate.

In most of the programs, payments for food, lodging, and travel are provided to facilitate the vocational rehabilitation of the worker. These payments are provided through the extension of the period for which regular compensation is payable, or are in addition to the payment of indemnity benefits, sometimes with time limitations.

Federal-State Vocational Rehabilitation Program

In addition to any special rehabilitation benefits and services provided under the workers' compensation laws, an injured worker may be eligible for the services provided by the Federal-State program of vocational rehabilitation. This program is operated by the State divisions of vocational rehabilitation and applies to disabled persons whether or not the disability is work connected. The services rendered include medical examination, medical and vocational diagnosis, counsel and guidance in selecting a suitable job, and training for and placement in that job.

SUBSEQUENT INJURY FUNDS

To help place injured workers in jobs and to relieve the fear of employers that their workers' compensation costs will be unduly burdened if they hire workers with disabilities, all but three states have some form of subsequent injury or second injury fund. When a subsequent injury occurs to a worker who has sustained a previous permanent injury, the employee is compensated for the disability resulting from the combined injuries. The current employer pays only for the last injury and the remainder of the award is paid from the second-injury fund.

The method of financing the subsequent injury fund differs among the various programs. Generally, financing is by assessment of insurance carriers, self-insurers, or employers. In some States, an assessment is made against certain types of compensation payments.

DEATH BENEFITS

As set forth above, compensation related to earnings and the number of dependents is payable to the survivors of workers who die from work injury. Generally, weekly or monthly death payments are made to the spouse for life or until remarriage, regardless of the spouse's age at the time of the death of the worker. All programs provide payments to children until age 18 or later if they are incapacitated or are students. In addition, all of the programs provide for payment of burial expenses subject to a specified maximum amount.

OFFSET PROVISION UNDER THE SOCIAL SECURITY AMENDMENTS

If you are permanently unable to return to work due to your disability, you may qualify for Social Security Disability benefits. These benefits are reserved for the most seriously disabled workers who, because of their injury or illness, are prevented from doing any "substantial gainful work." In addition, to be eligible, the worker's disability must be expected to last at least twelve months or result in the worker's death.

Social Security Disability Insurance (SSDI) and workers' compensation are the country's two largest disability programs. In 2002, the SSDI program paid $66 billion in benefits to 5.5 million disabled workers and their dependents. In the same year, workers' compensation paid out $53 billion—$29 billion in wage-loss compensation and $24 billion in medical benefits.

Because SSDI and workers' compensation are so large and have overlapping goals, it is not surprising that many people receive benefits from both programs. In some cases, however, overlapping benefits can create excessive wage replacement rates and the resulting disincentives for achieving self-sufficiency.

For this reason, the Social Security Amendments of 1965 established the workers' compensation offset provision. The offset provision assures that the combined amount of a disabled worker's and family's benefit from SSDI and workers' compensation will not exceed 80% of the worker's average current earnings. Under the offset provision, the SSDI benefit may be reduced for any month to fully or partially offset a worker's compensation benefit received for the same month.

Nevertheless, this reduction is made only if the total benefits payable to the worker, or his or her dependents, under the Social Security Act, plus those paid as workers' compensation, exceed the higher of 80% of the worker's "average current earnings" before the onset of the disability, or the family's total social security benefit before reduction.

If the total amount of these benefits exceeds 80% of the worker's average current earnings, the excess amount is deducted from the worker's social security benefit. The social security benefit will be reduced accordingly until the month the worker reaches age 65, or the month the workers' compensation benefits stop, whichever comes first.

> **EXAMPLE:** A worker's average current earnings before he became disabled were $4,000 per month. The worker's wife and two children would be eligible to receive a total of $2,200 per month in social security disability benefits. The worker also receives $2,000 per month from the workers' compensation program. Thus, the total amount of benefits the worker and his family would receive totals $4,200. However, eighty percent of the worker's average current earnings is $3,200. Under the formula, the worker's social security benefit would be reduced by the excess amount of $1000.

Nevertheless, the worker's SSDI benefit will not be reduced if the workers' compensation law provides for the reduction of the workers' compensation benefit when the worker is entitled to SSDI benefits.

Disabled workers receiving SSDI benefits are required to file a Workers' Compensation/Public Benefit Questionnaire (SSA Form 546) if they received, are receiving, or expect to receive disability-related benefits from any such programs.

The Workers' Compensation/Public Disability Benefit Questionnaire (Form SSA-546) is set forth in Appendix 22.

CHAPTER 4:
THE FEDERAL EMPLOYEES'
COMPENSATION PROGRAM

IN GENERAL

The Federal Employees' Compensation Program is administered by the Office of Workers' Compensation Programs pursuant to the authority contained in the Federal Employees' Compensation Act (5 U.S.C. §§ 8101 - 8193) ("FECA"). The OWCP maintains 12 district offices located across the United States.

The Federal Employees' Compensation Program is a highly cost-effective self-insurance system. Overhead is low, and because the system is non-adversarial, the Federal government avoids time-consuming and expensive litigation, which in some non-Federal workers' compensation systems can amount to as much as 46% of the payout.

Disputes under the program are resolved through informal conferences or formal reconsideration at the district office level, through administrative hearing, or review by the independent Employees' Compensation Appeals Board whose decision is final.

COVERED EMPLOYEES

The FECA provides compensation benefits to more than three million civilian employees of the United States who suffer disability due to work-related personal injury or illness. Included among the executive, legislative and judicial branch employees covered by the FECA are civilian defense workers, medical workers in veterans' hospitals, and the 800,000 workers of the Postal Service, the country's largest civilian employer.

Special legislation provides coverage to Peace Corps and VISTA volunteers; Federal petit or grand jurors; volunteer members of the Civil Air Patrol; Reserve Officer Training Corps Cadets; Job Corps; Neighborhood Youth Corps; and Youth Conservation Corps enrollees; and non-Federal law enforcement officers under certain circumstances involving crimes against the United States.

Contract employees, volunteers, and loaned employees are covered under some circumstances. Federal employees who are neither citizens nor residents of the United States or Canada are covered subject to certain special provisions governing their pay rates and computation of compensation payments.

Coverage under the program is extended to Federal employees regardless of the length of time on the job or the type of position held. Probationary, temporary, and term employees are covered on the same basis as permanent employees. Also, part-time, seasonal, and intermittent employees are covered.

TYPES OF FEDERAL WORKERS' COMPENSATION CLAIMS

Federal workers' compensation claims generally fall into the same three categories as claims under state workers' compensation statutes:

1. Traumatic Injury Claims;

2. Occupational Disease or Illness Claims; and

3. Death Claims.

Traumatic Injury Claims

A traumatic injury is a wound or other condition of the body caused by external force, including stress or strain. The injury must occur at a specific time and place, and it must affect a specific member or function of the body. The injury must be caused by a specific event or incident, or a series of events or incidents, within a single day or work shift.

Traumatic injuries include damage solely to or destruction of prostheses, such as dentures or artificial limbs. Traumatic injuries also include damage to or destruction of personal appliances, such as eyeglasses or hearing aids, when a personal injury requiring medical services occurred.

Occupational Disease or Illness Claims

An occupational disease or illness is a condition produced by the work environment over a period longer than one workday or shift. The condition may result from infection, repeated stress or strain, or repeated exposure to toxins, poisons, fumes or other continuing conditions of the work environment.

Death Claims

A death claim is one that is made by the survivors of an employee who died as a result of a work-related injury or illness. In order to recover, the survivors must prove that the death was caused by an injury or disease that was causally related to their decedent's employment.

BENEFITS

Benefits available to disabled federal employees are similar to those provided under state workers' compensation systems. Benefits include medical care and wage loss compensation, as well as rehabilitation and assistance in returning to work. The FECA also provides compensation to an employee's dependents if the injury or disease causes his or her death.

Employees are not entitled to any benefits if:

1. The injury or death is caused by the willful misconduct of the employee; or

2. The injury or death is caused by the employee's intention to bring about his or her injury or death or that of another; or

3. If intoxication by alcohol or drugs is the proximate cause of the employee's injury or death.

Wage Loss Compensation

Temporary Disability

The FECA provides non-taxable compensation benefits to federal employees for temporary disability due to work-related injury or disease. An injured employee is entitled to continuation of pay ("COP") from the employing agency for up to 45 days of disability after a three-day waiting period in a non-paid status. However, if the disability causing wage loss lasts longer than 14 days from the time compensation begins, no waiting period is required.

Continuation of pay benefits do not apply to occupational disease cases. However, the employee may use sick or annual leave or enter a leave without pay status and claim compensation.

Compensation is generally payable at the rate of two-thirds of the employee's pre-disability gross earnings if the employee has no dependents. Employees with dependents are generally entitled to compensation payable at the rate of three-fourths of pre-disability gross earnings.

The term "dependent" as defined in the FECA includes a husband, wife, unmarried child under 18 years of age, and a wholly dependent parent.

An unmarried child may qualify as a dependent after reaching the age of 18 if incapable of self-support by reason of mental or physical disability, or as long as the child continues to be a full-time student at an accredited institution, until he or she reaches the age of 23 or has completed four years of education beyond the high school level.

Permanent Disability

The FECA also provides compensation benefits for work-related loss, or loss of use of, specified members, organs, and functions of the body. Benefits are calculated based on scheduled awards and loss of earning capacity. For example, an award of 160 weeks of compensation is payable to an employee who loses total vision in one eye due to a work-related occurrence.

In addition, compensation for loss of earning capacity may be paid if the employee is unable to resume his or her usual work because of the work-related disability. This compensation is paid on the basis of the difference between (i) the employee's capacity to earn wages after an injury; and (ii) the wages of the job he or she held when injured.

Cost of Living Increases

Compensation payments on account of a disability or death that occurred more than one year before March 1 of each year, are increased on that date by any percentage change in the Consumer Price Index published for December of the preceding year.

Attachment and Garnishment of Compensation Payments

Under the FECA, assignment of a claim for compensation is void, and all compensation payments are exempt from the claims of creditors.

Nevertheless, disability compensation payments may be garnisheed for alimony and child support payments if allowed by state law, and the legal process is served according to state law.

Medical Benefits

In General

Under the FECA, a disabled employee is entitled to:

1. Medical services;

2. Surgical services;

3. Hospital services;

4. Necessary medical supplies; and

5. Transportation necessary to obtain medical care.

Seek Immediate Medical Attention

In case of injury, an employee should seek immediate medical attention even if the injury is minor. While many minor injuries heal without treatment, a few result in serious prolonged disability that could have been prevented had the employee received treatment when the injury occurred.

For traumatic injuries, the employer must authorize medical treatment prior to the employee's visit to the doctor.

For occupational disease or illness, an employer may authorize medical treatment for occupational illness only with the prior approval of OWCP.

Choosing a Physician

Initially, the injured employee is entitled to choose a physician or hospital to provide necessary treatment. If the physician selected has been excluded from participating in the Compensation Program, the OWCP District Office will advise the employee of the exclusion and the need to select another physician. The employee may also use agency medical facilities if available.

After the employee's initial choice of physician has been made, he or she may not change physicians without obtaining OWCP authorization. If the employee changes physicians without OWCP authorization, OWCP will not pay for such unauthorized treatment. However, this provision does not apply when the attending physician has referred the employee to another medical provider. In addition, an employee is entitled to a referral to a medical specialist for a second opinion examination where required by the worker's medical condition or the office's need for additional medical information.

An injured employee who is unable to return to his or her employment within a specified period of time is entitled to the services of a registered nurse. The nurse ensures that appropriate medical care is rendered and assists the worker in returning to employment.

If the employee's condition requires a constant attendant, an additional amount not to exceed $1500 per month may be allowed.

Covered Medical Providers

The term "physician" as used in the FECA includes surgeons, osteopathic practitioners, podiatrists, dentists, clinical psychologists, optometrists and chiropractors within the scope of their practice as defined by State law. Payment for chiropractic services is limited to treatment consisting of manual manipulation of the spine to correct a subluxation as demonstrated by x-ray to exist.

Submit Timely Medical Bills

The employee should submit medical bills promptly. Bills for medical treatment may not be paid if submitted to OWCP more than one year after the calendar year in which treatment was rendered, or in which the condition was accepted as compensable.

Vocational Rehabilitation

The employee is entitled to vocational rehabilitation services if he or she is unable to return to work at the employing agency, or in his or her previous job category. OWCP may provide a maintenance allowance not to exceed $200 per month. A disabled employee participating in an OWCP-approved training or vocational rehabilitation program is paid at the compensation rate for total disability.

Survivor Benefits

If an employee dies due to a work-related injury or illness, his or her family members are entitled to compensation, as follows:

1. If the employee had no eligible children, the surviving spouse's compensation is 50 percent of the employee's pay at the time of death.

2. If the employee had a child or children eligible for benefits, the surviving spouse is entitled to 45 percent of the employee's pay at the time of death, and each child is entitled to 15 percent.

3. If the employee's children are his or her sole survivors, 40 percent of the employee's pay at the time of death is paid to the first child and 15 percent for each additional child, to be shared equally.

4. Other related persons such as dependent parents, brothers, sisters, grandparents, and grandchildren may also be entitled to benefits.

In any event, the total compensation paid to the employee's survivors may not exceed 75 percent of the employee's pay, or the pay of the highest step for GS-15 of the General Schedule, except when such excess is created by authorized cost-of-living increases.

Termination Provisions

Compensation to an employee's surviving spouse terminates upon his or her death or remarriage, unless the remarriage takes place after the age of 55.

Awards to children, brothers, sisters and grandchildren terminate at the age of 18, unless the dependent is incapable of self-support, or continues to be a full-time student at an accredited institution, until he or she reaches the age of 23, or has completed four years of education beyond the high school level.

Burial Expenses

Burial expenses up to $800 are payable. If the Department of Veterans Affairs (VA) also pays a burial allowance, that allowance must be deducted. If the employee dies away from home, the cost of transporting the body to the place of burial will be paid in full. In addition, a $200 allowance will be paid for terminating the deceased's status as a Federal employee.

FILING A CLAIM UNDER THE FECA

Legal Representation

An employee does not need an attorney or other representative to file or pursue a claim for compensation. However, the employee may obtain the services of an attorney or other representative if desired. The employee must advise OWCP in writing of the name of the representative.

A Federal employee may not serve as a representative unless he or she is an immediate family member of the injured worker, or is acting in his or her official capacity as a union representative. An OWCP employee may not act as a representative under any circumstances.

If the employee hires an attorney, the employee is responsible for paying the fee. The OWCP will not direct the payment of a fee or help collect a fee. The employee and representative must resolve these matters.

The employee should not pay any legal fee until the OWCP has approved the amount. The OWCP will approve a fee based on an itemized statement submitted by the representative showing the work performed, along with a statement from the employee indicating his or her agreement, or lack of agreement, with the requested fee.

Written Notice Requirement

The employee should provide written notice of injury or illness to his or her supervisor on the appropriate forms as soon as possible. The supervisor is required to accept the notice and has no authority to accept or deny a claim. Only the OWCP may make this decision.

If a supervisor refuses to accept the notice of injury or illness, the OWCP should be notified, as this is a violation under the law, as follows:

Whoever, being an officer or employee of the United States charged with the responsibility for making the reports of the immediate superior specified by section 8120 of title 5, willfully fails, neglects, or refuses to make any of the reports, or knowingly files a false report, or induces, compels, or directs an injured employee to forego filing of any claim for compensation or other benefits provided under subchapter I of chapter 81 of title 5 or any extension or application thereof, or willfully retains any notice, report, claim, or paper which is required to be filed under that subchapter or any extension or application thereof, or regulations prescribed thereunder, shall be fined under this title or imprisoned not more than one year, or both. [18 U.S.C. 19220.

Written Notice of a Traumatic Injury

Every injury should be reported to the employee's supervisor. Written notice of a traumatic injury is required to be reported on Form CA-1. This form may be obtained from the federal employer or the OWCP office, and should be filed within 30 days. Any claim that is not submitted within 3 years will be barred by statutory time limitations unless the immediate superior had actual knowledge of the injury or death within 30 days of occurrence.

Further, Form CA-1 must be filed within the 30-day period to qualify for continuation of pay (COP) for a disabling traumatic injury. COP may be terminated if medical evidence of the injury-related disability is not submitted to the employer within 10 workdays. It is the employee's responsibility to make sure that the proper medical evidence is submitted to his or her employer.

The Federal Employee's Notice of Injury and Claim for Compensation (Form CA-1) is set forth in Appendix 23.

Written Notice of Occupational Illness or Disease

Written notice of an occupational disease or illness must be reported on Form CA-2. This form may also be obtained from the federal employer or the OWCP office, and should be filed within 30 days.

The Federal Employee's Notice of Occupational Disease and Claim for Compensation (Form CA-2) is set forth in Appendix 24.

Establish the Necessary Elements of the Claim

The employee must be able to establish the elements of his or her claim to prevail. For example:

1. The employee must prove that he or she is a covered employee under the FECA;

2. The employee must prove that benefits were applied for in a timely manner;

3. The employee must prove that the injury occurred as reported, and while in performance of duty; and

4. The employee must prove that his or her condition is causally related to the employment.

OWCP assists employees in gathering evidence and meeting their burden of proof on these elements.

Required Proof - Causal Relationship

The employee must prove that he or she actually sustained an injury or illness, as a result of his or her employment.

Time, Place and Manner

It must be shown that an incident occurred at the time and place and in the manner claimed. This is determined on the basis of factual evidence, including statements from the employee, the supervisor, and any witnesses. Nevertheless, an injury need not be witnessed to be compensable.

Medical Evidence

It must be shown that the employee has a medical condition that may be related to the incident. This is determined on the basis of the attending physician's statement. Opinions of the employee, supervisors or witnesses are not considered, nor is general medical information in published articles.

The fact that a condition appears during Federal employment does not establish causal relationship between the two. Likewise, the employee's belief that work factors caused or aggravated the condition does not establish causal relationship.

In addition, in order to be covered for aggravation of a pre-existing condition, the employee must submit medical and factual evidence showing that their employment aggravated, accelerated, or precipitated their disease or illness. Where a pre-existing condition involving the same part of the body is present, the physician must provide a medical opinion, which states both the effects of the work-related condition and those of the pre-existing condition.

Performance of Duty Requirement

In order to prevail on a federal workers' compensation claim, the employee is required to prove that the injury or illness occurred while the employee was performing his or her duties. Generally, this means that the injury or illness must occur on the employer's premises during working hours while the employee is performing assigned duties or engaging in an activity that is reasonably associated with the employment.

Workers who perform assigned duties away from the employer's premises are also covered. For example:

Lunch and Break Time

An employee is considered to be in performance of duty during a break or at lunch on the employer's premises, however, unless the employee is in travel status or is performing regular duties off the premises, an injury that occurs during lunch hour off the premises is not usually covered.

Recreational Activities

Injuries that occur during recreation which the employee is required to perform as a part of training or assigned duties, or which occur while the employee is in pay status, are considered to be in performance of duty for compensation purposes.

Injuries that occur during informal recreation on the employer's premises may also be covered, including injuries that may occur while an employee is engaged in activities approved as part of an individual plan developed under a formal physical fitness program managed by the employer.

Injuries that occur during informal recreation off the employer's premises, such as playing on an employer-sponsored baseball team, may also be covered. In that connection, the employer must explain what benefit it derived from the employee's participation, the extent to which the employer sponsored or directed the activity, and whether the employee's participation was required or not.

Travel Time

Employees are not generally covered for injuries that occur before they reach the employer's premises or after they have left it. However, coverage may be extended when the employer provides transportation to and from work, when the employee is required to travel during a curfew or an emergency, or when the employee is required to use his or her automobile during the workday.

Nevertheless, an employee considered to be in travel status is covered 24 hours a day for all activities incidental to the work assignment. Such activities include obtaining meals, using the hotel room, and traveling between the hotel and the work site. However, this does not include recreational or sightseeing trips.

Continuation of Pay Claim

If the employee continues to lose pay after the dates initially claimed, he or she must submit to his or her employer a Claim for Continuing Compensation on Account of Disability (Form CA-8), to claim additional compensation until he or she is able to return to work.

If the employee chooses to use leave time, he or she may, with the employer's approval, request to "buy back" their leave time. Any compensation payment is to be used to partially reimburse the employer for the leave pay.

The employee must also arrange to pay the employer the difference between the leave pay based on the full salary, and the compensation payment that was paid at 2/3 or 3/4 of the employee's salary. The employer will then re-credit the leave to the employee's leave record.

Time Limits in Adjudicating a Federal Compensation Claim

Injured Employees

Employees who suffer traumatic injuries generally receive a decision within 45 days of receipt of the claim, unless the case is particularly complex. If the case is accepted, and the medical evidence supports the disability, compensation payments are usually made within 14 days of submission to the OWCP district office by the employing agency.

Approved medical bills, whether submitted directly by the providers or as reimbursement requests by injured workers, are usually paid within 28 days of receipt.

Occupational Disease

A simple occupational disease claim is usually decided within 90 days of receipt of the claim. Decisions in cases that require more extensive evidentiary development may take up to six months. However, if the claim is particularly complex, it may take up to 10 months of receipt of the claim for a decision.

Appeal Rights

If the employee's claim is denied, the OWCP sends a written notice of the decision. The decision states the specific reason for denying the case and discusses the evidence that led to the decision. Copies of the decision are sent to the employer and to the employee's representative, if one has been retained.

An employee who disagrees with a final OWCP determination may appeal the decision. Appeal rights include the following:

1. The employee has the right to an oral hearing before an OWCP representative. The employee claiming benefits can testify and present written evidence. The hearing is held at a location near the employee's home. The employee may have legal representation at the hearing, but it is not necessary.

2. The employee has the right to a review of the written record by an OWCP representative. The employee claiming benefits will not be asked to attend or testify, but he or she may submit written evidence.

3. The employee has the right to reconsideration of a decision by district office staff that were not involved in making the decision. The request must clearly state the grounds for requesting reconsideration, and it must include evidence not submitted before or a legal argument not made before.

4. The employee has the right to a review by the Employees' Compensation Appeals Board (ECAB). The ECAB is part of the U.S. Department of Labor, but separate from the OWCP. Review by the ECAB is limited to the evidence of record, and no new evidence may be submitted. The individual claiming benefits may be represented by an attorney or by any other person authorized by that individual. The ECAB must approve any fee for such representation.

Unlike state workers' compensation systems, if the federal employee is dissatisfied with the decision reached on appeal, he or she cannot obtain review through a state or Federal court system.

Penalties for Filing a False Claim for Compensation

It is illegal to file a false claim for federal workers' compensation benefits:

Whoever knowingly and wilfully falsifies, conceals, or covers up a material fact, or makes a false, fictitious, or fraudulent statement or representation, or makes or uses a false statement or report knowing the same to contain any false, fictitious, or fraudulent statement or entry in connection with the application for or receipt of compensation or other benefit or payment under subchapter I or III of chapter 81 of title 5, shall be guilty of perjury, and on conviction thereof shall be punished by a fine under this title, or by imprisonment for not more than 5 years, or both; but if the amount of the benefits falsely obtained does not exceed $1,000, such person shall be punished by a fine under this title, or by imprisonment for not more than 1 year, or both. [18 U.S.C. 1920].

RETURN TO WORK PROVISIONS

Under the FECA, injured workers have the right to reclaim their Federal jobs within one year of the onset of wage loss. Thus, the employee should return to work as soon as he or she is able to do so.

Employees who fully or partially recover from their injuries are expected to return to work. The FECA provides vocational rehabilitation services to partially disabled employees for this purpose. If the employer gives the employee a written description of an available light duty job, he or she must provide a copy to the doctor and ask if and when the duties described could be performed, and if there are any work restrictions.

In any event, the employer is entitled to written verification of the doctor's return to work instructions for the employee. Compensation may be terminated if the employee refuses work that is within these medical restrictions without good cause, or if the employee fails to respond within specified time limits to a job offer from the employer.

In appropriate cases, the OWCP provides assistance in arranging for reassignment to lighter duties in cooperation with the employer. In addition, injured employees have certain other specified rights under the jurisdiction of the Office of Personnel Management, such as reemployment rights if the disability has been overcome within one year.

RECURRENCE OF A WORK-RELATED DISABILITY

A disability that is caused by a new incident with an identifiable cause is considered a new injury. Unlike a new injury, a recurrence of disability is defined as follows:

1. An inability to work after an employee has returned to work, when the inability is caused by a spontaneous change in a medical condition, which had resulted from a previous injury or illness, without an intervening injury or new exposure to the work environment that caused the illness.

2. An inability to work that occurs when a light-duty assignment made specifically to accommodate an employee's physical restriction due to his or her work-related injury or illness is withdrawn.

3. An inability to work that occurs when the physical requirements of the light-duty assignment are changed so that they exceed an employee's established medical restrictions.

If an injured employee sustains a recurrence of a disability as defined above, he or she should report the recurrence using Form CA-2a, "Notice of Recurrence." The form should be filed even if the recurrence occurs while the employer is paying continuation of pay (COP) compensation.

The employee must submit the factual and medical evidence required. If the recurrent disability is deemed to be related to the original injury, the employee is entitled to medical treatment and compensation.

OWCP RIGHT TO REIMBURSEMENT FROM THIRD PARTY CLAIM RECOVERY

If a third party, other than the United States, is liable to the employee for his or her work-related injury or death, the OWCP is entitled to a portion of the cost of compensation and other benefits paid by OWCP if there is any recovery from such third party. OWCP will assist in obtaining a settlement with the third party.

The FECA guarantees that the employee may retain a certain portion of the settlement after any attorney fees and costs are deducted, even if the cost of compensation and other benefits exceeds the amount of the settlement.

PRIVACY RIGHTS

While workers' compensation records are protected from release under the Privacy Act, the employer is considered a party to the claim. It may receive information in the employee's file under the "routine use" provision of the regulations under which the Privacy Act is administered. Such information includes medical reports. Employers are expected, however, to handle this information with care and to restrict access to those with a specific need to have it.

CHAPTER 5:
THE LONGSHORE AND HARBOR WORKERS' COMPENSATION PROGRAM

IN GENERAL

The Office of Workers' Compensation Programs ("OWCP") is responsible for administering The Longshore and Harbor Workers' Compensation Program pursuant to the Longshore and Harbor Workers' Compensation Act of 1927 (33 U.S.C. §§901-950) (LHWCA).

Covered Workers

The LHWCA offers compensation and medical care to approximately one-half million maritime workers injured or killed upon the navigable waters of the U.S., as well as employees working on adjoining piers, docks and terminals, plus a number of other groups.

The Act also covers a variety of other workers through the following extensions to the Act:

1. The Defense Base Act of 1941;

2. The Nonappropriated Fund Instrumentalities Act of 1952; and

3. The Outer Continental Shelf Lands Act of 1953.

Under these extensions to the Act, the following workers are covered:

1. Overseas employees of defense contractors;

2. Employees at military post exchanges;

3. Workers engaged in the extraction of natural resources on the outer continental shelf; and

4. Other classes of private industry workers that are entitled to compensation benefits.

Excluded Workers

The LHWCA does not cover the following individuals if they are covered by a state workers' compensation law:

1. Individuals employed exclusively to perform office clerical, secretarial, security, or data processing work;

2. Individuals employed by a club, camp, recreational operation, restaurant, museum, or retail outlet;

3. Individuals employed by a marina and who are not engaged in construction, replacement, or expansion of such marina;

4. Individuals who are: (a) employed by suppliers, transporters, or vendors; (b) temporarily doing business on the premises of a maritime employer; and (c) not engaged in work normally performed by employees of that employer covered under this Act;

5. Aquaculture workers;

6. Individuals employed to build, repair, or dismantle any recreational vessel under sixty-five feet in length;

7. A master or member of a crew of any vessel;

8. Any person engaged by a master to load or unload or repair any small vessel under eighteen tons net; and

9. Employees of the United States government or of any state or foreign government.

FILING A CLAIM

If you are injured on the job, you must notify your employer immediately. If you need medical treatment, ask your employer to give you the necessary forms that authorize treatment by a doctor of your choice. You should obtain medical treatment as soon as possible.

In any event, you must give written notice of your injury to your employer within 30 days of the date of injury. Notice of death must also be given within 30 days. Additional time is provided for certain hearing loss and occupational disease claims.

A written claim for compensation must be filed within one year after the date of injury or last payment of compensation, whichever is later. A claim for survivor benefits must be filed within one year after the date of death. The time for filing claims in certain occupational disease cases has been extended to two years.

A sample Notice of Employee's Injury or Death Under the Longshore and Harbor Workers' Compensation Act (Form LS-201) is set forth in Appendix 26.

BENEFITS

The LHWCA provides the following benefits to employees who suffer work-related injuries or illness:

1. Monetary compensation for lost wages;

2. Medical benefits;

3. Rehabilitation services; and

4. Death benefits to dependents if the injury causes the employee's death.

These benefits are paid by an insurance company or by an employer who is authorized by the OWCP to be self-insured. In some cases, benefits are paid from a special fund consisting of employer contributions.

The Division of Longshore and Harbor Workers' Compensation (DLHWC) is responsible for administering this special fund, and ensuring that disabled workers or their survivors receive the benefits they are entitled to in an expedient manner. The DLHWC is also responsible for providing authorization to qualified insurance carriers and self-insured employers.

The program pays out over $747 million in monetary, medical and vocational rehabilitation benefits in more than 66,000 cases annually. In addition the program maintains over $2.8 billion in securities to ensure the continuing provision of benefits for these injured workers in cases of employer insolvency.

Monetary Benefits

Disability is defined as the employee's inability to earn the same wages he or she was earning at the time of injury. Disability compensation is paid every two weeks during an employee's total disability because of a work-related injury. Compensation is paid at a lesser rate if the employee is only partially disabled for his regular work.

No compensation is allowed for the first three days of disability unless the disability lasts longer than fourteen days. In such cases, compensation is paid retroactively from the first day of wage loss. The first installment of compensation is due 14 days after the employee begins to lose time from work due to the injury, or as directed by the OWCP.

Compensation is payable for disabilities that are permanent total, temporary total, permanent partial, or temporary partial.

Permanent Total and Temporary Total Disability

Compensation under this category is two-thirds of the employee's average weekly wage, subject to a maximum amount. The maximum rate payable for temporary total disability changes each October 1, based on the current National Average Weekly Wage for the affected period. Compensation for permanent total disability is adjusted each October 1, based on the percentage change in the national average weekly wage from the previous year, subject to a maximum adjustment of 5%.

Permanent Partial Disability

Compensation under this category is payable for the permanent loss or loss of use of certain parts or functions of the body, such as the loss of the arm, hand, fingers, leg, foot, toes, hearing or vision. Compensation is payable for a certain number of weeks for each type of disability as specified in the Act. For example, total loss of use of a foot entitles the employee to 205 weeks of compensation.

Temporary Partial and Non-Scheduled Permanent Partial Disability

Compensation under this category is two-thirds of the employee's weekly wage loss or loss of wage-earning capacity.

Permanent Partial Disability for Retirees

If a worker suffers the onset of a latent occupational disease after retirement, compensation is two-thirds of the National Average Weekly Wage (NAWW) multiplied by the percentage of impairment resulting from the disease.

Medical Benefits

Medical benefits include all medical, surgical, and hospital treatment and other medical supplies and services required by the employment related injury, as well as the cost of travel and mileage incidental to such treatment.

The employee may obtain medical treatment from a physician of his or her choice. The term "physician" includes doctors of medicine (MD), surgeons, podiatrists, dentists, clinical psychologists, optometrists, and osteopathic practitioners within the scope of their practice as defined by state law. Chiropractors are also included only to the extent that their treatment consists of manual manipulation of the spine to correct subluxation.

An employee may not choose a physician who is currently not authorized by the Department of Labor to render medical care under the Act. The list of physicians not authorized is available from the local OWCP district office.

Vocational Rehabilitation

A disabled worker is entitled to vocational rehabilitation. Vocational rehabilitation may include evaluation, testing, counseling, selective placement, and retraining, if the employee is injured and cannot return to the former job. Rehabilitation services may include the cost of tuition, books and supplies. A maintenance allowance not to exceed $25.00 per week is also provided during retraining. The cost of vocational rehabilitation services is paid by the U. S. Department of Labor.

Death Benefits

Death benefits are paid to a surviving spouse or other eligible survivors if the injury causes the employee's death. Compensation payable under the Act may not exceed 200% of the national average weekly wage, applicable at the time of injury, or the employee's full average weekly wage, whichever is less.

Surviving Spouse

The employee's surviving spouse receives 50% of the average weekly wage of the deceased employee for life or until remarriage. Upon remarriage, a widow or widower receives a lump sum payment of compensation covering two years.

Children

Additional compensation is payable at a rate of 16-2/3% of the employee's average weekly wage for one or more children. If children are the sole survivors of the employee, 50% of the employee's average weekly wage is paid on behalf of the first child. Where more than one child is entitled to benefits, a maximum of 66-2/3% applies, shared equally.

Other Eligible Survivors

Other eligible survivors include parents, brothers, sisters, grandparents and grandchildren who were dependent on the employee.

Termination Provisions

Benefit payments to children, brothers, sisters, and grandchildren terminate when they reach 18, but may be extended to age 23 if the child or beneficiary is a student. Payments may continue indefinitely if a child remains incapable of self-support due to mental or physical disabilities.

Funeral Expenses

Reasonable funeral expenses are paid, up to a maximum of $3,000.

ALTERNATIVE DISPUTE RESOLUTION

A primary function of the Longshore and Harbor Workers' Compensation Program is to resolve claims through alternative dispute resolution methods. Claims that are resolved voluntarily in mediation are beneficial to all parties. Mediation avoids the delays encountered during the more formal procedures. Thus, the worker and his or her family do not have to suffer the financial difficulties associated with loss of income and benefits while their claims are pending.

In addition, mediation provides the employer a way to minimize litigation expenses. The government also saves money because mediation conferences are far less expensive than formal hearings. For example, an informal conference can be conducted for an estimated average of $300, while each formal hearing costs over $2,000. During fiscal year 2005, over 2,900 informal conferences were conducted in disputed claims.

If the parties cannot resolve their controversy through this informal method, they must request a formal hearing before an Administrative Law Judge.

CHAPTER 6:
THE BLACK LUNG BENEFITS PROGRAM

IN GENERAL

The Office of Workers' Compensation Programs ("OWCP") is responsible for administering The Black Lung Benefits Program.

The Federal Coal Mine Health and Safety Act of 1969 established a system for providing monthly cash payments and medical benefits to coal miners who suffer from pneumoconiosis—commonly referred to as "black lung disease"—a crippling respiratory condition, arising from their employment in or around the nation's coal mines. Surviving dependents of the miner are also entitled to benefits if he or she dies as a result of coal mine dust exposure.

The Black Lung Benefits Program was initially administered by the Social Security Administration (SSA) under Part B of the Act. However, in 1973, jurisdiction over new claims was transferred to the Department of Labor's Office of Workers' Compensation Programs ("OWCP"), under Part C of the Act, pursuant to the 1972 amendments to the Act. Claims filed prior to implementation of the 1972 amendments remain under the jurisdiction of the Social Security Administration.

Part B of the Act was set up as a temporary system to compensate past victims of coal mine dust exposure from government funds. Part C of the Act made the program permanent, and diverted the responsibility for payment of benefits from the U.S. Government to the coal mining industry.

In 1977, the Black Lung Benefits Reform Act (30 U.S.C. §§ 901–945) was enacted. Under the Act, monthly compensation payments and medical treatment are provided to coal miners who are totally disabled as a result of work-related black lung disease. In addition, if the disabled worker dies, his or her surviving dependents are eligible to receive benefits.

THE DIVISION OF COAL MINE WORKERS' COMPENSATION

The Division of Coal Mine Workers' Compensation ("DCMWC") has been set up to administer the Black Lung Benefits Program under the jurisdiction of the OWCP. The DCMWC adjudicates and processes disability compensation claims filed by the nation's coal miners and their survivors. There are 17 DCMWC offices nationwide, including a national office, nine district offices, and seven field stations.

The DCMWC accepts, reviews and makes eligibility determinations on benefit applications. Ninety-eight percent (98%) of the claims the DCMWC receives are decided within 180 days. The Division began fiscal year 2004 with 5,049 claims for benefits pending, and received an additional 4,489 claims during the year. Decisions were issued in 6,495 claims, leaving 3,149 determinations to be made. The Division also initiated payments to 1,549 survivors who were automatically entitled to benefits following the death of the miner. In 2004, a total of over 102,000 beneficiaries and 18,000 dependents received benefits.

A directory of Black Lung district offices and the jurisdictions they serve is set forth at Appendix 27.

INSURANCE REQUIREMENT

The Black Lung Benefits Act requires each coal mine operator to secure the payment of its benefits liability by either qualifying as a self-insurer or by purchasing and maintaining in force a commercial insurance contract, including a policy or contract procured from a State agency.

Any coal mine operator who is required to secure the payment of benefits and who fails to do so is subject to a civil penalty of up to $1,000 for each day of noncompliance. In addition, the president, treasurer and secretary of an uninsured coal mine operator that is a corporation may be liable for the payment of benefits owed to former employees.

Coal transportation and coal mine construction employers who are not also coal mine operators do not have to secure benefit payments in advance; however, once an employee is awarded benefits, the employer may be required to secure a bond or otherwise guarantee payment.

THE BLACK LUNG DISABILITY TRUST FUND

Generally, the last coal mine operator for whom the miner worked for a cumulative period of at least one year is usually responsible for the payment of benefits; however, the Black Lung Disability Trust Fund pays benefits when:

1. The miner's last coal mine employment was before January 1, 1970;

2. There is no liable coal mine operator; or

3. The miner's most recent employment of at least one year with an operator ended while the operator was authorized to self-insure, and such operator is no longer financially capable of securing benefit payments.

FILING A CLAIM UNDER THE BLACK LUNG ACT

To initiate a claim under the Black Lung Act, the worker must contact the DCMWC to fill out the appropriate claim forms. The DCMWC staff is available to assist disabled workers in completing the required forms. Claims may be filed by present and former coal miners and their surviving dependents, including surviving spouses, orphaned children, and totally dependent parents, brothers and sisters of the worker.

Once the claim has been opened, a medical examination of the worker will be held to determine whether he or she suffers from black lung disease. Under The Black Lung Amendments of 1981, certain presumptions of disease and disability were eliminated in claims filed on or after January 1, 1982.

The 1981 Amendments also eliminated presumptions of death due to pneumoconiosis in survivor claims. Thus, a survivor's claim filed on or after January 1, 1982, in which there has been no previous compensation award, must generally prove that the miner's death was causally related to pneumoconiosis.

Claims Processing Procedure

For all claims filed after January 19, 2001, following is the claims processing procedure.

Development of Evidence

When a claim for benefits is received, the district office obtains a complete history of the miner's employment from the claimant. They then gather other evidence regarding the nature and duration of the miner's employment, and any other information necessary to resolve the claim.

If the claim is filed by or on behalf of a miner, a complete pulmonary evaluation is authorized and paid for by the Black Lung Disability Trust

Fund. The miner must select a physician or medical facility to conduct the evaluation from a list provided by the district office. The list includes physicians and facilities located in the miner's state of residence and contiguous states who have been authorized to conduct complete pulmonary evaluations.

If the claim is filed by or on behalf of a survivor, the district office obtains whatever medical evidence is necessary and available to evaluate the claim.

Determination of Claim

In the event the district office determines that the evidence supports an award, and that there is no coal mine operator responsible ("Responsible Operator") for the payment of benefits, they will issue a proposed decision and order an award of benefits payable by the Trust Fund.

If the district office determines the evidence does not support an award, and that there is no operator responsible for the payment of benefits, they will issue a Schedule for the Submission of Additional Evidence. In that instance, the district office will be entitled to exercise the same rights as a responsible operator, subject to certain limitations.

In all cases where an operator may be liable for the payment of benefits, however, the district director will issue a Notice of Claim, set forth below.

Notice of Claim

If, after developing evidence related to the miner's employment history, the district office identifies one or more operators who may be liable for the payment of benefits should they be awarded, they send a Notice of Claim to those operators and their insurers of record. These operators are called "potentially liable operators."

The Notice advises the operators and insurers of the existence of the claim and that they have been made parties to the claim. The district office sends a copy of the claimant's application and all of the evidence that has developed pertaining to the miner's employment history along with the Notice.

An operator who receives a Notice of Claim must respond within 30 days of receipt of the Notice and indicate its intent to accept or contest its identification as a potentially liable operator. The operator must send a copy of its response to the claimant.

An operator who contests its potential liability must state the precise nature of its disagreement with its designation by accepting or denying that:

1. It was an operator for any period after June 30, 1973;

2. It employed the miner as a miner for a cumulative period of not less than one year;

3. The miner was exposed to coal mine dust while working for the operator;

4. It employed the miner at least one day after December 31, 1969;

5. It is capable of assuming liability for the payment of benefits.

If a notified operator fails to respond within 30 days, it will not be allowed to contest its liability for the payment of benefits in later proceedings on any of these five grounds, although it will retain the right to assert that another operator is liable for the particular claim involved.

Within 90 days of the date on which it receives the Notice of Claim, an operator may submit documentary evidence in support of its position. Documentary evidence relevant to the five grounds listed above must be submitted to the district office. If the operator does not submit the documentary evidence, it will not be admitted in any further proceedings absent a showing of exceptional circumstances.

The 30 and 90-day response periods may be extended for good cause shown if an extension request is filed with the district office before the response period expires.

Submission of Additional Evidence

Once the district office completes the development of medical evidence and receives responses and evidence regarding liability from potentially liable operators, they will issue a Schedule for the Submission of Additional Evidence ("Schedule"). The district office will send a copy of the Schedule, together with a copy of the evidence developed, to the claimant and all designated potentially liable operators.

The Schedule will include:

1. A summary of the results of the initial complete pulmonary evaluation or, for survivors' claims, a summary of the medical evidence developed;

2. The preliminary analysis of the medical evidence;

3. The designation of the "responsible operator" liable for the payment of benefits; and

4. A notice to the claimant and the designated responsible operator that they have a right to submit evidence on the claimant's entitlement to benefits and the responsible operator's liability for them.

The responsible operator named in the Schedule must respond to the schedule within 30 days of issuance indicating whether it agrees or disagrees with its designation as the responsible operator liable for the payment of benefits. If it does not timely respond, the responsible operator will be deemed to have accepted liability should benefits be awarded, and to have waived its right to challenge its liability in any further proceedings.

On the merits of the claim, the responsible operator may file a statement accepting the claimant's entitlement to benefits; otherwise, the responsible operator will be deemed to have contested the claim.

The Schedule will give the claimant and the responsible operator no less than 60 days to submit additional evidence on both the liability and entitlement issues, and will allow an additional 30 days within which to respond to evidence the other party submits. These time periods may be extended for good cause if an extension request is filed with the district office before the time period expires.

Development of Evidence by the Claimant and the Responsible Operator

Evidence Regarding Liability

During the time periods set out in the Schedule for the submission of affirmative and rebuttal evidence, the responsible operator may submit evidence to the district office demonstrating it is not the potentially liable operator that most recently employed the miner. Other parties as well may submit evidence regarding the designated responsible operator's liability.

There is no limitation on the amount of evidence regarding liability a party may submit. A copy of any documentary evidence submitted must be mailed to all other parties. Absent extraordinary circumstances, no documentary evidence pertaining to this aspect of the liability determination shall be admitted in any further proceeding conducted with respect to the claim unless it is submitted to the district office in compliance with the schedule for the submission of additional evidence.

Medical Evidence

Documentary medical evidence is treated differently. A party may submit medical evidence either to the district office in compliance with the Schedule, or to the assigned judge up to 20 days before the hearing, as discussed below.

The amount of documentary medical evidence a party may submit is limited. Each side may submit two chest x-ray interpretations, the results of two pulmonary function tests, two arterial blood gas studies and two medical reports as its affirmative case. Each side may also submit one autopsy report and one report of each biopsy.

In addition, each party may submit one piece of evidence in rebuttal of each piece of medical evidence submitted by the opposing party. In a case in which rebuttal evidence has been submitted, the party that originally submitted the evidence subjected to rebuttal may submit one additional statement to rehabilitate its evidence.

Documentary medical evidence exceeding these limits will not be admitted absent a showing of good cause. Notwithstanding these limitations, any record of a miner's hospitalization or medical treatment for a respiratory or pulmonary or related disease may be submitted. Each party must serve a copy of any documentary medical evidence it submits on all other parties. If the claimant is unrepresented, the district office will mail copies of the claimant's evidence to the other parties.

Claim Review

At the end of the period for submission of additional evidence, the district office will review the claim on the basis of all evidence submitted. They may notify additional operators of their potential liability, issue a new schedule for the submission of additional evidence identifying another potentially liable operator as the responsible operator, schedule an informal conference, issue a proposed Decision and Order, or take any other action that is considered appropriate. If the district office chooses to designate a different operator as the responsible operator, they will suspend development of medical evidence until the operator issue is resolved.

Informal Conference

The district office may determine that an informal conference is not warranted in a particular case. In that instance, they will generally issue a proposed Decision and Order at the conclusion of the period allowed for submission of evidence. The district office may, however, conduct an informal conference in any claim where it appears that a conference will assist in the voluntary resolution of any issue raised with respect to the claim.

The district office must hold the conference no later than 90 days after the conclusion of the period for submission of additional evidence unless a party, based on good cause shown, obtains an extension. A conference may be held only if all parties have representation. A coal mine operator that is either self-insured or covered by a commercial insurance policy for the claim in question, is considered represented.

The unexcused failure of any party to appear at an informal conference will be grounds for the imposition of sanctions: if the claimant does not appear, the claim may be denied as abandoned; if the operator does not appear, it will be deemed to have waived its right to contest its liability and, within the district office's discretion, to have waived its right to contest the claimant's eligibility.

At the end of the conference, the district office will prepare, and all parties will sign, a stipulation of contested and uncontested issues. Within 20 days after the termination of all conference proceedings, the district office will prepare and send to the parties a proposed Decision and Order.

Proposed Decision and Order

A proposed Decision and Order is a document, generally issued by the district office after the evidentiary development of the claim is completed, which attempts to resolve the claim on the basis of all of the evidence. The proposed Decision and Order will set forth the district office's determination of the merits of the claim, i.e., an award or a denial of benefits.

The proposed Decision and Order will also contain the district office's final designation of the responsible operator liable for the payment of benefits, and will dismiss all other potentially liable operators. The proposed Decision and Order will advise the parties of their right to request a formal hearing before the Department of Labor's Office of Administrative Law Judges.

If a party requests a hearing before the district office concludes it's adjudication of the claim, and the later determination is adverse to that party, the district office will forward the claim to the Office of Administrative Law Judges unless the party affirmatively states that it no longer desires a hearing.

Otherwise, within 30 days after the date the proposed Decision and Order is issued, any party may request a revision of the proposed Decision and Order or a hearing. Such requests must be made in writing to the district office and served on all other parties. If any party requests a hearing within the 30-day period, the district office will refer the claim to the Office of Administrative Law Judges. If no party responds to a proposed Decision and Order, it will become final and effective upon the expiration of the applicable 30-day period.

Administrative Hearing

Once a case is forwarded to the Office of Administrative Law Judges for hearing, it is assigned to an Administrative Law Judge (ALJ). In most cases, the ALJ will hold an oral hearing, receive testimony and other evidence in accordance with all applicable rules, and render a written decision on the claim.

The decision will address the relevant issues in dispute between the parties and adjudicate the claim. If the ALJ awards benefits, the responsible coal mine operator must begin paying monthly benefits to the claimant, and pay any retroactive benefits to which the claimant is entitled.

Reconsideration and Appeal

Any party dissatisfied with the ALJ's decision has 30 days from the date the decision is filed with OWCP either to: (1) ask the ALJ to reconsider their decision; or (2) appeal to the Department of Labor's Benefits Review Board.

The Board reviews the ALJ's decision to determine whether it is supported by substantial evidence and in accordance with law, and issues a written decision disposing of the appeal.

Any party adversely affected or aggrieved by the Board's decision may, within 60 days of its issuance, petition the court of appeals where the miner was exposed to coal mine dust for review of the Board's decision.

Finally, a party may seek review of the court's decision in the Supreme Court. If the award becomes final, the responsible coal mine operator must reimburse the Trust Fund for any benefits paid to the claimant on an interim basis.

Final Decision

Once a decision becomes final, there are no rights to further proceedings with respect to the claim except for filing a request for modification. At any time before one year after the decision becomes final, or within one year of the last payment of benefits, a party may request modification of the Decision and Order based upon a change in conditions or because of a mistake in a determination of fact.

A claimant whose previous claim was finally denied more than one year earlier may file a subsequent claim for benefits. The subsequent claim will be processed and adjudicated in the same manner as an initial claim, except that the claim will be denied unless the claimant demonstrates that one of the applicable conditions of entitlement has changed since the date on which the order denying the prior claim became final.

BENEFITS UNDER THE BLACK LUNG ACT

Monetary Benefits

Once eligibility under the Black Lung Benefits Act has been established, a totally disabled miner is eligible to receive monthly benefits. Benefit payments are generally equal to a portion of the monthly pay rate for federal employees.

The Black Lung Monthly Benefits Rate for 2007

On January 1, 2007, new monthly rates went into effect for Black Lung benefits that include a 1.7% increase over the 2006 benefit amounts. Benefit rates are set in accordance with the Federal Coal Mine Health and Safety Act, as amended, Section 412(a)(1). The new rates are set forth below.

Part-B Black Lung Monthly Benefit Rates

Payments for Part B claims approved by the Social Security Administration are received around the 3rd of each month. The new rates are as follows:

Primary beneficiary—$584.00

Primary beneficiary and one dependent—$876.00

Primary beneficiary and two dependents—$1022.00

Primary beneficiary and three or more dependents—$1,168.00

Part-C Black Lung Monthly Benefit Rates

Payments for Part C claims approved by the U.S. Department of Labor are received around the 15th of each month. The new rates are as follows:

Primary beneficiary—$584.40

Primary beneficiary and one dependent—$876.50

Primary beneficiary and two dependents—$1022.60

Primary beneficiary and three or more dependents—$1,168.70

Medical Benefits

In addition to the monetary payments, the Act provides for the payment of medical and rehabilitation benefits to the miner for respiratory conditions related to treatment for black lung disease. The medical benefits are payable for the life of the miner and include not only treatment and rehabilitative measures but also the reasonable cost of travel to acquire medical attention.

Two types of medical services related to black lung disease are provided:

Diagnostic Testing

Miner-claimants are entitled to diagnostic testing to determine the presence or absence of black lung disease and the degree of associated disability. Diagnostic testing includes a chest x-ray, pulmonary function study (breathing test), arterial blood gas study, and a physical examination.

Medical Coverage

Miners who receive monthly benefits are also entitled to medical coverage for treatment of black lung disease and disability. Medical coverage includes, but is not limited to, costs for prescription drugs, office visits, and hospitalizations.

Also provided, with specific approval, are items of durable medical equipment, such as hospital beds, home oxygen, and nebulizers; outpatient pulmonary rehabilitation therapy; and home nursing visits.

In fiscal year 2004, approximately 336,000 medical treatment bills were processed. Medical treatment bills are monitored and subject to audit to ensure that the requested treatments are necessary and that payments are correct.

Death Benefits

If the miner succumbs to black lung disease, the miner's survivors are entitled to monthly benefit payments as set forth above. The miner's surviving widow is entitled to receive the same monthly benefit payment as the deceased miner. If the miner has no surviving widow, a single surviving child will also receive the same monthly benefit amount. The benefit amount increases incrementally with each subsequent surviving child.

If there is no surviving widow or child, the miner's dependent parents or siblings will receive a monthly benefit amount at the same rate as the children. The miner's surviving widow and dependents are not eligible for the medical or rehabilitation benefits.

CHAPTER 7:
THE ENERGY EMPLOYEES'
OCCUPATIONAL ILLNESS COMPENSATION
PROGRAM

IN GENERAL

The Energy Employees Occupational Illness Compensation Program (EEOICP) provides benefits authorized by the Energy Employees Occupational Illness Compensation Program Act (EEOICPA). The EEOICP began on July 31, 2001 with the implementation of Part B of the program. Part E of the Program went into effect on October 28, 2004.

The mission of the program is to provide lump-sum compensation and health benefits to eligible employees and former employees of the Department of Energy (DOE) and its predecessor agencies, as well as contractors and subcontractors involved in nuclear weapons production and testing programs, who have suffered certain illnesses caused by exposure to radiation, beryllium or silica. In addition, certain survivors of deceased workers may be entitled to lump sum compensation.

The Department of Labor's Office of Workers' Compensation Programs (OWCP) is responsible for adjudicating and administering the program.

ELIGIBILITY

A worker or former worker may be eligible for benefits if:

1. He or she has or had radiation-induced cancers, beryllium diseases or silicosis; and

2. He or she was exposed to radiation, beryllium or silica while working in the nuclear weapons industry for DOE or its contractors or subcontractors.

In addition, uranium miners, millers and ore transporters may be eligible for benefits if they have received an award of benefits under Section 5 of the Radiation Exposure Compensation Act from the Department of Justice.

Survivorship Rules

If a covered worker is deceased at the time of payment, certain survivors are eligible to receive benefits, as follows:

1. If the deceased employee is survived by a spouse for at least one year immediately before the death of that individual, the spouse receives the entire lump-sum benefit.

2. If the covered employee is also survived by at least one child of the covered employee who is (a) living and a minor at the time of payment; and (b) not a recognized natural child or adopted child of the surviving spouse, then half of the compensation shall be paid to the surviving spouse, and the other half of the compensation shall be paid in equal shares to each child of the deceased covered employee who is a minor at the time of payment.

3. If the covered employee is not survived by a spouse but is survived by a child, including a recognized natural child, a stepchild who lived with an individual in a regular parent-child relationship, and an adopted child, all of the children of the covered employee who are living at the time of payment share the lump sum equally.

4. If the covered employee is not survived by a spouse or children, but is survived by a parent, including fathers and mothers through adoption, the parents of the covered employee who are living at the time of payment share the lump sum equally.

5. If the covered employee is not survived by a spouse, children, or parents, but is survived by grandchildren, the grandchildren of the covered employee who are living at the time of payment share the lump sum equally.

6. If the covered employee is not survived by a spouse, children, parents, or grandchildren but is survived by grandparents, the grandparents of the covered employee who are living at the time of payment share the lump sum equally.

Total survivor compensation under the program cannot exceed $175,000.

PART B BENEFITS

Lump Sum of $150,000 and Medical Expenses

Under Part B of the program, compensation of $150,000, and payment of medical expenses from the date a claim is filed is available to the following covered individuals:

1. Employees of the Department of Energy (DOE), its contractors or subcontractors, and atomic weapons employers with radiation-induced cancer if:

(a) The employee developed cancer after working at a covered facility of the Department of Energy, its contractors and subcontractors; and

(b) The employee's cancer is determined at least as likely as not related to that employment in accordance with guidelines issued by the Department of Health and Human Services; or

(c) The employee is determined to be a member of the Special Exposure Cohort. The Special Exposure Cohort includes employees who worked at least 250 days before February 1, 1992, for the Department of Energy or its contractors or subcontractors at one or more of the three Gaseous Diffusion Plants located at Oak Ridge, TN, Paducah, KY or Portsmouth, OH or who were exposed to radiation related to certain underground nuclear tests at Amchitka, AK, and developed one of certain listed cancers.

2. Employees of the Department of Energy, its contractors and subcontractors, and designated beryllium vendors who worked at covered facilities where they were exposed to beryllium produced or processed for the Department of Energy who developed Chronic Beryllium Disease; and

3. Employees of the Department of Energy or its contractors and subcontractors who worked at least 250 days during the mining of tunnels at underground nuclear weapons tests sites in Nevada or Alaska and who developed chronic silicosis.

Lump Sum of $50,000 and Medical Expenses

Compensation of $50,000 and payment of medical expenses from the date a claim is filed is available for

1. Uranium workers, or their survivors, previously awarded benefits by the Department of Justice under Section 5 of the Radiation Exposure Compensation Act.

2. Employees of the Department of Energy, its contractors and subcontractors who were exposed to beryllium on the job and now have beryllium sensitivity will receive medical monitoring to check for Chronic Beryllium Disease.

PART E BENEFITS

Under Part E of the program, compensation and payment of medical expenses is available to employees of DOE contractors and subcontractors, or their survivors, who develop an illness due to exposure to toxic substances at certain DOE facilities.

Uranium miners, millers, and ore transporters are also eligible for benefits if they develop an illness as a result of toxic exposure and worked at a facility covered under Section 5 of the Radiation Exposure Compensation Act (RECA).

Under Part E, a toxic substance is not limited to radiation but includes things such as chemicals, solvents, acids and metals.

Variable Compensation

Under the program, variable compensation up to $250,000 is determined based on wage loss, impairment, and survivorship. Medical expenses are not included in the $250,000 cap.

Wage Loss

Wage loss is based on the number of years that the employee was either (1) unable to work; or (2) sustained a reduction in earnings as a result of the illness. Wage loss compensation is payable for years of lost wages that are prior to regular Social Security Retirement age—usually age 65.

Wage loss compensation is calculated as follows:

1. $10,000 for each year in which wages were 25–50% less than the Average Annual Wage (AAW). The AAW is the average earnings for the 12 quarters (36 months) prior to the first quarter of wage loss; and

2. $15,000 for each year in which wages were less than 50% of the AAW.

Impairment

Impairment is a decrease in the functioning of a body part or organ as it affects the whole body, as a result of the illness. An impairment rating is performed once the claimant has reached Maximum Medical

Improvement—i.e. the condition is stabilized and is unlikely to improve with additional medical treatment.

Impairment compensation is calculated as $2500 for each one percent of whole body impairment. Survivor benefits include compensation of at least $125,000.

If the employee sustained wage loss as a result of the covered illness, and that wage loss was prior to Social Security Retirement age, additional compensation may be awarded as follows:

1. $0—If the employee had less than 10 years of wage loss;

2. $25,000—If the employee had between 10 and 19 years of wage loss; or

3. $50,000—If the employee had 20 years or more wage loss.

Survivorship

Eligible survivors may receive compensation if the employee's death was caused, contributed to or aggravated by the covered illness.

FILING A CLAIM

Eligible claimants are required to file certain forms in order for the OWCP to adjudicate the claim. These forms provide the OWCP with basic information.

1. Workers and former workers must complete Form EE-1 (Claim for Benefits under Energy Employees Occupational Illness Compensation Program Act).

2. Survivors must complete Form EE-2 (Claim for Survivor Benefits under Energy Employees Occupational Illness Compensation Program Act).

In addition to the above forms, the claimant must also submit the following forms:

1. A completed Form EE-3 (Employment History for Claim under Energy Employees Occupational Illness Compensation Program Act).

2. Medical evidence of the illness as outlined in Form EE-7 (Medical Requirements under the Energy Employees Occupational Illness Compensation Program Act (EEOICPA)). Each written medical document must be a clear readable copy.

In addition to information about a deceased worker's employment history and illness, a survivor will need proof of his or her relationship to the deceased employee, such as marriage or birth certificates, and a death certificate.

Once a claim is submitted, the OWCP will seek information from the Department of Energy (DOE) and its contractors concerning the employment history claimed on Form EE-3. The DOE will certify that it agrees or disagrees with the employment information provided on the EE-3 or that it has no relevant records.

In the event that additional information is required, the OWCP will ask the claimant to provide any employment records in their possession and, if necessary, assist the claimant in obtaining records from other sources such as social security records, pension and union records, or statements by co-workers or other contacts.

The OWCP has established district offices and resource centers where workers and their families can receive assistance in filing claim forms for the program.

Directories of the EEOICP district offices and resource centers administering the program are set forth in Appendix 28 and 29 respectively.

In addition, claim forms may be obtained by calling and requesting the forms, or downloading the forms on the internet, as follows:

1. Toll-Free Call Center: 1-866-888-3322; or

2. Internet: www.dol.gov/esa/regs/compliance/owcp/eeoicp/main.htm

The claim for benefits may be filed in person at the district office or resource center, or it can be mailed to the district office having jurisdiction over the state where the covered employee last worked. There is no deadline for filing a claim, however, medical benefits for any job-related illness start from the date the claim is filed.

THE CLAIMS PROCESS

After the district office receives the claims package, it reviews the medical evidence and employment verification. A "Recommended Decision" is then made by the district office. The Recommended Decision explains the basis for the proposed decision and allows the claimant the opportunity to request a hearing, a review of the written record, or a waiver of additional review.

Recommended Decisions are then referred to the Final Adjudication Branch for a Final Decision. The Final Decision results in the payment of compensation or the denial of the claim.

Lump Sum Payment

At the time a Final Decision accepting the claim is issued by the Final Adjudication Branch, the claimant will be informed of the amount of the award and sent an "Acceptance of Payment" form.

Obtaining Medical Benefits

Once a determination has been made that a covered employee is entitled to medical benefits, the OWCP will cover all medical costs related to the accepted condition. This includes necessary medical services, prescriptions, appliances, or supplies that a qualified physician prescribes or recommends, retroactive to the date the claim was filed, but not before July 31, 2001—the start date of the program.

If there is any doubt as to whether a specific service, appliance or supply is necessary to treat the occupational illness, the claimant should consult the district office prior to obtaining it.

Any qualified physician or qualified hospital may provide services, appliances and supplies. A qualified provider of medical support services may also furnish appropriate services, appliances, and supplies. Prescription medications may also be covered.

The claimant will receive a medical benefits identification card, which he or she will need to show to their physician and any other authorized medical provider treating his or her condition. The card is accompanied with instructions and a phone number to call to activate the card. This card will instruct any physician, hospital, durable medical equipment supplier or other health care providers to bill the EEOICP directly so that the claimant will not have to pay for medical treatment covered under the program.

To bill the EEOICP directly, providers must be enrolled in the EEOICP. For information about enrollment and billing, providers can contact the DOL at 1-866-272-2682. The OWCP will explain the program to the provider(s) and give them the necessary forms required for submitting their bills for reimbursement.

To seek reimbursement for out-of-pocket expenses for medical treatment, prescription medication and medical supplies, the claimant must complete and submit Form EE-915, (Claim for Medical Reimbursement under Energy Employees Occupational Illness Compensation Program Act).

Medical treatment that was provided to an employee who dies before a claim is accepted will be paid, as long as such treatment was provided on or after the date the employee filed the claim, and a survivor may receive payment.

A sample Claim for Benefits Under the Energy Employees' Occupational Illness Compensation Act (Form EE-1) is set forth in Appendix 30.

CHAPTER 8:
ADDITIONAL FEDERAL DISABILITY PROGRAMS

THE FEDERAL EMPLOYMENT LIABILITY ACT

In 1908, Congress passed the Federal Employers' Liability Act (FELA). The goal of FELA is to provide railroad employees with a safe place to work, and provide benefits to employees and the families if a railroad employee is injured on the job.

Unlike the worker's compensation programs discussed in this Almanac, FELA is not a "no-fault" statute, and benefits are not awarded automatically. As set forth below, FELA requires the injured employee to prove that the railroad was liable for causing his or her injury. Once the employee proves that the employer is liable, he or she is entitled to full compensation.

Under the law, a railroad employee is entitled to damages when: (1) The road on which the employee works is engaged in interstate commerce, e.g., it runs across state lines or handles interstate freight; and (2) injury to the worker is the result of the negligence of any officer, agent or employee of the railroad, or the injury is caused by any defect in the cars, engines, appliances, machinery, track, road bed, or any other equipment of the road.

Under FELA, injured employees can seek compensation for wage loss, future wage loss, medical expenses and treatments, pain and suffering, and for partial or permanent disability. If an employee is killed on the job, survivors are entitled to recover death benefits.

Damages

The amount of money an injured railroad employee may recover depends on (1) the seriousness of his or her injuries, and (2) whether the injured employee can demonstrate that the injury was caused by the negligence of the railroad or its employees in failing to provide a safe workplace, or by a defect in the equipment.

The contributory negligence of the railroad employee is not a bar to recovery, although compensation may be reduced in proportion to the employee's degree of negligence unless the employee's injuries were caused by the employer's violation of a safety statute designed to protect employees. In addition, the injured employee cannot be held to have assumed the risks of employment if their injury or death was caused by negligence or the violation of a safety statute.

Filing a Claim

You should immediately report the accident and your injury to your union. You should also notify your employer. You are required to complete an accident report, however, you should not sign any statements concerning the accident until you have first consulted with a legal representative familiar with FELA, who can advise you of your rights. Most union agreements with railroads provide that an employee is entitled to representation. In addition, under FELA, an injured employee has the right to representation during all stages of their claim.

Although you are required to complete the accident report as soon as possible, if you are in extreme pain, you may be able to delay filling out the form. You do not want to unwittingly defeat your case by signing a statement that contains inaccuracies that may undermine your claim of negligence against the employer. Request copies of every document you sign, at the time you sign them, including the accident report and any written statements concerning the accident. You will need copies of these documents to pursue your claim.

Insofar as you will be required to demonstrate negligence or unsafe working conditions, it is important to keep a journal which details the facts surrounding the accident. This includes the exact time and place of the accident, and the manner in which the accident happened. You should obtain the names and addresses of any witnesses to the accident. If permitted, you should photograph the scene of the accident. It is also important to document your physical condition after the accident; therefore, you should have your injuries photographed.

You do not have to fear retaliation if you report your accident and injury. Under the law, employers are prohibited from retaliating against an employee who files a claim for benefits:

§ 60. Penalty for suppression of voluntary information incident to accidents.

"Any contract, rule, regulation, or device whatsoever, the purpose, intent, or effect of which shall be to prevent employees of any common carrier from furnishing voluntarily information to a person in interest as to the facts incident to the injury or death of any employee, shall be void, and whoever, by threat, intimidation, order, rule, contract, regulation, or device whatsoever, shall attempt to prevent any person from furnishing voluntarily such information to a person in interest, or whoever discharges or otherwise disciplines or attempts to discipline any employee for furnishing voluntarily such information to a person in interest, shall, upon conviction thereof, be punished by a fine of not more than $1,000 or imprisoned for not more than one year, or by both such fine and imprisonment, for each offense ..."

Settlement

If you are able to establish your injury claim by showing that the employer's negligence or an unsafe workplace caused your accident, the following factors must be taken into account when considering a settlement offer:

1. The seriousness of your injury, e.g., permanent, temporary, total or partial disability.

2. The amount of your past lost wages and the amount of wages you will likely lose in the future due to your injury.

3. The amount of money you have spent on medical treatment, including medical bills, medication, hospitalization, surgery, etc.

4. The amount of money you expect to spend on future medical treatment.

5. Vocational evaluation and retraining, if necessary.

6. A sum of money that represents your past, present and future pain and suffering.

If you are unable to settle your injury claim, you can bring a lawsuit in either a state court or Federal court. You are entitled to a trial by jury.

THE MERCHANT MARINE ACT

The Merchant Marine Act—also called "The Jones Act"—is a federal law enacted in 1920 that provides seaman with workers' compensation coverage. Under the Act, maritime workers are provided the same protection from employer negligence as the Federal Employment Liability Act affords railroad workers discussed above.

Covered Employees

In 1995, the U.S. Supreme Court ruled that any worker who spends more than thirty percent of his time in the service of a vessel on navigable waters qualifies as a seaman under the Merchant Marine Act. [Chandris, Inc., v. Latsis, 515 U.S. 347, 115 S.Ct. 2172 (1995)]

Requirements for U.S. Flagged Vessels

The Merchant Marine Act requires U.S.-flagged vessels to be built in the United States, owned by United States citizens, and documented under the laws of the United States. To be documented in the United States means that the vessel is registered, enrolled, or licensed under the laws of the United States. In addition, 75% of the crew and all of the officers of the vessel must be United States citizens. Vessels that meet the above requirements are designated the "Jones Act fleet."

Workers' Compensation Provisions

Under the Merchant Marine Act, injured seaman may recover damages for pain and suffering from their ship owner or employer if the ship owner, captain, or fellow crew members are determined to be negligent. An action under the Act may be brought either in a U.S. federal court or in a state court.

The Merchant Marine Act expands coverage of the Federal Employment Liability Act that pertains to recovery by railroad workers, by making it applicable to sailors. The applicable provision reads as follows:

> Any seaman who shall suffer personal injury in the course of his employment may, at his election, maintain an action for damages at law, with the right of trial by jury, and in such action all statutes of the United States modifying or extending the common-law right or remedy in cases of personal injury to railway employees shall apply; and in case of the death of any seaman as a result of any such personal injury the personal representative of such seaman may maintain an action for damages at law with the right of trial by jury, and in such action all statutes of the United States conferring or regulating the right of action for death in the case of railway employees shall be applicable. [46 U.S.C. 688(a)].

The Merchant Marine Act entitles injured sailors to "transportation, wages, maintenance, and cure." This means that the ship owner or employer must transport the injured sailor home; pay the sailor his or her wages while unable to work; and provide medical care for the sailor's injuries until the sailor has recovered to the degree possible.

VETERANS' DISABILITY PROGRAMS

If you were injured while serving in the United States military, you may be entitled to a number of disability benefits. The United States Department of Veterans Affairs (VA) administers disability programs for service members who are disabled as a result of their military service.

Information regarding specific benefit programs may be obtained from the Veterans Administration, by calling 1-800-827-1000.

Disability Compensation

Disability compensation is a benefit paid to a veteran because of injuries or diseases that happened while he or she was on active duty in the military. Disability compensation is also paid to a veteran if an injury or illness was made worse by active military service. There is no deadline to apply for disability benefits.

Eligibility

You may be eligible for disability compensation benefits if:

1. You were discharged under other than dishonorable conditions; and

2. You have a service-related disability.

Amount of Benefits

The disability compensation program pays monthly benefits to military veterans who are determined to be at least 10% degree disabled as a result of their military service. The degree of disability determination attempts to represent the average loss in wages resulting from service-connected injuries and diseases, and their complications in civil occupations. Generally, the degrees of disability specified are also designed to compensate for considerable loss of working time from exacerbations or illnesses.

The amount of the basic disability compensation benefit based on the 2006 rates ranges from $115 to $2,471 per month, depending on your degree of disability. Disability compensation benefits are tax-free. You may be entitled to an additional amount in certain cases, e.g., (1) if you have a severe disability or loss of limb(s); (2) you have a spouse, children or dependent parents; or (3) you have a seriously disabled spouse.

Applying for Disability Compensation Benefits

You can apply for disability compensation benefits by filing an Application for Compensation or Pension (VA Form 21-526). The following items must accompany your application, if applicable:

1. Dependency records, such as your marriage certificate or your child's birth certificate.

2. Medical evidence of your disability, such as doctor and hospital reports.

Related Benefits

Related benefits to which you may be entitled include:

1. Priority Medical Care

2. Vocational Rehabilitation

3. Clothing Allowance

4. Service-Disabled Veterans Insurance

5. Grants for Specially Adapted Housing

6. Automobile Grant & Adaptive Equipment

7. Federal Employment Preference

8. State/Local Veterans Benefits

9. Military Exchange & Commissary Privileges

Disability Compensation for Sexual or Personal Trauma

The VA has established a disability compensation program to assist male and female veterans who have suffered sexual or other personal trauma while serving on active military duty. Sexual or personal trauma is defined as events of human design that threaten or inflict harm, including rape, physical assault, domestic battering, and stalking.

Veterans who have experienced sexual or personal trauma may struggle with fear, anxiety, embarrassment, or profound anger as a result of their experiences. They are often diagnosed with post traumatic stress disorder (PTSD) secondary to sexual or personal trauma. Post traumatic stress disorder is defined as a recurrent emotional reaction to a terrifying, uncontrollable or life-threatening event. The symptoms may develop immediately after the event, or may be delayed for years. The symptoms include:

1. Sleep disturbances and nightmares;

2. Emotional instability;

3. Feelings of fear and anxiety;

4. Impaired concentration;

5. Flashbacks; and

6. Problems in intimate and other interpersonal relations.

Eligibility

You may be eligible for disability compensation benefits if:

1. You were discharged under other than dishonorable conditions; and

2. You are currently suffering from disabling symptoms related to sexual or personal trauma.

Amount of Benefits

The disability compensation program pays monthly benefits to military veterans who are suffering from disabilities due to sexual or personal trauma.

Applying for Disability Compensation Benefits

You can apply for disability compensation benefits relating to sexual or personal trauma by filing an Application for Compensation or Pension (VA Form 21-526). In addition, VA counselors are available for assistance.

Disability Pension

The VA also pays a monthly disability pension to wartime veterans who have limited income and are no longer able to work. There is no deadline to apply for a disability pension.

Eligibility

You may be eligible for disability compensation benefits if:

1. You were discharged under other than dishonorable conditions; and

2. You served 90 days or more of active duty with at least 1 day during a period of war time. However, anyone who enlists after September 7, 1980 generally has to serve at least 24 months or the full period for which a person was called or ordered to active duty in order to receive any benefits based on that period of service;

3. You are permanently and totally disabled, or are age 65 or older; and

4. Your countable family income is below a yearly limit set by law.

Amount of Benefits

The VA pays the difference between your countable family income and the yearly income limit established by the VA for your family size. This amount is generally paid in 12 equal monthly payments.

Applying for Disability Pension Benefits

You can apply for disability pension benefits by filing an Application for Compensation or Pension (VA Form 21-526). The following items must accompany your application, if applicable:

1. Dependency records, such as your marriage certificate or your child's birth certificate.

2. Medical evidence of your disability, such as doctor and hospital reports.

Related Benefits

Related benefits to which you may be entitled include:

1. Vocational Rehabilitation Program; and

2. Medical Care.

Vocational Rehabilitation

The VA operates a vocational rehabilitation program to assist eligible disabled veterans find and maintain suitable employment. The VA also helps seriously disabled veterans achieve independence in daily living. Some of the services the VA provides include:

1. Job Search—The VA operates a job search program that prepares veterans with service-connected disabilities for their return to work. Veterans are also given assistance in finding and maintaining suitable employment.

2. Vocational Evaluation—The VA conducts an evaluation of the disabled veteran's abilities, skills, interests and needs.

3. Career Exploration—The VA offers the disabled veteran vocational counseling and planning.

4. Vocational Training—The VA provides disabled veterans with training, such as on-the-job training and non-paid work experience, if needed.

5. Education Training—The VA provides disabled veterans with educational training so that they can accomplish their rehabilitation goal.

6. Rehabilitation Service—The VA offers supportive rehabilitation and counseling services and, for veterans who have more serious disabilities.

Services generally last up to 48 months, but they can be extended in certain instances.

Eligibility

To be eligible for vocational rehabilitation services, you must meet the following criteria:

1. You must first be awarded a monthly VA disability compensation payment, with limited exceptions;

2. You must have served in the military on or after September 16, 1940;

3. Your service-connected disabilities must be rated at least 20% disabled by the VA or 10% disabled if you have a serious employment handicap; and

4. It has been less than 12 years since the VA notified you of your eligibility status, unless certain conditions prevented you from vocational rehabilitation training, in which case your eligibility for this benefit may be extended.

Amount of Benefits

If you need vocational rehabilitation training, the VA will pay for the training costs, including tuition and fees, books, supplies, equipment, and special services, if needed. The VA also pays a monthly benefit—called a subsistence allowance—to help you with your living expenses while you are in training.

Applying for Vocational Rehabilitation Benefits

You can apply for vocational rehabilitation benefits by filing a Disabled Veterans Application for Vocational Rehabilitation (VA Form 28-1900).

Related Benefits

Related benefits to which you may be entitled include:

1. Work Study Allowance;

2. Tutorial Assistance; and

3. Revolving Fund Loan.

Housing Assistance for Disabled Veterans and Military Personnel

In addition to the guaranteed loans available to eligible veterans and military personnel, the VA offers special grants to certain disabled veterans and military personnel, in order to acquire housing suitable, or adapt current housing, according to their needs. There is no time limit for a veteran to apply for a VA home loan.

Burial Benefits

The VA offers certain benefits and services for deceased veterans. All eligible veterans are entitled to: (1) a headstone to mark the veteran's grave; (2) a presidential memorial certificate; (3) an American flag to drape the veteran's casket; (4) a $300 allowance for burial and funeral expenses; (5) a $300 allowance for a plot or burial in a VA national cemetery.

In addition, the burial allowance for veterans who die due to a service-related cause is increased to $2,000.

There is no time limitation for making a claim for reimbursement of burial expenses for a service-related death. In all other cases, a reimbursement claim must be filed within 2 years of the date of the veteran's burial.

Dependents and Survivors Benefits

The VA pays dependency and indemnity compensation to certain survivors of: (1) service members who died while on active duty; (2) veterans who died from service-related disabilities; and (3) certain veterans who were being paid a 100% disability compensation at their time of death.

In addition, a death pension is payable to some surviving spouses and children of deceased wartime veterans. This benefit is based on the financial need of the family.

There is no time limit to apply for the dependents' and survivors' benefits.

Health Care Services

The VA provides a variety of health care services, including:

1. Hospital, outpatient medical, dental, pharmacy, and prosthetic services.

2. Domiciliary, nursing home, and community-based residential care.

3. Sexual trauma counseling.

4. Specialized health care for women veterans.

5. Health and rehabilitation programs for homeless veterans.

6. Readjustment counseling.

7. Alcohol and drug dependency treatment.

8. Medical evaluation for military service exposure, including Gulf War, Agent Orange, radiation, or other environmental hazards.

In addition to the above, the VA will provide combat veterans with free medical care for any illness that is possibly associated with service against a hostile force in a war after the Gulf War or during a period of hostility after November 11, 1998. This benefit may be provided for two years from the veteran's release from active duty.

Service-Disabled Veterans Insurance

Service-Disabled Veterans Insurance—also called "RH Insurance—is life insurance for service-disabled veterans. The basic coverage is $10,000. However, if the premium payments for the basic policy are waived due to the veteran's total disability, he or she may be eligible for a supplemental policy of up to $20,000. Veterans have two years after being notified of their service-connected disability to apply for basic insurance coverage.

Benefits for Selected Reserve and National Guard Members

Active Duty Service

Selected Reserve and National Guard members who served on regular active duty are eligible for the same VA benefits as other veterans, as discussed above. The member must also meet the same length of service requirement for any benefit.

Non-Active Duty Service

Selected Reserve and National Guard members may be eligible for the following VA benefits based on non-active duty service:

Compensation

Selected Reserve and National Guard members are eligible for a monthly benefit paid for disabilities that resulted from a disease or injury incurred while on active duty for training, or an injury, heart attack or stroke incurred during inactive duty for training. These disabilities are considered "service-connected" disabilities.

Medical Care

Selected Reserve and National Guard members are entitled to medical care for service-connected disabilities.

Vocational Rehabilitation

Selected Reserve and National Guard members who have service-connected disabilities are entitled to services and assistance in finding and maintaining suitable employment. The VA also helps members with serious service-connected disabilities achieve independence in daily living.

SOCIAL SECURITY DISABILITY INSURANCE

The Social Security Amendments of 1954 initiated a disability insurance program that provides workers with additional coverage against economic insecurity if they have to stop working at any time before age 65 due to health reasons. Under the social security disability insurance program, you may be eligible for benefits if:

1. You meet the Social Security Administration (SSA) standard for disability; and

2. You are deemed "insured" because you have worked the required number of quarters for a person your age, and you contributed to the Social Security system.

If you are deemed disabled, benefits may start as early as five months after you become disabled. In addition, you may be entitled to retroactive benefits for up to one year, depending on how much time elapsed between the onset of your disability and the date you filed your application for benefits.

APPENDIX 1:
DIRECTORY OF OFFICE OF WORKERS' COMPENSATION PROGRAMS (OWCP) DISTRICT OFFICES

DISTRICT	AREA COVERED	ADDRESS	TELEPHONE	INTERACTIVE VOICE RESPONSE SYSTEM
District Office 1— Boston	Connecticut, Maine, Massachusetts, New Hampshire, Rhode Island, and Vermont	JFK Federal Building Rm. E-260 Boston, MA 02203	617-565-2137	617-565-1931
District Office 2— New York	New Jersey, New York, Puerto Rico, and the Virgin Islands	201 Varick Street Room 740 New York, NY 10014	212-337-2075	Same
District Office 3— Philadelphia	Delaware, Pennsylvania, and West Virginia	Gateway Building Room 15200 3535 Market Street, Philadelphia, PA 19104	215-596-1457	Same

DISTRICT	AREA COVERED	ADDRESS	TELEPHONE	INTERACTIVE VOICE RESPONSE SYSTEM
District Office 6— Jackson Ville	Alabama, Florida, Georgia, Kentucky, Mississippi, No. Carolina, So. Carolina, and Tennessee	214 North Hogan Street Suite 1006 Jacksonville, FL 32202	904-357-4777	904-357-4778
District Office 9— Cleve Land	Indiana, Michigan, and Ohio	1240 East Ninth Street, Room 851 Cleveland, OH 44199	216-522-3800	216-522-2867
District Office 10— Chicago	Illinois, Minnesota, and Wisconsin	230 South Dearborn Street Eighth Floor Chicago, IL 60604	312-353-5656	Same
District 11— Kansas City	Iowa, Kansas, Missouri, and Nebraska; all employees of the Department of Labor, except Job Corps enrollees, and their relatives	City Center Square 1100 Main Street Suite 750 Kansas City, MO 64105	816-426-2195	Same
District 12— Denver	Colorado, Montana, No. Dakota, So. Dakota, Utah, and Wyoming	1801 California Street Suite 915 Denver, CO 80202-2614	303-844-1310	Same
District 13— San Francisco	Arizona, California, Hawaii, and Nevada	71 Stevenson Street San Francisco, CA 94105	415-975-4090	Same

DISTRICT	AREA COVERED	ADDRESS	TELEPHONE	INTERACTIVE VOICE RESPONSE SYSTEM
District Office 14— Seattle	Alaska, Idaho, Oregon, and Washington	1111 Third Avenue Suite 615 Seattle, WA 98101-3212	206-553-5508	Same
District Office 16— Dallas	Arkansas, Louisiana, New Mexico, Oklahoma, and Texas	525 Griffin Street Room 100 Dallas, TX 75202	214-767-4707	214-767-4360
District Office 25— Washington, D.C.	District of Columbia, Maryland, and Virginia; all areas outside the U.S., its possessions, territories, and trust territories; and all special claims	800 N. Capitol Street NW Room 800 Washington, D.C. 20211	202-565-9770	Same

APPENDIX 2:
THE FEDERAL EMPLOYEES'
COMPENSATION ACT—SELECTED
PROVISIONS
[5 U.S.C. §§ 8101 – 8193]

§8101. Definitions [Omitted]

§8102. Compensation for disability or death of employee

(a) The United States shall pay compensation as specified by this sub-chapter for the disability or death of an employee resulting from personal injury sustained while in the performance of his duty, unless the injury or death is—

(1) caused by willful misconduct of the employee;

(2) caused by the employee's intention to bring about the injury or death of himself or of another; or

(3) proximately caused by the intoxication of the injured employee.

(b) Disability or death from a war-risk hazard or during or as a result of capture, detention, or other restraint by a hostile force or individual, suffered by an employee who is employed outside the continental United States or in Alaska or in the areas and installations in the Republic of Panama made available to the United States pursuant to the Panama Canal Treaty of 1977 and related agreements (as described in section 3(a) of the Panama Canal Act of 1979), is deemed to have resulted from personal injury sustained while in the performance of his duty, whether or not the employee was engaged in the course of employment when the disability or disability resulting in death occurred or when he was taken by the hostile force or individual. This subsection does not apply to an individual—

(1) whose residence is at or in the vicinity of the place of his employment and who was not living there solely because of the exigencies of his employment, unless he was injured or taken while engaged in the course of his employment; or

(2) who is a prisoner of war or a protected individual under the Geneva Conventions of 1949 and is detained or utilized by the United States.

This subsection does not affect the payment of compensation under this subchapter derived otherwise than under this subsection, but compensation for disability or death does not accrue for a period for which pay, other benefit, or gratuity from the United States accrues to the disabled individual or his dependents on account of detention by the enemy or because of the same disability or death, unless that pay, benefit, or gratuity is refunded or renounced.

§8103. Medical services and initial medical and other benefits

(a) The United States shall furnish to an employee who is injured while in the performance of duty, the services, appliances, and supplies prescribed or recommended by a qualified physician, which the Secretary of Labor considers likely to cure, give relief, reduce the degree or the period of disability, or aid in lessening the amount of the monthly compensation. These services, appliances, and supplies shall be furnished—

(1) whether or not disability has arisen;

(2) notwithstanding that the employee has accepted or is entitled to receive benefits under subchapter III of chapter 83 of this title or another retirement system for employees of the Government; and

(3) by or on the order of United States medical officers and hospitals, or, at the employee's option, by or on the order of physicians and hospitals designated or approved by the Secretary. The employee may initially select a physician to provide medical services, appliances, supplies, in accordance with such regulations and instructions as the Secretary considers necessary, and may be furnished necessary and reasonable transportation and expenses incident to the securing of such services, appliances, and supplies. These expenses, when authorized or approved by the Secretary, shall be paid from the Employees' Compensation Fund.

(b) The Secretary, under such limitations or conditions as he considers necessary, may authorize the employing agencies to provide for the initial furnishing of medical and other benefits under this section.

The Secretary may certify vouchers for these expenses out of the Employees' Compensation Fund when the immediate superior of the employee certifies that the expense was incurred in respect to an injury which was accepted by the employing agency as probably compensable under this subchapter.

The Secretary shall prescribe the form and content of the certificate.

§8104. Vocational rehabilitation

(a) The Secretary of Labor may direct a permanently disabled individual whose disability is compensable under this subchapter to undergo vocational rehabilitation. The Secretary shall provide for furnishing the vocational rehabilitation services. In providing for these services, the Secretary, insofar as practicable, shall use the services or facilities of State agencies and corresponding agencies which cooperate with the Secretary of Health, Education, and Welfare in carrying out the purposes of chapter 4 of title 29, except to the extent that the Secretary of Labor provides for furnishing these services under section 8103 of this title. The cost of providing these services to individuals undergoing vocational rehabilitation under this section shall be paid from the Employees' Compensation Fund. However, in reimbursing a State or corresponding agency under an arrangement pursuant to this section the cost to the agency reimbursable in full under section 32(b)(1) of title 29 is excluded.

(b) Notwithstanding section 8106, individuals directed to undergo vocational rehabilitation by the Secretary shall, while undergoing such rehabilitation, receive compensation at the rate provided in sections 8105 and 8110 of this title, less the amount of any earnings received from remunerative employment, other than employment undertaken pursuant to such rehabilitation.

§8105. Total disability

(a) If the disability is total, the United States shall pay the employee during the disability monthly monetary compensation equal to 66 2/3 percent of his monthly pay, which is known as his basic compensation for total disability.

(b) The loss of use of both hands, both arms, both feet, or both legs, or the loss of sight of both eyes, is prima facie permanent total disability.

§8106. Partial disability

(a) If the disability is partial, the United States shall pay the employee during the disability monthly monetary compensation equal to 66 2/3 percent of the difference between his monthly pay and his monthly wage-earning capacity after the beginning of the partial disability, which is known as his basic compensation for partial disability.

(b) The Secretary of Labor may require a partially disabled employee to report his earnings from employment or self-employment, by affidavit or otherwise, in the manner and at the times the Secretary specifies. The employee shall include in the affidavit or report the value of housing, board, lodging, and other advantages which are part of his earnings in employment or self-employment and which can be estimated in money. An employee who—

(1) fails to make an affidavit or report when required; or

(2) knowingly omits or understates any part of his earnings; forfeits his right to compensation with respect to any period for which the affidavit or report was required. Compensation forfeited under this subsection, if already paid, shall be recovered by a deduction from the compensation payable to the employee or otherwise recovered under section 8129 of this title, unless recovery is waived under that section.

(c) A partially disabled employee who—

(1) refuses to seek suitable work; or

(2) refuses or neglects to work after suitable work is offered to, procured by, or secured for him; is not entitled to compensation.

§8107. Compensation schedule

(a) If there is permanent disability involving the loss, or loss of use, of a member or function of the body or involving disfigurement, the employee is entitled to basic compensation for the disability, as provided by the schedule in subsection (c) of this section, at the rate of 66 2/3 percent of his monthly pay. The basic compensation is—

(1) payable regardless of whether the cause of the disability originates in a part of the body other than that member;

(2) payable regardless of whether the disability also involves another impairment of the body; and

(3) in addition to compensation for temporary total or temporary partial disability.

(b) With respect to any period after payments under subsection (a) of this section have ended, an employee is entitled to compensation as provided by—

(1) section 8105 of this title if the disability is total; or

(2) section 8106 of this title if the disability is partial.

(c) The compensation schedule is as follows:

(1) Arm lost, 312 weeks' compensation.

(2) Leg lost, 288 weeks' compensation.

(3) Hand lost, 244 weeks' compensation.

(4) Foot lost, 205 weeks' compensation.

(5) Eye lost, 160 weeks' compensation.

(6) Thumb lost, 75 weeks' compensation.

(7) First finger lost, 46 weeks' compensation.

(8) Great toe lost, 38 weeks' compensation.

(9) Second finger lost, 30 weeks' compensation.

(10) Third finger lost, 25 weeks' compensation.

(11) Toe other than great toe lost, 16 weeks' compensation.

(12) Fourth finger lost, 15 weeks' compensation.

(13) Loss of hearing—

(A) complete loss of hearing of one ear, 52 weeks' compensation; or

(B) complete loss of hearing of both ears, 200 weeks' compensation.

(14) Compensation for loss of binocular vision or for loss of 80 percent or more of the vision of an eye is the same as for loss of the eye.

(15) Compensation for loss of more than one phalanx of a digit is the same as for loss of the entire digit. Compensation for loss of the first phalanx is one-half of the compensation for loss of the entire digit.

(16) If, in the case of an arm or a leg, the member is amputated above the wrist or ankle, compensation is the same as for loss of the arm or leg, respectively.

(17) Compensation for loss of use of two or more digits, or one or more phalanges of each of two or more digits, of a hand or foot, is proportioned to the loss of use of the hand or foot occasioned thereby.

(18) Compensation for permanent total loss of use of a member is the same as for loss of the member.

(19) Compensation for permanent partial loss of use of a member may be for proportionate loss of use of the member. The degree of loss of vision or hearing under this schedule is determined without regard to correction.

(20) In case of loss of use of more than one member or parts of more than one member as enumerated by this schedule, the compensation is for loss of use of each member or part thereof, and the awards run consecutively. However, when the injury affects only two or more digits of the same hand or foot, paragraph (17) of this subsection applies, and when partial bilateral loss of hearing is involved, compensation is computed on the loss as affecting both ears.

(21) For serious disfigurement of the face, head, or neck of a character likely to handicap an individual in securing or maintaining employment, proper and equitable compensation not to exceed $3,500 shall be awarded in addition to any other compensation payable under this schedule.

(22) For permanent loss or loss of use of any other important external or internal organ of the body as determined by the Secretary, proper and equitable compensation not to exceed 312 weeks' compensation for each organ so determined shall be paid in addition to any other compensation payable under this schedule.

* * *

§8109. Beneficiaries of awards unpaid at death; order of precedence

(a) If an individual—

(1) has sustained disability compensable under section 8107(a) of this title;

(2) has filed a valid claim in his lifetime; and

(3) dies from a cause other than the injury before the end of the period specified by the schedule; the compensation specified by the schedule that is unpaid at his death, whether or not accrued or due at his death, shall be paid—

(A) under an award made before or after the death;

(B) for the period specified by the schedule;

(C) to and for the benefit of the persons then in being within the classes and proportions and on the conditions specified by this section; and

(D) in the following order of precedence:

(i) If there is no child, to the widow or widower.

(ii) If there are both a widow or widower and a child or children, one-half to the widow or widower and one-half to the child or children.

(iii) If there is no widow or widower, to the child or children.

(iv) If there is no survivor in the above classes, to the parent or parents wholly or partly dependent for support on the decedent, or to other wholly dependent relatives listed by section 8133 (a)(5) of this title, or to both in proportions provided by regulation.

(v) If there is no survivor in the above classes and no burial allowance is payable under section 8134 of this title, an amount not exceeding that which would be expendable under section 8134 of this title if applicable shall be paid to reimburse a person equitably entitled thereto to the extent and in the proportion that he has paid the burial expenses, but a compensated insurer or other person obligated by law or contract to pay the burial expenses or a State or political subdivision or entity is deemed not equitably entitled.

(b) Payments under subsection (a) of this section, except for an amount payable for a period preceding the death of the individual, are at the basic rate of compensation for permanent disability specified by section 8107(a) of this title even if at the time of death the individual was entitled to the augmented rate specified by section 8110 of this title.

(c) A surviving beneficiary under subsection (a) of this section, except one under subsection (a)(D)(v), does not have a vested right to payment and must be alive to receive payment.

(d) A beneficiary under subsection (a) of this section, except one under subsection (a)(D)(v), ceases to be entitled to payment on the happening of an event which would terminate his right to compensation for death under section 8133 of this title. When that entitlement ceases, compensation remaining unpaid under subsection (a) of this section is payable to the surviving beneficiary in accordance with subsection (a) of this section.

§8110. Augmented compensation for dependents

(a) For the purpose of this section, "dependent" means—

(1) a wife, if—

(A) she is a member of the same household as the employee;

(B) she is receiving regular contributions from the employee for her support; or

(C) the employee has been ordered by a court to contribute to her support;

(2) a husband, if—

(A) he is a member of the same household as the employee; or

(B) he is receiving regular contributions from the employee for his support; or

(C) the employee has been ordered by a court to contribute to his support;

(3) an unmarried child, while living with the employee or receiving regular contributions from the employee toward his support, and who is—

(A) under 18 years of age; or

(B) over 18 years of age and incapable of self-support because of physical or mental disability; and

(4) a parent, while wholly dependent on and supported by the employee.

Notwithstanding paragraph (3) of this subsection, compensation payable for a child that would otherwise end because the child has reached 18 years of age shall continue if he is a student as defined by section 8101 of this title at the time he reaches 18 years of age for so long as he continues to be such a student or until he marries.

(b) A disabled employee with one or more dependents is entitled to have his basic compensation for disability augmented—

(1) at the rate of 8 1/3 percent of his monthly pay if that compensation is payable under section 8105 or 8107(a) of this title; and

(2) at the rate of 8 1/3 percent of the difference between his monthly pay and his monthly wage-earning capacity if that compensation is payable under section 8106(a) of this title.

§8111. Additional compensation for services of attendants or vocational rehabilitation

(a) The Secretary of Labor may pay an employee who has been awarded compensation an additional sum of not more than $1,500 a month, as the Secretary considers necessary, when the Secretary finds that the service of an attendant is necessary constantly because the employee is totally blind, or has lost the use of both hands or both feet, or is paralyzed and unable to walk, or because of other disability resulting from the injury making him so helpless as to require constant attendance.

(b) The Secretary may pay an individual undergoing vocational rehabilitation under section 8104 of this title additional compensation necessary for his maintenance, but not to exceed $200 a month.

§8112. Maximum and minimum monthly payments

(a) Except as provided by section 8138 of this title, the monthly rate of compensation for disability, including augmented compensation under section 8110 of this title but not including additional compensation under section 8111 of this title, may not be more than 75 percent of the monthly pay of the maximum rate of basic pay for GS-15, and in case of total disability may not be less than 75 percent of the monthly pay of the minimum rate of basic pay for GS-2 or the amount of the monthly pay of the employee, whichever is less.

(b) The provisions of subsection (a) shall not apply to any employee whose disability is a result of an assault which occurs during an assassination or attempted assassination of a Federal official described under section 351(a) or 1751(a) of title 18, and was sustained in the performance of duty.

§8113. Increase or decrease of basic compensation

(a) If an individual—

(1) was a minor or employed in a learner's capacity at the time of injury; and

(2) was not physically or mentally handicapped before the injury; the Secretary of Labor, on review under section 8128 of this title after the time the wage-earning capacity of the individual would probably have increased but for the injury, shall recompute prospectively the monetary compensation payable for disability on the basis of an assumed monthly pay corresponding to the probable increased wage-earning capacity.

(b) If an individual without good cause fails to apply for and undergo vocational rehabilitation when so directed under section 8104 of this title, the Secretary, on review under section 8128 of this title and after finding that in the absence of the failure the wage-earning capacity of the individual would probably have substantially increased, may reduce prospectively the monetary compensation of the individual in accordance with what would probably have been his wage-earning capacity in the absence of the failure, until the individual in good faith complies with the direction of the Secretary.

§8114. Computation of pay

(a) For the purpose of this section—

(1) "overtime pay" means pay for hours of service in excess of a statutory or other basic workweek or other basic unit of worktime, as observed by the employing establishment; and

(2) "year" means a period of 12 calendar months, or the equivalent thereof as specified by regulations prescribed by the Secretary of Labor.

(b) In computing monetary compensation for disability or death on the basis of monthly pay, that pay is determined under this section.

(c) The monthly pay at the time of injury is deemed one-twelfth of the average annual earnings of the employee at that time. When compensation is paid on a weekly basis, the weekly equivalent of the monthly pay is deemed one-fifty-second of the average annual earnings. However, for so much of a period of total disability as does not exceed 90 calendar days from the date of the beginning of compensable disability, the compensation, in the discretion of the Secretary of Labor, may be computed on the basis of the actual daily wage of the employee at the time of injury in which event he may be paid compensation for the days he would have worked but for the injury.

(d) Average annual earnings are determined as follows:

(1) If the employee worked in the employment in which he was employed at the time of his injury during substantially the whole year immediately preceding the injury and the employment was in a position for which an annual rate of pay—

(A) was fixed, the average annual earnings are the annual rate of pay; or

(B) was not fixed, the average annual earnings are the product obtained by multiplying his daily wage for the particular employment, or the average thereof if the daily wage has fluctuated, by 300 if he was employed on the basis of a 6-day workweek, 280 if employed on the basis of a 5 1/2-day week, and 260 if employed on the basis of a 5-day week.

(2) If the employee did not work in employment in which he was employed at the time of his injury during substantially the whole year immediately preceding the injury, but the position was one

which would have afforded employment for substantially a whole year, the average annual earnings are a sum equal to the average annual earnings of an employee of the same class working substantially the whole immediately preceding year in the same or similar employment by the United States in the same or neighboring place, as determined under paragraph (1) of this subsection.

(3) If either of the foregoing methods of determining the average annual earnings cannot be applied reasonably and fairly, the average annual earnings are a sum that reasonably represents the annual earning capacity of the injured employee in the employment in which he was working at the time of the injury having regard to the previous earnings of the employee in Federal employment, and of other employees of the United States in the same or most similar class working in the same or most similar employment in the same or neighboring location, other previous employment of the employee, or other relevant factors. However, the average annual earnings may not be less than 150 times the average daily wage the employee earned in the employment during the days employed within 1 year immediately preceding his injury.

(4) If the employee served without pay or at nominal pay, paragraphs (1), (2), and (3) of this subsection apply as far as practicable, but the average annual earnings of the employee may not exceed the minimum rate of basic pay for GS-15. If the average annual earnings cannot be determined reasonably and fairly in the manner otherwise provided by this section, the average annual earnings shall be determined at the reasonable value of the service performed but not in excess of $3,600 a year.

(e) The value of subsistence and quarters, and of any other form of remuneration in kind for services if its value can be estimated in money, and premium pay under section 5545(c)(1) of this title are included as part of the pay, but account is not taken of—

(1) overtime pay;

(2) additional pay or allowance authorized outside the United States because of differential in cost of living or other special circumstances; or

(3) bonus or premium pay for extraordinary service including bonus or pay for particularly hazardous service in time of war.

§8115. Determination of wage-earning capacity

(a) In determining compensation for partial disability, except permanent partial disability compensable under sections 8107—8109 of this title, the wage-earning capacity of an employee is determined by his actual earnings if his actual earnings fairly and reasonably represent his wage-earning capacity. If the actual earnings of the employee do not fairly and reasonably represent his wage-earning capacity or if the employee has no actual earnings, his wage-earning capacity as appears reasonable under the circumstances is determined with due regard to—

(1) the nature of his injury;

(2) the degree of physical impairment;

(3) his usual employment;

(4) his age;

(5) his qualifications for other employment;

(6) the availability of suitable employment; and

(7) other factors or circumstances which may affect his wage-earning capacity in his disabled condition.

(b) Section 8114(d) of this title is applicable in determining the wage-earning capacity of an employee after the beginning of partial disability.

§8116. Limitations on right to receive compensation

(a) While an employee is receiving compensation under this subchapter, or if he has been paid a lump sum in commutation of installment payments until the expiration of the period during which the installment payments would have continued, he may not receive salary, pay, or remuneration of any type from the United States, except—

(1) in return for service actually performed;

(2) pension for service in the Army, Navy, or Air Force;

(3) other benefits administered by the Department of Veterans Affairs unless such benefits are payable for the same injury or the same death; and

(4) retired pay, retirement pay, retainer pay, or equivalent pay for service in the Armed Forces or other uniformed services, subject to the reduction of such pay in accordance with section 5532(b) of title 5, United States Code.

However, eligibility for or receipt of benefits under subchapter III of chapter 83 of this title, or another retirement system for employees of the Government, does not impair the right of the employee to compensation for scheduled disabilities specified by section 8107(c) of this title.

(b) An individual entitled to benefits under this subchapter because of his injury, or because of the death of an employee, who also is entitled to receive from the United States under a provision of statute other than this subchapter payments or benefits for that injury or death (except proceeds of an insurance policy), because of service by him (or in the case of death, by the deceased) as an employee or in the armed forces, shall elect which benefits he will receive. The individual shall make the election within 1 year after the injury or death or within a further time allowed for good cause by the Secretary of Labor. The election when made is irrevocable, except as otherwise provided by statute.

(c) The liability of the United States or an instrumentality thereof under this subchapter or any extension thereof with respect to the injury or death of an employee is exclusive and instead of all other liability of the United States or the instrumentality to the employee, his legal representative, spouse, dependents, next of kin, and any other person otherwise entitled to recover damages from the United States or the instrumentality because of the injury or death in a direct judicial proceeding, in a civil action, or in admiralty, or by an administrative or judicial proceeding under a workmen's compensation statute or under a Federal tort liability statute. However, this subsection does not apply to a master or a member of a crew of a vessel.

(d) Notwithstanding the other provisions of this section, an individual receiving benefits for disability or death under this subchapter who is also receiving benefits under subchapter III of chapter 84 of this title or benefits under title II of the Social Security Act shall be entitled to all such benefits, except that—

(1) benefits received under section 223 of the Social Security Act (on account of disability) shall be subject to reduction on account of benefits paid under this subchapter pursuant to the provisions of section 224 of the Social Security Act; and

(2) in the case of benefits received on account of age or death under title II of the Social Security Act, compensation payable under this subchapter based on the Federal service of an employee shall be reduced by the amount of any such social security benefits payable that are attributable to Federal service of that employee covered by chapter 84 of this title. However, eligibility for or receipt of benefits under chapter 84 of this title, or benefits under title II of the Social Security Act by virtue of service covered by chapter 84 of this title,

does not affect the right of the employee to compensation for scheduled disabilities specified by section 8107(c) of this title.

§8117. Time of accrual of right

An employee is not entitled to compensation for the first 3 days of temporary disability, except—

(1) when the disability exceeds 14 days;

(2) when the disability is followed by permanent disability; or

(3) as provided by sections 8103 and 8104 of this title.

§8118. Continuation of pay; election to use annual or sick leave

(a) The United States shall authorize the continuation of pay of an employee, as defined in section 8101(1) of this title (other than those referred to in clause (B) or (E)), who has filed a claim for a period of wage loss due to a traumatic injury with his immediate superior on a form approved by the Secretary of Labor within the time specified in section 8122(a)(2) of this title.

(b) Continuation of pay under this subchapter shall be furnished—

(1) without a break in time unless controverted under regulations of the Secretary;

(2) for a period not to exceed 45 days; and

(3) under accounting procedures and such other regulations as the Secretary may require.

(c) An employee may use annual or sick leave to his credit at the time the disability begins, but his compensation for disability does not begin, and the time periods specified by section 8117 of this title do not begin to run, until termination of pay as set forth in subsections (a) and (b) or the use of annual or sick leave ends.

(d) If a claim under subsection (a) is denied by the Secretary, payments under this section shall, at the option of the employee, be charged to sick or annual leave or shall be deemed overpayments of pay within the meaning of section 5584 of title 5, United States Code.

(e) Payments under this section shall not be considered as compensation as defined by section 8101(12) of this title.

§8119. Notice of injury or death

An employee injured in the performance of his duty, or someone on his behalf, shall give notice thereof. Notice of a death believed to be related to the employment shall be given by an eligible beneficiary specified in section 8133 of this title, or someone on his behalf. A notice of injury or death shall—

(a) be given within 30 days after the injury or death;

(b) be given to the immediate superior of the employee by personal delivery or by depositing it in the mail properly stamped and addressed;

(c) be in writing;

(d) state the name and address of the employee;

(e) state the year, month, day, and hour when and the particular locality where the injury or death occurred;

(f) state the cause and nature of the injury, or, in the case of death, the employment factors believed to be the cause; and

(g) be signed by and contain the address of the individual giving the notice.

§8120. Report of injury

Immediately after an injury to an employee which results in his death or probable disability, his immediate superior shall report to the Secretary of Labor. The Secretary may—

(1) prescribe the information that the report shall contain;

(2) require the immediate superior to make supplemental reports; and

(3) obtain such additional reports and information from employees as are agreed on by the Secretary and the head of the employing agency.

§8121. Claim

Compensation under this subchapter may be allowed only if an individual or someone on his behalf makes claim therefor. The claim shall—

(1) be made in writing within the time specified by section 8122 of this title;

(2) be delivered to the office of the Secretary of Labor or to an individual whom the Secretary may designate by regulation, or deposited in the mail properly stamped and addressed to the Secretary or his designee;

(3) be on a form approved by the Secretary;

(4) contain all information required by the Secretary;

(5) be sworn to by the individual entitled to compensation or someone on his behalf; and

(6) except in case of death, be accompanied by a certificate of the physician of the employee stating the nature of the injury and the nature and probable extent of the disability.

The Secretary may waive paragraphs (3)–(6) of this section for reasonable cause shown.

§8122. Time for making claim

(a) An original claim for compensation for disability or death must be filed within 3 years after the injury or death. Compensation for disability or death, including medical care in disability cases, may not be allowed if claim is not filed within that time unless—

(1) the immediate superior had actual knowledge of the injury or death within 30 days. The knowledge must be such to put the immediate superior reasonably on notice of an on-the-job injury or death; or

(2) written notice of injury or death as specified in section 8119 of this title was given within 30 days.

(b) In a case of latent disability, the time for filing claim does not begin to run until the employee has a compensable disability and is aware, or by the exercise of reasonable diligence should have been aware, of the causal relationship of the compensable disability to his employment. In such a case, the time for giving notice of injury begins to run when the employee is aware, or by the exercise of reasonable diligence should have been aware, that his condition is causally related to his employment, whether or not there is a compensable disability.

(c) The timely filing of a disability claim because of injury will satisfy the time requirements for a death claim based on the same injury.

(d) The time limitations in subsections (a) and (b) of this section do not—

(1) begin to run against a minor until he reaches 21 years of age or has had a legal representative appointed; or

(2) run against an incompetent individual while he is incompetent and has no duly appointed legal representative; or

(3) run against any individual whose failure to comply is excused by the Secretary on the ground that such notice could not be given because of exceptional circumstances.

§8123. Physical examinations

(a) An employee shall submit to examination by a medical officer of the United States, or by a physician designated or approved by the Secretary of Labor, after the injury and as frequently and at the times and places as may be reasonably required. The employee may have a physician designated and paid by him present to participate in the examination. If there is disagreement between the physician making the examination for the United States and the physician of the employee, the Secretary shall appoint a third physician who shall make an examination.

(b) An employee is entitled to be paid expenses incident to an examination required by the Secretary which in the opinion of the Secretary are necessary and reasonable, including transportation and loss of wages incurred in order to be examined. The expenses, when authorized or approved by the Secretary, are paid from the Employees' Compensation Fund.

(c) The Secretary shall fix the fees for examinations held under this section by physicians not employed by or under contract to the United States to furnish medical services to employees. The fees, when authorized or approved by the Secretary, are paid from the Employees' Compensation Fund.

(d) If an employee refuses to submit to or obstructs an examination, his right to compensation under this subchapter is suspended until the refusal or obstruction stops. Compensation is not payable while a refusal or obstruction continues, and the period of the refusal or obstruction is deducted from the period for which compensation is payable to the employee.

§8124. Findings and award; hearings

(a) The Secretary of Labor shall determine and make a finding of facts and make an award for or against payment of compensation under this subchapter after—

(1) considering the claim presented by the beneficiary and the report furnished by the immediate superior; and

(2) completing such investigation as he considers necessary.

(b) (1) Before review under section 8128(a) of this title, a claimant for compensation not satisfied with a decision of the Secretary under subsection (a) of this section is entitled, on request made within 30 days after the date of the issuance of the decision, to a hearing on his claim before a representative of the Secretary. At the hearing, the claimant is entitled to present evidence in further support of his claim. Within 30 days after the hearing ends, the Secretary shall notify the claimant in writing of his further decision and any modifications of the award he may make and of the basis of his decision.

(2) In conducting the hearing, the representative of the Secretary is not bound by common law or statutory rules of evidence, by technical or formal rules of procedure, or by section 554 of this title except as provided by this subchapter, but may conduct the hearing in such manner as to best ascertain the rights of the claimant. For this purpose, he shall receive such relevant evidence as the claimant adduces and such other evidence as he determines necessary or useful in evaluating the claim.

* * *

§8133. Compensation in case of death

(a) If death results from an injury sustained in the performance of duty, the United States shall pay a monthly compensation equal to a percentage of the monthly pay of the deceased employee in accordance with the following schedule:

(1) To the widow or widower, if there is no child, 50 percent.

(2) To the widow or widower, if there is a child, 45 percent and in addition 15 percent for each child not to exceed a total of 75 percent for the widow or widower and children.

(3) To the children, if there is no widow or widower, 40 percent for one child and 15 percent additional for each additional child not to exceed a total of 75 percent, divided among the children share and share alike.

(4) To the parents, if there is no widow, widower, or child, as follows:

(A) 25 percent if one parent was wholly dependent on the employee at the time of death and the other was not dependent to any extent;

(B) 20 percent to each if both were wholly dependent; or

(C) a proportionate amount in the discretion of the Secretary of Labor if one or both were partly dependent.

If there is a widow, widower, or child, so much of the percentages are payable as, when added to the total percentages payable to the widow, widower, and children, will not exceed a total of 75 percent.

(5) To the brothers, sisters, grandparents, and grandchildren, if there is no widow, widower, child, or dependent parent as follows:

(A) 20 percent if one was wholly dependent on the employee at the time of death;

(B) 30 percent if more than one was wholly dependent, divided among the dependents share and share alike; or

(C) 10 percent if no one is wholly dependent but one or more is partly dependent, divided among the dependents share and share alike.

If there is a widow, widower, or child, or dependent parent, so much of the percentages are payable as, when added to the total percentages payable to the widow, widower, children, and dependent parents, will not exceed a total of 75 percent.

(b) The compensation payable under subsection (a) of this section is paid from the time of death until—

(1) a widow, or widower dies or remarries before reaching age 55;

(2) a child, a brother, a sister, or a grandchild dies, marries, or becomes 18 years of age, or if over age 18 and incapable of self-support becomes capable of self-support; or

(3) a parent or grandparent dies, marries, or ceases to be dependent.

Notwithstanding paragraph (2) of this subsection, compensation payable to or for a child, a brother or sister, or grandchild that would otherwise end because the child, brother or sister, or grandchild has reached 18 years of age shall continue if he is a student as defined by section 8101 of this title at the time he reaches 18 years of age for so long as he continues to be such a student or until he marries. A widow or widower who has entitlements to benefits under this title derived from more than one husband or wife shall elect one entitlement to be utilized.

(c) On the cessation of compensation under this section to or on account of an individual, the compensation of the remaining individuals entitled to compensation for the unexpired part of the period during which their compensation is payable, is that which they would have received if they had been the only individuals entitled to compensation at the time of the death of the employee.

(d) When there are two or more classes of individuals entitled to compensation under this section and the apportionment of compensation under this section would result in injustice, the Secretary may modify the apportionment to meet the requirements of the case.

(e) In computing compensation under this section, the monthly pay is deemed not less than the minimum rate of basic pay for GS-2. However, the total monthly compensation may not exceed—

(1) the monthly pay computed under section 8114 of this title, except for increases authorized by section 8146a of this title; or

(2) 75 percent of the monthly pay of the maximum rate of basic pay for GS-15.

(f) Notwithstanding any funeral and burial expenses paid under section 8134, there shall be paid a sum of $200 to the personal representative of a deceased employee within the meaning of section 8101(1) of this title for reimbursement of the costs of termination of the decedent's status as an employee of the United States.

§8134. Funeral expenses; transportation of body

(a) If death results from an injury sustained in the performance of duty, the United States shall pay, to the personal representative of the deceased or otherwise, funeral and burial expenses not to exceed $800, in the discretion of the Secretary of Labor.

(b) The body of an employee whose home is in the United States, in the discretion of the Secretary, may be embalmed and transported in a hermetically sealed casket to his home or last place of residence at the expense of the Employees' Compensation Fund if—

(1) the employee dies from—

(A) the injury while away from his home or official station or outside the United States; or

(B) from other causes while away from his home or official station for the purpose of receiving medical or other services, appliances, supplies, or examination under this subchapter; and

(2) the relatives of the employee request the return of his body.

If the relatives do not request the return of the body of the employee, the Secretary may provide for its disposition and incur and pay from the Employees' Compensation Fund the necessary and reasonable transportation, funeral, and burial expenses.

§8135. Lump-sum payment

(a) The liability of the United States for compensation to a beneficiary in the case of death or of permanent total or permanent partial disability may be discharged by a lump-sum payment equal to the present value of all future payments of compensation computed at 4 percent true discount compounded annually if—

(1) the monthly payment to the beneficiary is less than $50 a month;

(2) the beneficiary is or is about to become a nonresident of the United States; or

(3) the Secretary of Labor determines that it is for the best interest of the beneficiary.

The probability of the death of the beneficiary before the expiration of the period during which he is entitled to compensation shall be determined according to the most current United States Life Tables, as developed by the United States Department of Health, Education, and Welfare, which shall be updated from time to time, but the lump-sum payment to a widow or widower of the deceased employee may not exceed 60 months' compensation. The probability of the happening of any other contingency affecting the amount or duration of compensation shall be disregarded.

(b) On remarriage before reaching age 55, a widow or widower entitled to compensation under section 8133 of this title, shall be paid a lump sum equal to twenty-four times the monthly compensation payment (excluding compensation on account of another individual) to which he was entitled immediately before the remarriage.

* * *

§8151. Civil service retention rights

(a) In the event the individual resumes employment with the Federal Government, the entire time during which the employee was receiving compensation under this chapter shall be credited to the employee for the purposes of within-grade step increases, retention purposes, and other rights and benefits based upon length of service.

APPENDIX 3:
THE LONGSHORE AND HARBOR WORKERS' COMPENSATION ACT [33 U.S.C. §§901-950]—SELECTED PROVISIONS

SEC. 901. SHORT TITLE; THIS ACT MAY BE CITED AS THE "LONGSHORE AND HARBOR WORKERS' COMPENSATION ACT".

* * *

SEC. 903. COVERAGE

(a) Disability or death; injuries occurring upon navigable waters of United States

Except as otherwise provided in this section, compensation shall be payable under this chapter in respect of disability or death of an employee, but only if the disability or death results from an injury occurring upon the navigable waters of the United States (including any adjoining pier, wharf, dry dock, terminal, building way, marine railway, or other adjoining area customarily used by an employer in loading, unloading, repairing, dismantling, or building a vessel).

(b) Governmental officers and employees

No compensation shall be payable in respect of the disability or death of an officer or employee of the United States, or any agency thereof, or of any State or foreign government, or any subdivision thereof.

(c) Intoxication; willful intention to kill

No compensation shall be payable if the injury was occasioned solely by the intoxication of the employee or by the willful intention of the employee to injure or kill himself or another.

(d) Small vessels

(1) No compensation shall be payable to an employee employed at a facility of an employer if, as certified by the Secretary, the facility is engaged in the business of building, repairing, or dismantling exclusively small vessels (as defined in paragraph (3) of this subsection), unless the injury occurs while upon the navigable waters of the United States or while upon any adjoining pier, wharf, dock, facility over land for launching vessels, or facility over land for hauling, lifting, or dry-docking vessels.

(2) Notwithstanding paragraph (1), compensation shall be payable to an employee—

(A) who is employed at a facility which is used in the business of building, repairing, or dismantling small vessels if such facility receives Federal maritime subsidies; or

(B) if the employee is not subject to coverage under a State workers' compensation law.

(3) For purposes of this subsection, a small vessel means—

(A) a commercial barge which is under 900 lightship displacement tons; or

(B) a commercial tugboat, towboat, crew boat, supply boat, fishing vessel, or other work vessel which is under 1,600 tons gross as measured under section 14502 of title 46, or an alternate tonnage measured under section 14302 of that title as prescribed by the Secretary under section 14104 of that title.

(e) Credit for benefits paid under other laws

Notwithstanding any other provision of law, any amounts paid to an employee for the same injury, disability, or death for which benefits are claimed under this chapter pursuant to any other workers' compensation law or section 688 of title 46, Appendix (relating to recovery for injury to or death of seamen), shall be credited against any liability imposed by this chapter.

SEC. 904. LIABILITY FOR COMPENSATION

(a) Every employer shall be liable for and shall secure the payment to his employees of the compensation payable under sections 907, 908, and 909 of this title. In the case of an employer who is a subcontractor, only if such subcontractor fails to secure the payment of compensation shall the contractor be liable for and be required to secure the payment of compensation. A subcontractor shall not be deemed to have failed to secure the payment of compensation if the contractor has provided insurance for such compensation for the benefit of the subcontractor.

(b) Compensation shall be payable irrespective of fault as a cause for the injury.

SEC. 905. EXCLUSIVENESS OF LIABILITY

(a) Employer liability; failure of employer to secure payment of compensation

The liability of an employer prescribed in section 904 of this title shall be exclusive and in place of all other liability of such employer to the employee, his legal representative, husband or wife, parents, dependents, next of kin, and anyone otherwise entitled to recover damages from such employer at law or in admiralty on account of such injury or death, except that if an employer fails to secure payment of compensation as required by this chapter, an injured employee, or his legal representative in case death results from the injury, may elect to claim compensation under the chapter, or to maintain an action at law or in admiralty for damages on account of such injury or death. In such action the defendant may not plead as a defense that the injury was caused by the negligence of a fellow servant, or that the employee assumed the risk of his employment, or that the injury was due to the contributory negligence of the employee. For purposes of this subsection, a contractor shall be deemed the employer of a subcontractor's employees only if the subcontractor fails to secure the payment of compensation as required by section 904 of this title.

(b) Negligence of vessel

In the event of injury to a person covered under this chapter caused by the negligence of a vessel, then such person, or anyone otherwise entitled to recover damages by reason thereof, may bring an action against such vessel as a third party in accordance with the provisions of section 933 of this title, and the employer shall not be liable to the vessel for such damages directly or indirectly and any agreements or warranties to the contrary shall be void. If such person was employed by the vessel to provide stevedoring services, no such action shall be permitted if the injury was caused by the negligence of persons engaged in providing stevedoring services to the vessel. If such person was employed to provide shipbuilding, repairing, or breaking services and such person's employer was the owner, owner pro hac vice, agent, operator, or charterer of the vessel, no such action shall be permitted, in whole or in part or directly or indirectly, against the injured person's employer (in any capacity, including as the vessel's owner, owner pro hac vice, agent, operator, or charterer) or against the employees of the employer. The liability of the vessel under this subsection shall not be based upon the warranty of seaworthiness or a breach thereof at the time the injury occurred. The remedy provided in this subsection shall be exclusive of all other remedies against the vessel except remedies available under this chapter.

(c) Outer Continental Shelf

In the event that the negligence of a vessel causes injury to a person entitled to receive benefits under this Act by virtue of section 1333 of title 43, then such person, or anyone otherwise entitled to recover damages by reason thereof, may bring an action against such vessel in accordance with the provisions of subsection (b) of this section. Nothing contained in subsection (b) of this section shall preclude the enforcement according to its terms of any reciprocal indemnity provision whereby the employer of a person entitled to receive benefits under this chapter by virtue of section 1333 of title 43 and the vessel agree to defend and indemnify the other for cost of defense and loss or liability for damages arising out of or resulting from death or bodily injury to their employees.

SEC. 906. COMPENSATION

(a) Time for commencement

No compensation shall be allowed for the first three days of the disability, except the benefits provided for in section 907 of this title: Provided, however, That in case the injury results in disability of more than fourteen days the compensation shall be allowed from the date of the disability.

(b) Maximum rate of compensation

(1) Compensation for disability or death (other than compensation for death required by this chapter to be paid in a lump sum) shall not exceed an amount equal to 200 per centum of the applicable national average weekly wage, as determined by the Secretary under paragraph (3).

(2) Compensation for total disability shall not be less than 50 per centum of the applicable national average weekly wage determined by the Secretary under paragraph (3), except that if the employee's average weekly wages as computed under section 910 of this title are less than 50 per centum of such national average weekly wage,

he shall receive his average weekly wages as compensation for total disability.

(3) As soon as practicable after June 30 of each year, and in any event prior to October 1 of such year, the Secretary shall determine the national average weekly wage for the three consecutive calendar quarters ending June 30. Such determination shall be the applicable national average weekly wage for the period beginning with October 1 of that year and ending with September 30 of the next year. The initial determination under this paragraph shall be made as soon as practicable after October 27, 1972.

(c) Applicability of determinations

Determinations under subsection (b)(3) of this section with respect to a period shall apply to employees or survivors currently receiving compensation for permanent total disability or death benefits during such period, as well as those newly awarded compensation during such period.

SEC. 907. MEDICAL SERVICES AND SUPPLIES

(a) General requirement

The employer shall furnish such medical, surgical, and other attendance or treatment, nurse and hospital service, medicine, crutches, and apparatus, for such period as the nature of the injury or the process of recovery may require.

(b) Physician selection; administrative supervision; change of physicians and hospitals

The employee shall have the right to choose an attending physician authorized by the Secretary to provide medical care under this chapter as hereinafter provided. If, due to the nature of the injury, the employee is unable to select his physician and the nature of the injury requires immediate medical treatment and care, the employer shall select a physician for him. The Secretary shall actively supervise the medical care rendered to injured employees, shall require periodic reports as to the medical care being rendered to injured employees, shall have authority to determine the necessity, character, and sufficiency of any medical aid furnished or to be furnished, and may, on his own initiative or at the request of the employer, order a change of physicians or hospitals when in his judgment such change is desirable or necessary in the interest of the employee or where the charges exceed those prevailing within the community for the same or similar services or exceed the provider's customary charges. Change of physicians at the request of employees shall be permitted in accordance with regulations of the Secretary.

(c) Physicians and health care providers not authorized to render medical care or provide medical services

(1) (A) The Secretary shall annually prepare a list of physicians and health care providers in each compensation district who are not authorized to render medical care or provide medical services under this chapter. The names of physicians and health care providers contained on the list required under this subparagraph shall be made available to employees and employers in each compensation district through posting and in such other forms as the Secretary may prescribe.

(B) Physicians and health care providers shall be included on the list of those not authorized to provide medical care and medical services pursuant to subparagraph (A) when the Secretary determines under this section, in accordance with the procedures provided in subsection (j) of this section, that such physician or health care provider—

(i) has knowingly and willfully made, or caused to be made, any false statement or misrepresentation of a material fact for use in a claim for compensation or claim for reimbursement of medical expenses under this chapter;

(ii) has knowingly and willfully submitted, or caused to be submitted, a bill or request for payment under this chapter containing a charge which the Secretary finds to be substantially in excess of the charge for the service, appliance, or supply prevailing within the community or in excess of the provider's customary charges, unless the Secretary finds there is good cause for the bill or request containing the charge;

(iii) has knowingly and willfully furnished a service, appliance, or supply which is determined by the Secretary to be substantially in excess of the need of the recipient thereof or to be of a quality which substantially fails to meet professionally recognized standards;

(iv) has been convicted under any criminal statute (without regard to pending appeal thereof) for fraudulent activities in connection with any Federal or State program for which payments are made to physicians or providers of similar services, appliances, or supplies; or

(v) has otherwise been excluded from participation in such program.

(C) Medical services provided by physicians or health care providers who are named on the list published by the Secretary pursuant to subparagraph (A) of this section shall not be reimbursable under this chapter; except that the Secretary shall direct the reimbursement of medical claims for services rendered by such physicians or health care providers in cases where the services were rendered in an emergency.

(D) A determination under subparagraph (B) shall remain in effect for a period of not less than three years and until the Secretary finds and gives notice to the public that there is reasonable assurance that the basis for the determination will not reoccur.

(E) A provider of a service, appliance, or supply shall provide to the Secretary such information and certification as the Secretary may require to assure that this subsection is enforced.

(2) Whenever the employer or carrier acquires knowledge of the employee's injury, through written notice or otherwise as prescribed by the chapter, the employer or carrier shall forthwith authorize medical treatment and care from a physician selected by an employee pursuant to subsection (b) of this section. An employee may not select a physician who is on the list required by paragraph (1) of this subsection. An employee may not change physicians after his initial choice unless the employer, carrier, or deputy commissioner has given prior consent for such change. Such consent shall be given in cases where an employee's initial choice was not of a specialist whose services are necessary for and appropriate to the proper care and treatment of the compensable injury or disease. In all other cases, consent may be given upon a showing of good cause for change.

(d) Request of treatment or services prerequisite to recovery of expenses; formal report of injury and treatment; suspension of compensation for refusal of treatment or examination; justification

(1) An employee shall not be entitled to recover any amount expended by him for medical or other treatment or services unless—

(A) the employer shall have refused or neglected a request to furnish such services and the employee has complied with subsections (b) and (c) of this section and the applicable regulations; or

(B) the nature of the injury required such treatment and services and the employer or his superintendent or foreman having knowledge of such injury shall have neglected to provide or authorize same.

(2) No claim for medical or surgical treatment shall be valid and enforceable against such employer unless, within ten days following the first treatment, the physician giving such treatment furnishes to the employer and the deputy commissioner a report of such injury or treatment, on a form prescribed by the Secretary. The Secretary may excuse the failure to furnish such report within the ten-day period whenever he finds it to be in the interest of justice to do so.

(3) The Secretary may, upon application by a party in interest, make an award for the reasonable value of such medical or surgical treatment so obtained by the employee.

(4) If at any time the employee unreasonably refuses to submit to medical or surgical treatment, or to an examination by a physician selected by the employer, the Secretary or administrative law judge may, by order, suspend the payment of further compensation during such time as such refusal continues, and no compensation shall be paid at any time during the period of such suspension, unless the circumstances justified the refusal.

(e) Physical examination; medical questions; report of physical impairment; review or reexamination; costs

In the event that medical questions are raised in any case, the Secretary shall have the power to cause the employee to be examined by a physician employed or selected by the Secretary and to obtain from such physician a report containing his estimate of the employee's physical impairment and such other information as may be appropriate. Any party who is dissatisfied with such report may request a review or reexamination of the employee by one or more different physicians employed or selected by the Secretary. The Secretary shall order such review or reexamination unless he finds that it is clearly unwarranted. Such review or reexamination shall be completed within two weeks from the date ordered unless the Secretary finds that because of extraordinary circumstances a longer period is required. The Secretary shall have the power in his discretion to charge the cost of examination or review under this subsection to the employer, if he is a self-insurer, or to the insurance company which is carrying the risk, in appropriate cases, or to the special fund in section 944 of this title.

(f) Place of examination; exclusion of physicians other than examining physician of Secretary; good cause for conclusions of other physicians respecting impairment; examination by employer's physician; suspension of proceedings and compensation for refusal of examination

An employee shall submit to a physical examination under subsection (e) of this section at such place as the Secretary may require. The place, or places, shall be designated by the Secretary and shall be reasonably convenient for the employee. No physician selected by the employer, carrier, or employee shall be present at or participate in any manner in such examination, nor shall conclusions of such physicians as to the nature or extent of impairment or the cause of impairment be available to the examining physician unless otherwise ordered, for good cause, by the Secretary. Such employer or carrier shall, upon request, be entitled to have the employee examined immediately thereafter and upon the same premises by a qualified physician or physicians in the presence of such physician as the employee may select, if any. Proceedings shall be suspended and no compensation shall be payable for any period during which the employee may refuse to submit to examination.

(g) Fees and charges for examinations, treatment, or service; limitation; regulations

All fees and other charges for medical examinations, treatment, or service shall be limited to such charges as prevail in the community for such treatment, and shall be subject to regulation by the Secretary. The Secretary shall issue regulations limiting the nature and extent of medical expenses chargeable against the employer without authorization by the employer or the Secretary.

(h) Third party liability

The liability of an employer for medical treatment as herein provided shall not be affected by the fact that his employee was injured through the fault or negligence of a third party not in the same employ, or that suit has been brought against such third party. The employer shall, however, have a cause of action against such third party to recover any amounts paid by him for such medical treatment in like manner as provided in section 933 (b) of this title.

(i) Physicians' ineligibility for subsection (e) physical examinations and reviews because of workmen's compensation claim employment or fee acceptance or participation

Unless the parties to the claim agree, the Secretary shall not employ or select any physician for the purpose of making examinations or reviews under subsection (e) of this section who, during such employment, or during the period of two years prior to such employment, has been employed by, or accepted or participated in any fee relating to a workmen's compensation claim from any insurance carrier or any self-insurer.

(j) Procedure; judicial review

(1) The Secretary shall have the authority to make rules and regulations and to establish procedures, not inconsistent with the provisions of this chapter, which are necessary or appropriate to carry out the provisions of subsection (c) of this section, including the nature and extent of the proof and evidence necessary for actions under this section and the methods of taking and furnishing such proof and evidence.

(2) Any decision to take action with respect to a physician or health care provider under this section shall be based on specific findings of fact by the Secretary. The Secretary shall provide notice of these findings and an opportunity for a hearing pursuant to section 556 of title 5 for a provider who would be affected by a decision under this section. A request for a hearing must be filed with the Secretary within thirty days after notice of the findings is received by the provider making such request. If a hearing is held, the Secretary shall, on the basis of evidence adduced at the hearing, affirm, modify, or reverse the findings of fact and proposed action under this section.

(3) For the purpose of any hearing, investigation, or other proceeding authorized or directed under this section, the provisions of section [1] 49 and 50 of title 15 (relating to the attendance of witnesses and the production of books, papers, and documents) shall apply to the jurisdiction, powers, and duties of the Secretary or any officer designated by him.

(4) Any physician or health care provider, after any final decision of the Secretary made after a hearing to which he was a party, irrespective of the amount in controversy, may obtain a review of such decision by a civil action commenced within sixty days after the mailing to him of notice of such decision, but the pendency of such review shall not operate as a stay upon the effect of such decision. Such action shall be brought in the court of appeals of the United States for the judicial circuit in which the plaintiff resides or has his principal place of business, or the Court of Appeals for the District of Columbia. As part of his answer, the Secretary shall file a certified copy of the transcript of the record of the hearing, including all evidence submitted in connection therewith. The findings of fact of the Secretary, if based on substantial evidence in the record as a whole, shall be conclusive.

(k) Refusal of treatment on religious grounds

(1) Nothing in this chapter prevents an employee whose injury or disability has been established under this chapter from relying in good faith on treatment by prayer or spiritual means alone, in accordance with the tenets and practice of a recognized church or religious denomination, by an accredited practitioner of such recognized church or religious denomination, and on nursing services rendered in accordance with such tenets and practice, without suffering loss or diminution of the compensation or benefits under this chapter. Nothing in this subsection shall be construed to except an employee from all physical examinations required by this chapter.

(2) If an employee refuses to submit to medical or surgical services solely because, in adherence to the tenets and practice of a recognized church or religious denomination, the employee relies upon prayer or spiritual means alone for healing, such employee shall not be considered to have unreasonably refused medical or surgical treatment under subsection (d) of this section.

SEC. 908. COMPENSATION FOR DISABILITY

Compensation for disability shall be paid to the employee as follows:

(a) Permanent total disability: In case of total disability adjudged to be permanent 662/3 per centum of the average weekly wages shall be paid to the employee during the continuance of such total disability. Loss of both hands, or both arms, or both feet, or both legs, or both eyes, or of any two thereof shall, in the absence of conclusive proof to the contrary, constitute permanent total disability. In all other cases permanent total disability shall be determined in accordance with the facts.

(b) Temporary total disability: In case of disability total in character but temporary in quality 662/3 per centum of the average weekly wages shall be paid to the employee during the continuance thereof.

(c) Permanent partial disability: In case of disability partial in character but permanent in quality the compensation shall be 662/3 per centum of the average weekly wages, which shall be in addition to compensation for temporary total disability or temporary partial disability paid in accordance with subsection (b) or subsection (e) of this section, respectively, and shall be paid to the employee, as follows:

(1) Arm lost, three hundred and twelve weeks' compensation.

(2) Leg lost, two hundred and eighty-eight weeks' compensation.

(3) Hand lost, two hundred and forty-four weeks' compensation.

(4) Foot lost, two hundred and five weeks' compensation.

(5) Eye lost, one hundred and sixty weeks' compensation.

(6) Thumb lost, seventy-five weeks' compensation.

(7) First finger lost, forty-six weeks' compensation.

(8) Great toe lost, thirty-eight weeks' compensation.

(9) Second finger lost, thirty weeks' compensation.

(10) Third finger lost, twenty-five weeks' compensation.

(11) Toe other than great toe lost, sixteen weeks' compensation.

(12) Fourth finger lost, fifteen weeks' compensation.

(13) Loss of hearing:

(A) Compensation for loss of hearing in one ear, fifty-two weeks.

(B) Compensation for loss of hearing in both ears, two-hundred weeks.

(C) An audiogram shall be presumptive evidence of the amount of hearing loss sustained as of the date thereof, only if

(i) such audiogram was administered by a licensed or certified audiologist or a physician who is certified in otolaryngology,

(ii) such audiogram, with the report thereon, was provided to the employee at the time it was administered, and

(iii) no contrary audiogram made at that time is produced.

(D) The time for filing a notice of injury, under section 912 of this title, or a claim for compensation, under section 913 of this title, shall not begin to run in connection with any claim for loss of hearing under this section, until the employee has received an audiogram, with the accompanying report thereon, which indicates that the employee has suffered a loss of hearing.

(E) Determinations of loss of hearing shall be made in accordance with the guides for the evaluation of permanent impairment as promulgated and modified from time to time by the American Medical Association.

(14) Phalanges: Compensation for loss of more than one phalange of a digit shall be the same as for loss of the entire digit. Compensation for loss of the first phalange shall be one-half of the compensation for loss of the entire digit.

(15) Amputated arm or leg: Compensation for an arm or a leg, if amputated at or above the elbow or the knee, shall be the same as for a loss of the arm or leg; but, if amputated between the elbow and the wrist or the knee and the ankle, shall be the same as for loss of a hand or foot.

(16) Binocular vision or per centum of vision: Compensation for loss of binocular vision or for 80 per centum or more of the vision of an eye shall be the same as for loss of the eye.

(17) Two or more digits: Compensation for loss of two or more digits, or one or more phalanges of two or more digits, of a hand or foot may be proportioned to the loss of use of the hand or foot occasioned thereby, but shall not exceed the compensation for loss of a hand or foot.

(18) Total loss of use: Compensation for permanent total loss of use of a member shall be the same as for loss of the member.

(19) Partial loss or partial loss of use: Compensation for permanent partial loss or loss of use of a member may be for proportionate loss or loss of use of the member.

(20) Disfigurement: Proper and equitable compensation not to exceed $7,500 shall be awarded for serious disfigurement of the face, head, or neck or of other normally exposed areas likely to handicap the employee in securing or maintaining employment.

(21) Other cases: In all other cases in the class of disability, the compensation shall be 66 2/3 per centum of the difference between the average weekly wages of the employee and the employee's wage-earning capacity thereafter in the same employment or otherwise, payable during the continuance of partial disability.

(22) In any case in which there shall be a loss of, or loss of use of, more than one member or parts of more than one member set forth in paragraphs (1) to (19) of this subsection, not amounting to permanent total disability, the award of compensation shall be for the loss of, or loss of use of, each such member or part thereof, which awards shall run consecutively, except that where the injury affects only two or more digits of the same hand or foot, paragraph (17) of this subsection shall apply.

(23) Notwithstanding paragraphs (1) through (22), with respect to a claim for permanent partial disability for which the average weekly wages are determined under section 910 (d)(2) of this title, the compensation shall be 66 2/3 per centum of such average weekly wages multiplied by the percentage of permanent impairment, as determined under the guides referred to in section 902 (10) of this title, payable during the continuance of such impairment.

(d) (1) If an employee who is receiving compensation for permanent partial disability pursuant to subsection (c)(1)–(20) of this section dies from causes other than the injury, the total amount of the award unpaid at the time of death shall be payable to or for the benefit of his survivors, as follows:

(A) if the employee is survived only by a widow or widower, such unpaid amount of the award shall be payable to such widow or widower,

(B) if the employee is survived only by a child or children, such unpaid amount of the award shall be paid to such child or children in equal shares,

(C) if the employee is survived by a widow or widower and a child or children, such unpaid amount of the award shall be payable to such survivors in equal shares,

(D) if there be no widow or widower and no surviving child or children, such unpaid amount of the award shall be paid to the survivors specified in section 909 (d) of this title (other than a wife, husband, or child); and the amount to be paid each such survivor shall be determined by multiplying such unpaid amount of the award by the appropriate percentage specified in section 909 (d) of this title, but if the aggregate amount to which all such survivors are entitled, as so determined, is less than such unpaid amount of the award, the excess amount shall be divided among such survivors pro rata according to the amount otherwise payable to each under this subparagraph.

(2) Notwithstanding any other limitation in section 909 of this title, the total amount of any award for permanent partial disability pursuant to subsection (c)(1)–(20) of this section unpaid at time of death shall be payable in full in the appropriate distribution.

(3) An award for disability may be made after the death of the injured employee. Except where compensation is payable under subsection (c)(21) of this section if there be no survivors as

prescribed in this section, then the compensation payable under this subsection shall be paid to the special fund established under section 944 (a) of this title.

(e) Temporary partial disability:

In case of temporary partial disability resulting in decrease of earning capacity the compensation shall be two-thirds of the difference between the injured employee's average weekly wages before the injury and his wage-earning capacity after the injury in the same or another employment, to be paid during the continuance of such disability, but shall not be paid for a period exceeding five years.

(f) Injury increasing disability:

(1) In any case in which an employee having an existing permanent partial disability suffers injury, the employer shall provide compensation for such disability as is found to be attributable to that injury based upon the average weekly wages of the employee at the time of the injury. If following an injury falling within the provisions of subsection (c)(1)–(20) of this section, the employee is totally and permanently disabled, and the disability is found not to be due solely to that injury, the employer shall provide compensation for the applicable prescribed period of weeks provided for in that section for the subsequent injury, or for one hundred and four weeks, whichever is the greater, except that, in the case of an injury falling within the provisions of subsection (c)(13) of this section, the employer shall provide compensation for the lesser of such periods. In all other cases of total permanent disability or of death, found not to be due solely to that injury, of an employee having an existing permanent partial disability, the employer shall provide in addition to compensation under subsections (b) and (e) of this section, compensation payments or death benefits for one hundred and four weeks only. If following an injury falling within the provisions of subsection (c)(1)–(20) of this section, the employee has a permanent partial disability and the disability is found not to be due solely to that injury, and such disability is materially and substantially greater than that which would have resulted from the subsequent injury alone, the employer shall provide compensation for the applicable period of weeks provided for in that section for the subsequent injury, or for one hundred and four weeks, whichever is the greater, except that, in the case of an injury falling within the provisions of subsection (c)(13) of this section, the employer shall provide compensation for the lesser of such periods.

In all other cases in which the employee has a permanent partial disability, found not to be due solely to that injury, and such disability is materially and substantially greater than that which would have resulted from the subsequent injury alone, the employer shall provide in addition to compensation under subsections (b) and (e) of this section, compensation for one hundred and four weeks only.

(2) (A) After cessation of the payments for the period of weeks provided for herein, the employee or his survivor entitled to benefits shall be paid the remainder of the compensation that would be due out of the special fund established in section 944 of this title, except that the special fund shall not assume responsibility with respect to such benefits (and such payments shall not be subject to cessation) in the case of any employer who fails to comply with section 932 (a) of this title.

(B) After cessation of payments for the period of weeks provided for in this subsection, the employer or carrier responsible for payment of compensation shall remain a party to the claim, retain access to all records relating to the claim, and in all other respects retain all rights granted under this chapter prior to cessation of such payments.

(3) Any request, filed after September 28, 1984, for apportionment of liability to the special fund established under section 944 of this title for the payment of compensation benefits, and a state-ment of the grounds therefore, shall be presented to the deputy commissioner prior to the consideration of the claim by the deputy commissioner. Failure to present such request prior to such consideration shall be an absolute defense to the special fund's liability for the payment of any benefits in connection with such claim, unless the employer could not have reasonably anticipated the liability of the special fund prior to the issuance of a compensation order.

(g) Maintenance for employees undergoing vocational rehabilitation:

An employee who as a result of injury is or may be expected to be totally or partially incapacitated for a remunerative occupation and who, under the direction of the Secretary as provided by section 939 (c) of this title, is being rendered fit to engage in a remunerative occupation, shall receive additional compensation necessary for his maintenance, but such additional compensation shall not exceed $25 a week. The expense shall be paid out of the special fund established in section 944 of this title.

(h) The wage-earning capacity of an injured employee in cases of partial disability under subsection (c)(21) of this section or under subsection (e) of this section shall be determined by his actual earnings if such actual earnings fairly and reasonably represent his wage-earning capacity: Provided, however, That if the employee has no actual earnings or his actual earnings do not fairly and reasonably represent his wage-earning capacity, the deputy commissioner may, in the interest of justice, fix such wage-earning capacity as shall be reasonable, having due regard to the nature of his injury, the degree of physical impairment, his usual employment, and any other factors or circumstances in the case which may affect his capacity to earn wages in his disabled condition, including the effect of disability as it may naturally extend into the future.

(i) (1) Whenever the parties to any claim for compensation under this chapter, including survivors benefits, agree to a settlement, the deputy commissioner or administrative law judge shall approve the settlement within thirty days unless it is found to be inadequate or procured by duress. Such settlement may include future medical benefits if the parties so agree. No liability of any employer, carrier, or both for medical, disability, or death benefits shall be discharged unless the application for settlement is approved by the deputy commissioner or administrative law judge. If the parties to the settlement are represented by counsel, then agreements shall be deemed approved unless specifically disapproved within thirty days after submission for approval.

(2) If the deputy commissioner disapproves an application for settlement under paragraph (1), the deputy commissioner shall issue a written statement within thirty days containing the reasons for disapproval. Any party to the settlement may request a hearing before an administrative law judge in the manner prescribed by this chapter. Following such hearing, the administrative law judge shall enter an order approving or rejecting the settlement.

(3) A settlement approved under this section shall discharge the liability of the employer or carrier, or both. Settlements may be agreed upon at any stage of the proceeding including after entry of a final compensation order.

(4) The special fund shall not be liable for reimbursement of any sums paid or payable to an employee or any beneficiary under such settlement, or otherwise voluntarily paid prior to such settlement by the employer or carrier, or both.

(j) (1) The employer may inform a disabled employee of his obligation to report to the employer not less than semiannually any earnings from employment or self-employment, on such forms as the Secretary shall specify in regulations.

(2) An employee who—

(A) fails to report the employee's earnings under paragraph (1) when requested, or

(B) knowingly and willfully omits or understates any part of such earnings, and who is determined by the deputy commissioner to have violated clause (A) or (B) of this paragraph, forfeits his right to compensation with respect to any period during which the employee was required to file such report.

(3) Compensation forfeited under this subsection, if already paid, shall be recovered by a deduction from the compensation payable to the employee in any amount and on such schedule as determined by the deputy commissioner.

SEC. 909. COMPENSATION FOR DEATH

If the injury causes death, the compensation therefore shall be known as a death benefit and shall be payable in the amount and to or for the benefit of the persons following:

(a) Reasonable funeral expenses not exceeding $3,000.

(b) If there be a widow or widower and no child of the deceased, to such widow or widower 50 per centum of the average wages of the deceased, during widowhood, or dependent widowerhood, with two years' compensation in one sum upon remarriage; and if there be a surviving child or children of the deceased, the additional amount of 16 2/3 per centum of such wages for each such child; in case of the death or remarriage of such widow or widower, if there be one surviving child of the deceased employee, such child shall have his compensation increased to 50 per centum of such wages, and if there be more than one surviving child of the deceased employee, to such children, in equal parts, 50 per centum of such wages increased by 16 2/3 per centum of such wages for each child in excess of one: Provided, That the total amount payable shall in no case exceed 66 2/3 per centum of such wages. The deputy commissioner having jurisdiction over the claim may, in his discretion, require the appointment of a guardian for the purpose of receiving the compensation of a minor child. In the absence of such a requirement the appointment of a guardian for such purposes shall not be necessary.

(c) If there be one surviving child of the deceased, but no widow or widower, then for the support of such child 50 per centum of the wages of the deceased; and if there be more than one surviving child of the deceased, but no widow or dependent husband, then for the support of such children, in equal parts 50 per centum of such wages increased by 16 2/3 per centum of such wages for each child in excess of one: Provided, That the total amount payable shall in no case exceed 66 2/3 per centum of such wages.

(d) If there be no surviving wife or husband or child, or if the amount payable to a surviving wife or husband and to children shall be less in the aggregate than 66 2/3 per centum of the average wages of the deceased; then for the support of grandchildren or brothers and sisters, if dependent upon the deceased at the time of the injury, and any other persons who satisfy the definition of the term "dependent" in section 152 of title 26, but are not otherwise eligible under this section, 20 per centum of such wages for the support of each such person during such dependency and for the support of each parent, or grandparent, of the deceased if dependent upon him at the time of the injury, 25 per centum of such wages during such dependency. But in no case shall the aggregate amount payable under this subsection exceed the difference between 66 2/3 per centum of such wages and the amount payable as hereinbefore provided to widow or widower and for the support of surviving child or children.

(e) In computing death benefits, the average weekly wages of the deceased shall not be less than the national average weekly wage as prescribed in section 906 (b) of this title, but—

(1) the total weekly benefits shall not exceed the lesser of the average weekly wages of the deceased or the benefit which the deceased employee would have been eligible to receive under section 906 (b)(1) of this title; and

(2) in the case of a claim based on death due to an occupational disease for which the time of injury (as determined under section 910 (i) of this title) occurs after the employee has retired, the total weekly benefits shall not exceed one fifty-second part of the employee's average annual earnings during the 52-week period preceding retirement.

(f) All questions of dependency shall be determined as of the time of the injury.

(g) Aliens: Compensation under this chapter to aliens not residents (or about to become nonresidents) of the United States or Canada shall be the same in amount as provided for residents, except that dependents in any foreign country shall be limited to surviving wife and child or children, or if there be no surviving wife or child or children, to surviving father or mother whom the employee has supported, either wholly or in part, for the period of one year prior to the date of the injury, and except that the Secretary may, at his option or upon the application of the insurance carrier shall, commute all future installments of compensation to be paid to such aliens by paying or causing to be paid to them one-half of the commuted amount of such future installments of compensation as determined by the Secretary.

* * *

SEC. 913. FILING OF CLAIMS

(a) Time to file

Except as otherwise provided in this section, the right to compensation for disability or death under this chapter shall be barred unless a claim therefore is filed within one year after the injury or death. If payment of compensation has been made without an award on account of such injury or death, a claim may be filed within one year after the date of the last payment. Such claim shall be filed with the deputy commissioner in the compensation district in which such injury or death occurred. The time for filing a claim shall not begin to run until the employee or beneficiary is aware, or by the exercise of reasonable diligence should have been aware, of the relationship between the injury or death and the employment.

(b) Failure to file

(1) Notwithstanding the provisions of subsection (a) of this section failure to file a claim within the period prescribed in such subsection shall not be a bar to such right unless objection to such failure is made at the first hearing of such claim in which all parties in interest are given reasonable notice and opportunity to be heard.

(2) Notwithstanding the provisions of subsection (a) of this section, a claim for compensation for death or disability due to an occupational disease which does not immediately result in such death or disability shall be timely if filed within two years after the employee or claimant becomes aware, or in the exercise of reasonable diligence or by reason of medical advice should have been aware, of the relationship between the employment, the disease, and the death or disability, or within one year of the date of the last payment of compensation, whichever is later.

(c) Effect on incompetents and minors

If a person who is entitled to compensation under this chapter is mentally incompetent or a minor, the provisions of subsection (a) of this section shall not be applicable so long as such person has no guardian or other authorized representative, but shall be applicable in the case of a person who is mentally incompetent or a minor from the date of appointment of such guardian or other representative, or in the case of a minor, if no guardian is appointed before he becomes of age, from the date he becomes of age.

(d) Tolling provision

Where recovery is denied to any person, in a suit brought at law or in admiralty to recover damages in respect of injury or death, on the ground that such person was an employee and that the defendant was an employer within the meaning of this chapter and that such employer had secured compensation to such employee under this chapter, the limitation of time prescribed in subsection (a) of this section shall begin to run only from the date of termination of such suit.

SEC. 914. PAYMENT OF COMPENSATION

(a) Manner of payment

Compensation under this chapter shall be paid periodically, promptly, and directly to the person entitled thereto, without an award, except where liability to pay compensation is controverted by the employer.

(b) Period of installment payments

The first installment of compensation shall become due on the fourteenth day after the employer has been notified pursuant to section 912 of this title, or the employer has knowledge of the injury or death, on which date all compensation then due shall be paid. Thereafter compensation shall be paid in installments, semimonthly, except where the deputy commissioner determines that payment in installments should be made monthly or at some other period.

(c) Notification of commencement or suspension of payment

Upon making the first payment, and upon suspension of payment for any cause, the employer shall immediately notify the deputy commissioner, in accordance with a form prescribed by the Secretary, that payment of compensation has begun or has been suspended, as the case may be.

(d) Right to compensation controverted

If the employer controverts the right to compensation he shall file with the deputy commissioner on or before the fourteenth day after he has knowledge of the alleged injury or death, a notice, in accordance with a form prescribed by the Secretary stating that the right to compensation is controverted, the name of the claimant, the name of the employer, the date of the alleged injury or death, and the grounds upon which the right to compensation is controverted.

(e) Additional compensation for overdue installment payments payable without award

If any installment of compensation payable without an award is not paid within fourteen days after it becomes due, as provided in subsection (b) of this section, there shall be added to such unpaid installment an amount equal to 10 per centum thereof, which shall be paid at the same time as, but in addition to, such installment, unless notice is filed under subsection (d) of this section, or unless such nonpayment is excused by the deputy commissioner after a showing by the employer that owing to conditions over which he had no control such installment could not be paid within the period prescribed for the payment.

(f) Additional compensation for overdue installment payments payable under terms of award

If any compensation, payable under the terms of an award, is not paid within ten days after it becomes due, there shall be added to such unpaid compensation an amount equal to 20 per centum thereof, which shall be paid at the same time as, but in addition to, such compensation, unless review of the compensation order making such award is had as provided in section 921 of this title and an order staying payment has been issued by the Board or court.

(g) Notice of payment; penalty

Within sixteen days after final payment of compensation has been made, the employer shall send to the deputy commissioner a notice, in accordance with a form prescribed by the Secretary, stating that such final payment has been made, the total amount of compensation paid, the name of the employee and of any other person to whom compensation has been paid, the date of the injury or death, and the date to which compensation has been paid. If the employer fails to so notify the deputy commissioner within such time the Secretary shall assess against such employer a civil penalty in the amount of $100.

(h) Investigations, examinations, and hearings for controverted, stopped, or suspended payments

The deputy commissioner

(1) may upon his own initiative at any time in a case in which payments are being made without an award, and

(2) shall in any case where right to compensation is controverted, or where payments of compensation have been stopped or suspended, upon receipt of notice from any person entitled to compensation, or

from the employer, that the right to compensation is controverted, or that payments of compensation have been stopped or suspended, make such investigations, cause such medical examinations to be made, or hold such hearings, and take such further action as he considers will properly protect the rights of all parties.

(i) Deposit by employer

Whenever the deputy commissioner deems it advisable he may require any employer to make a deposit with the Treasurer of the United States to secure the prompt and convenient payment of such compensation, and payments therefrom upon any awards shall be made upon order of the deputy commissioner.

(j) Reimbursement for advance payments

If the employer has made advance payments of compensation, he shall be entitled to be reimbursed out of any unpaid installment or installments of compensation due.

(k) Receipt for payment

An injured employee, or in case of death his dependents or personal representative, shall give receipts for payment of compensation to the employer paying the same and such employer shall produce the same for inspection by the deputy commissioner, whenever required.

* * *

SEC. 934. COMPENSATION NOTICE

Every employer who has secured compensation under the provisions of this chapter shall keep posted in a conspicuous place or places in and about his place or places of business typewritten or printed notices, in accordance with a form prescribed by the Secretary, stating that such employer has secured the payment of compensation in accordance with the provisions of this chapter. Such notices shall contain the name and address of the carrier, if any, with whom the employer has secured payment of compensation and the date of the expiration of the policy.

APPENDIX 4:
THE BLACK LUNG BENEFITS ACT
[30 U.S.C. §§901-945]—SELECTED
PROVISIONS

SEC. 901. CONGRESSIONAL FINDINGS AND DECLARATION OF PURPOSE; SHORT TITLE

* * *

(a) Congress finds and declares that there are a significant number of coal miners living today who are totally disabled due to pneumoconiosis arising out of employment in one or more of the Nation's coal mines; that there are a number of survivors of coal miners whose deaths were due to this disease; and that few States provide benefits for death or disability due to this disease to coal miners or their surviving dependents. It is, therefore, the purpose of this subchapter to provide benefits, in cooperation with the States, to coal miners who are totally disabled due to pneumoconiosis and to the surviving dependents of miners whose death was due to such disease; and to ensure that in the future adequate benefits are provided to coal miners and their dependents in the event of their death or total disability due to pneumoconiosis.

(b) This subchapter may be cited as the "Black Lung Benefits Act".

SEC. 922. PAYMENT OF BENEFITS

(a) Schedules

Subject to the provisions of subsection (b) of this section, benefit payments shall be made by the Secretary under this part as follows:

(1) In the case of total disability of a miner due to pneumoconiosis, the disabled miner shall be paid benefits during the disability at a

rate equal to 37 1/2 per centum of the monthly pay rate for Federal employees in grade GS-2, step 1.

(2) In the case of death of a miner due to pneumoconiosis or, except with respect to a claim filed under part C of this subchapter on or after the effective date of the Black Lung Benefits Amendments of 1981, of a miner receiving benefits under this part, benefits shall be paid to his widow (if any) at the rate the deceased miner would receive such benefits if he were totally disabled.

(3) In the case of the child or children of a miner whose death is due to pneumoconiosis or, except with respect to a claim filed under part C of this subchapter on or after the effective date of the Black Lung Benefits Amendments of 1981, of a miner who is receiving benefits under this part at the time of his death or who was totally disabled by pneumoconiosis at the time of his death, in the case of the child or children of a widow who is receiving benefits under this part at the time of her death, and in the case of any child or children entitled to the payment of benefits under paragraph (5) of section 921(c) of this title, benefits shall be paid to such child or children as follows: If there is one such child, he shall be paid benefits at the rate specified in paragraph (1). If there is more than one such child, the benefits paid shall be divided equally among them and shall be paid at a rate equal to the rate specified in paragraph (1), increased by 50 per centum of such rate if there are two such children, by 75 per centum of such rate if there are three such children, and by 100 per centum of such rate if there are more than three such children: Provided, That benefits shall only be paid to a child for so long as he meets the criteria for the term 'child' contained in section 902(g) of this title: And provided further, That no entitlement to benefits as a child shall be established under this paragraph (3) for any month for which entitlement to benefits as a widow is established under paragraph (2).

(4) In the case of an individual entitled to benefit payments under clause (1) or (2) of this subsection who has one or more dependents, the benefit payments shall be increased at the rate of 50 per centum of such benefit payments, if such individual has one dependent, 75 per centum if such individual has two dependents, and 100 per centum if such individual has three or more dependents.

(5) In the case of the dependent parent or parents of a miner whose death is due to pneumoconiosis, or, except with respect to a claim filed under part C of this subchapter on or after the effective date of the Black Lung Benefits Amendments of 1981, of a miner who is

receiving benefits under this part at the time of his death or who was totally disabled by pneumoconiosis at the time of death, and who is not survived at the time of his death by a widow or a child, in the case of the dependent surviving brother(s) or sister(s) of such a miner who is not survived at the time of his death by a widow, child, or parent, in the case of the dependent parent or parents of a miner (who is not survived at the time of his or her death by a widow or a child) who are entitled to the payment of benefits under paragraph (5) of section 921(c) of this title, or in the case of the dependent surviving brother(s) or sister(s) of a miner (who is not survived at the time of his or her death by a widow, child, or parent) who are entitled to the payment of benefits under paragraph (5) of section 921(c) of this title, benefits shall be paid under this part to such parent(s), or to such brother(s), or sister(s), at the rate specified in paragraph (3) (as if such parent(s) or such brother(s) or sister(s), were the children of such miner). In determining for purposes of this paragraph whether a claimant bears the relationship as the miner's parent, brother, or sister, the Secretary shall apply legal standards consistent with those applicable to relationship determination under title II of the Social Security Act (42 U.S.C. 401 et seq.). No benefits to a sister or brother shall be payable under this paragraph for any month beginning with the month in which he or she receives support from his or her spouse, or marries. Benefits shall be payable under this paragraph to a brother only if he is—

(1) (A) under eighteen years of age, or

(B) under a disability as defined in section 223(d) of the Social Security Act 423(d)) which began before the age specified in section 202(d)(1)(B)(ii) of such Act (42 U.S.C. 402(d)(1)(B)(ii)), or in the case of a student, before he ceased to be a student, or

(C) a student as defined in section 902(g) of this title; or

(2) who is, at the time of the miner's death, disabled as determined in accordance with section 223(d) of the Social Security Act (42 U.S.C. 423(d)), during such disability. Any benefit under this paragraph for a month prior to the month in which a claim for such benefit is filed shall be reduced to any extent that may be necessary, so that it will not render erroneous any benefit which, before the filing of such claim, the Secretary has certified for payment for such prior months. As used in this paragraph, 'dependent' means that during the one year period prior to and ending with such miner's death, such parent, brother, or sister

was living in the miner's household, and was, during such period, totally dependent on the miner for support. Proof of such support shall be filed by such claimant within two years after May 1972, or within two years after the miner's death, whichever is the later. Any such proof which is filed after the expiration of such period shall be deemed to have been filed within such period if it is shown to the satisfaction of the Secretary that there was good cause for failure to file such proof within such period. The determination of what constitutes 'living in the miner's household', 'totally dependent upon the miner for support,' and 'good cause,' shall for purposes of this paragraph be made in accordance with regulations of the Secretary. Benefit payments under this paragraph to a parent, brother, or sister, shall be reduced by the amount by which such payments would be reduced on account of excess earnings of such parent, brother, or sister, respectively, under section 203(b)-(l) of the Social Security Act (42 U.S.C. 403(b)-(l)), as if the benefit under this paragraph were a benefit under section 202 of such Act (42 U.S.C. 402).

. . . .

(6) If an individual's benefits would be increased under paragraph (4) of this subsection because he or she has one or more dependents, and it appears to the Secretary that it would be in the interest of any such dependent to have the amount of such increase in benefits (to the extent attributable to such dependent) certified to a person other than such individual, then the Secretary may, under regulations prescribed by him, certify the amount of such increase in benefits (to the extent so attributable) not to such individual but directly to such dependent or to another person for the use and benefit of such dependent; and any payment made under this clause, if otherwise valid under this subchapter, shall be a complete settlement and satisfaction of all claims, rights, and interests in and to such payment.

(b) Reduction of benefits

Notwithstanding subsection (a) of this section, benefit payments under this section to a miner or his widow, child, parent, brother, or sister shall be reduced, on a monthly or other appropriate basis, by an amount equal to any payment received by such miner or his widow, child, parent, brother, or sister under the workmen's compensation, unemployment compensation, or disability insurance laws of his State on account of the disability of such miner due to pneumoconiosis, and the amount by which such payment would be reduced on account of excess earnings of such miner under section 203(b) through (l) of the Social Security Act (42 U.S.C. 403(b) to (l)) if the amount paid were a benefit payable under section 202 of such Act (42 U.S.C. 402). This part shall not be considered a workmen's compensation law or plan for purposes of section 224 of such Act (42 U.S.C. 424a).

(c) Reporting of income

Benefits payable under this part shall be deemed not to be income for purposes of the Internal Revenue Code of 1986.

SEC. 923. FILING OF NOTICE OF CLAIM

(a) Promulgation of regulations; time requirement

Except as otherwise provided in section 924 of this title, no payment of benefits shall be made under this part except pursuant to a claim filed therefor on or before December 31, 1973, in such manner, in such form, and containing such information, as the Secretary shall by regulation prescribe.

(b) Utilization of personnel and procedures; evidence required to establish claim; medical evidence; affidavits; autopsy reports; reimbursement of expenses

In carrying out the provisions of this part, the Secretary shall to the maximum extent feasible (and consistent with the provisions of this part) utilize the personnel and procedures he uses in determining entitlement to disability insurance benefit payments under section 223 of the Social Security Act (42 U.S.C. 423), but no claim for benefits under this part shall be denied solely on the basis of the results of a chest roentgenogram. In determining the validity of claims under this part, all relevant evidence shall be considered, including, where relevant, medical tests such as blood gas studies, X-ray examination, electrocardiogram, pulmonary function studies, or physical performance tests, and any medical history, evidence submitted by the claimant's physician, or his wife's affidavits, and in the case of a deceased miner, other appropriate affidavits of persons with knowledge of the miner's physical condition, and other supportive materials. Where there is no medical or other relevant evidence in the case of a deceased miner, such affidavits, from persons not eligible for benefits in such case with respect to claims filed on or after the effective date of the Black Lung Benefits Amendments of 1981, shall be considered to be sufficient to establish that the miner was totally disabled due to pneumoconiosis or that his or her death was due to pneumoconiosis. In any case, other than that involving a claim filed on or after the effective date of the

Black Lung Benefits Amendments of 1981, in which there is other evidence that a miner has a pulmonary or respiratory impairment, the Secretary shall accept a board certified or board eligible radiologist's interpretation of a chest roentgenogram which is of a quality sufficient to demonstrate the presence of pneumoconiosis submitted in support of a claim for benefits under this subchapter if such roentgenogram has been taken by a radiologist or qualified technician, except where the Secretary has reason to believe that the claim has been fraudulently represented. In order to insure that any such roentgenogram is of adequate quality to demonstrate the presence of pneumoconiosis, and in order to provide for uniform quality in the roentgenograms, the Secretary of Labor may, by regulation, establish specific requirements for the techniques used to take roentgenograms of the chest. Unless the Secretary has good cause to believe that an autopsy report is not accurate, or that the condition of the miner is being fraudulently misrepresented, the Secretary shall accept such autopsy report concerning the presence of pneumoconiosis and the stage of advancement of pneumoconiosis. Claimants under this part shall be reimbursed for reasonable medical expenses incurred by them in establishing their claims. For purposes of determining total disability under this part, the provisions of subsections (a), (b), (c), (d), and (g) of section 221 of such Act (42 U.S.C. 421(a) to (d), (g)) shall be applicable. The provisions of sections 204, 205(a), (b), (d), (e),

(c) Filing of claim for workmen's compensation; necessity; exceptions

No claim for benefits under this section shall be considered unless the claimant has also filed a claim under the applicable State workmen's compensation law prior to or at the same time his claim was filed for benefits under this section; except that the foregoing provisions of this paragraph shall not apply in any case in which the filing of a claim under such law would clearly be futile because the period within which such a claim may be filed thereunder has expired or because pneumoconiosis is not compensable under such law, or in any other situation in which, in the opinion of the Secretary, the filing of a claim would clearly be futile.

(d) Employment termination and benefits entitlement

No miner who is engaged in coal mine employment shall (except as provided in section 921(c)(3) of this title) be entitled to any benefits under this part while so employed. Any miner who has been determined to be eligible for benefits pursuant to a claim filed while such miner was engaged in coal mine employment shall be entitled to such benefits if his or her employment terminates within one year after the date such determination becomes final.

SEC. 924. TIME FOR FILING CLAIMS

(a) Claims filed before December 31, 1973

(1) No claim for benefits under this part on account of total disability of a miner shall be considered unless it is filed on or before December 31, 1973, or, in the case of a claimant who is a widow, within six months after the death of her husband or by December 31, 1973, whichever is the later.

(2) In the case of a claim by a child this paragraph shall apply, notwithstanding any other provision of this part.

(A) If such claim is filed within six months following May 1972, and if entitlement to benefits is established pursuant to such claim, such entitlement shall be effective retroactively from December 30, 1969, or from the date such child would have been first eligible for such benefit payments had section 922(a)(3) of this title been applicable since December 30, 1969, whichever is the lesser period. If on the date such claim is filed the claimant is not eligible for benefit payments, but was eligible at any period of time during the period from December 30, 1969, to the date such claim is filed, entitlement shall be effective for the duration of eligibility during such period.

(B) If such claim is filed after six months following May 1972, and if entitlement to benefits is established pursuant to such claim, such entitlement shall be effective retroactively from a date twelve months preceding the date such claim is filed, or from the date such child would have been first eligible for such benefit payments had section 922(a)(3) of this title been applicable since December 30, 1969, whichever is the lesser period. If on the date such claim is filed the claimant is not eligible for benefit payments, but was eligible at any period of time during the period from a date twelve months preceding the date such claim is filed, to the date such claim is filed, entitlement shall be effective for the duration of eligibility during such period.

(C) No claim for benefits under this part, in the case of a claimant who is a child, shall be considered unless it is filed within six months after the death of his father or mother (whichever last occurred) or by December 31, 1973, whichever is the later.

(D) Any benefit under subparagraph (A) or (B) for a month prior to the month in which a claim is filed shall be reduced, to any extent that may be necessary, so that it will not render erroneous any benefit which, before the filing of such claim, the Secretary has certified for payment for such prior month.

(3) No claim for benefits under this part, in the case of a claimant who is a parent, brother, or sister shall be considered unless it is filed within six months after the death of the miner or by December 31, 1973, whichever is the later.

(b) Filing of claims after June 30, 1973

No benefits shall be paid under this part after December 31, 1973, if the claim therefor was filed after June 30, 1973.

(c) Effective date of claims

No benefits under this part shall be payable for any period prior to the date a claim therefor is filed.

(d) Reduction of State benefits

No benefits shall be paid under this part to the residents of any State which, after December 30, 1969, reduces the benefits payable to persons eligible to receive benefits under this part, under its State laws which are applicable to its general work force with regard to workmen's compensation, unemployment compensation, or disability insurance.

(e) Conditions upon payment

No benefits shall be payable to a widow, child, parent, brother, or sister under this part on account of the death of a miner unless

(1) benefits under this part were being paid to such miner with respect to disability due to pneumoconiosis prior to his death,

(2) the death of such miner occurred prior to January 1, 1974, or

(3) any such individual is entitled to benefits under paragraph (5) of section 921(c) of this title.

SEC. 924A. NOTIFICATION TO MINERS OF ELIGIBILITY FOR MEDICAL SERVICES AND SUPPLIES; PERIOD FOR FILING CLAIM

The Secretary of Health and Human Services shall notify each miner receiving benefits under this part on account of his or her total disability who such Secretary has reason to believe became eligible for medical services and supplies on January 1, 1974, of his or her possible eligibility for such benefits. Where such Secretary so notifies a miner, the period during which he or she may file a claim for medical services and supplies under part C of this subchapter shall not terminate before six months after such notification is made.

***

943. Black lung insurance program

(a) Authorization to establish and carry out

The Secretary is authorized to establish and carry out a black lung insurance program which will enable operators of coal mines to purchase insurance covering their obligations under section 932 of this title.

(b) Non-availability of other insurance coverage

The Secretary may exercise his or her authority under this section only if, and to the extent that, insurance coverage is not otherwise available, at reasonable cost, to operators of coal mines.

(c) Agreements with coal mine operators; reinsurance agreements

(1) The Secretary may enter into agreements with operators of coal mines who may be liable for the payment of benefits under section 932 of this title, under which the Black Lung Compensation Insurance Fund established under subsection (a) of this section (hereinafter in this section referred to as the 'insurance fund') shall assume all or part of the liability of such operator in return for the payment of premiums to the insurance fund, and on such terms and conditions as will fully protect the financial solvency of the insurance fund. During any period in which such agreement is in effect the operator shall be deemed in compliance with the requirements of section 933 of this title with respect to the risks covered by such agreement.

(2) The Secretary may also enter into reinsurance agreements with one or more insurers or pools of insurers under which, in return for the payment of premiums to the insurance fund, and on such terms and conditions as will fully protect the financial solvency of the insurance fund, the insurance fund shall provide reinsurance coverage for benefits required to be paid under section 932 of this title.

(d) Terms and conditions of insurability

The Secretary may by regulation provide for general terms and conditions of insurability as applicable to operators of coal mines or insurers eligible for insurance or reinsurance under this section, including—

(1) the types, classes, and locations of operators or facilities which shall be eligible for such insurance or reinsurance;

(2) the classification, limitation, and rejection of any operator or facility which may be advisable;

(3) appropriate premiums for different classifications of operators or facilities;

(4) appropriate loss deductibles;

(5) experience rating; and

(6) any other terms and conditions relating to insurance or reinsurance coverage or exclusion which may be appropriate to carry out the purposes of this section.

(e) Premium schedule studies and investigations

The Secretary may undertake and carry out such studies and investigations, and receive or exchange such information, as may be necessary to formulate a premium schedule which will enable the insurance and reinsurance authorized by this section to be provided on a basis which is (1) in accordance with accepted actuarial principles; and (2) fair and equitable.

(f) Regulations relating to premium rates

(1) On the basis of estimates made by the Secretary in formulating a premium schedule under subsection (e) of this section, and such other information as may be available, the Secretary shall from time to time prescribe by regulation the chargeable premium rates for types and classes of insurers, operators of coal mines, and facilities for which insurance or reinsurance coverage shall be available under this section and the terms and conditions under which, and the area within which, such insurance or reinsurance shall be available and such rates shall apply.

(2) Such premium rates shall be (A) based on a consideration of the risks involved, taking into account differences, if any, in risks based on location, type of operations, facilities, type of coal, experience, and any other matter which may be considered under accepted actuarial principles; and (B) adequate, on the basis of accepted actuarial principles, to provide reserves for anticipated losses.

(3) All premiums received by the Secretary shall be paid into the insurance fund.

(g) Black Lung Compensation Insurance Fund

(1) The Secretary may establish in the Department of Labor a Black Lung Compensation Insurance Fund which shall be available, without fiscal year limitation—

(A) to pay claims of miners for benefits covered by insurance or reinsurance issued under this section;

(B) to pay the administrative expenses of carrying out the black lung compensation insurance program under this section; and

(C) to repay to the Secretary of the Treasury such sums as may be borrowed in accordance with the authority provided in subsection (i) of this section.

(2) The insurance fund shall be credited with—

(A) premiums, fees, or other charges which may be collected in connection with insurance or reinsurance coverage provided under this section;

(B) such amounts as may be advanced to the insurance fund from appropriations in order to maintain the insurance fund in an operative condition adequate to meet its liabilities; and

(C) income which may be earned on investments of the insurance fund pursuant to paragraph (3).

(3) If, after all outstanding current obligations of the insurance fund have been liquidated and any outstanding amounts which may have been advanced to the insurance fund from appropriations authorized under subsection (i) of this section have been credited to the appropriation from which advanced, the Secretary determines that the moneys of the insurance fund are in excess of current needs, he or she may request the investment of such amounts as he or she deems advisable by the Secretary of the Treasury in public debt securities with maturities suitable for the needs of the insurance fund and bearing interest at prevailing market rates.

(h) Annual report to Congress

The Secretary shall report to the Congress not later than the first day of April of each year on the financial condition of the insurance fund and the results of the operations of the insurance fund during the preceding fiscal year and on its expected condition and operations during the fiscal year in which the report is made.

(i) Authorization of appropriations

There are authorized to be appropriated to the insurance fund, as repayable advances, such sums as may be necessary to meet obligations incurred under subsection (g) of this section. All such sums shall remain available without fiscal year limitation. Advances made pursuant to this subsection shall be repaid, with interest, to the general fund of the Treasury when the Secretary determines that moneys are available in the insurance fund for such repayments. Interest on such advances shall be computed in the same manner as provided in subsection (b)(2) of section 934a of this title.

APPENDIX 5:
DIRECTORY OF STATE WORKERS' COMPENSATION BOARDS

STATE	ADDRESS	TELEPHONE
Alabama	Workers' Compensation Division Department of Industrial Relations Industrial Relations Building Montgomery, AL 36131	(334) 242-2868
Alaska	Workers' Compensation Division Department of Labor 1111 West 8th Street, Suite 307 P.O. Box 25512 Juneau, AK 99802-5512	(907) 465-2790
Arizona	Industrial Commission 800 West Washington Street P. O. Box 19070 Phoenix, AZ 85005-9070	(602) 542-4411
Arkansas	Workers' Compensation Commission 324 S. Spring Street P. O. Box 950 Little Rock, AR 72203-9050	(501) 682-3930
California	Division of Workers' Compensation 455 Golden Gate Avenue, 9th Floor San Francisco, CA 94102	(415) 703-4600
Colorado	Division of Workers' Compensation 1515 Arapahoe Street Tower 2, Suite 400 Denver, CO 80202	(303) 575-8814
Connecticut	Workers' Compensation Commission 21 Oak Street Hartford, CT 06106	(860) 493-1500

STATE	ADDRESS	TELEPHONE
Delaware	Industrial Accident Board 4425 N. Market Street, 3rd Floor Wilmington, DE 19802	(302) 761-8200
District Of Columbia	Office of Workers' Compensation 441 4th St NW, Suite 1010 South Washington, DC 20001	(202) 727-8600
Florida	Division of Workers' Compensation 2012 Capital Circle SE Tallahassee, FL 32399-0680	(850) 488-2514
Georgia	Board of Workers' Compensation 270 Peachtree Street NW Atlanta, GA 30303-1205	(404) 656-3875
Hawaii	Disability Compensation Division Department of Labor and Industrial Relations 830 Punchbowl Street, Room 211 P. O. Box 3769 Honolulu, HI 96812	(808) 586-9151
Idaho	Industrial Commission Statehouse Mail 317 Main Street P. O. Box 83720 Boise, ID 83720-0041	(208) 334-6000
Illinois	Industrial Commission 100 West Randolph Street Suite 8-200 Chicago, IL 60601	(312) 814-6611
Indiana	Workers' Compensation Board 402 West Washington Street Room W-196 Indianapolis, IN 46204	(317) 232-3808
Iowa	Division of Workers' Compensation Workforce Development Department 1000 East Grand Avenue Des Moines, IA 50319	(515) 242-6070
Kansas	Division of Workers' Compensation Department of Human Resources 800 SW Jackson Street Suite 600 Topeka, KS 66612-1227	(785-296-3441

STATE	ADDRESS	TELEPHONE
Kentucky	Department of Workers Claims 1270 Louisville Road Perimeter Park West, Bldg. C Frankfort, KY 40601	(502) 564-5550
Louisiana	Office of Workers' Compensation 1001 North 23rd Street P. O. Box 94040 Baton Rouge, LA 70802-9040	(225) 342-7555
Maine	Workers' Compensation Board 27 State House Station Augusta, ME 04333-0027	(207) 287-7086
Maryland	Workers' Compensation Commission 10 E. Baltimore Street Baltimore, MD 21202-1641	(410) 864-5100
Massachusetts	Dept. of Industrial Accidents 600 Washington Street, 7th Floor Boston, MA 02111	(617) 727-4900
Michigan	Bureau of Workers' Disability Compensation 7150 Harris Drive P. O. Box 30016 Lansing, MI 48909	(517) 322-1296
Minnesota	Division of Workers' Compensation Department of Labor and Industry 443 Lafayette Road North St. Paul, MN 55155-4319	(651) 284-5017
Mississippi	Workers' Compensation Commission 1428 Lakeland Drive P. O. Box 5300 Jackson, MS 39296-5300	(601) 987-4200
Missouri	Division of Workers' Compensation Department of Labor and Industrial Relations P. O. Box 58 Jefferson City, MO 65102-0058	(573) 751-4231
Montana	Employment Relations Division Department of Labor and Industry 1805 Prospect Avenue P. O. Box 8011 Helena, MT 59604-8011	(406) 444-1555
Nebraska	Workers' Compensation Court Capitol Building P. O. Box 98908 Lincoln, NE 68509-8908	(402) 471-6468

STATE	ADDRESS	TELEPHONE
Nevada	Division of Industrial Insurance Relations 400 W. King Street, Suite 400 Carson City, NV 89703	(775) 886-1000
New Hampshire	Workers' Compensation Division Department of Labor 95 Pleasant Street Concord, NH 03301	(603) 271-3176
New Jersey	Division of Workers' Compensation P.O. Box 381 Trenton, NJ 08625-0381	(609) 292-2414
New Mexico	Workers' Compensation Administration 2410 Centre Drive SE P. O. Box 27198 Albuquerque, NM 87125-7198	(505) 841-6006
New York	Workers' Compensation Board 100 Broadway-Menands Albany, NY 12241	(518) 474-6670
North Carolina	Industrial Commission Dobbs Building 430 North Salisbury Street Raleigh, NC 27611	(919) 807-2500
North Dakota	Workers' Compensation Bureau 500 East Front Avenue Bismarck, ND 58504-5685	(701) 328-3800
Ohio	Bureau of Workers' Compensation 30 West Spring Street Columbus, OH 43266-0581	(614) 466-8751
Oklahoma	Workers' Compensation Court 1915 North Stiles Avenue Oklahoma City, OK 73105-4904	(405) 522-8600
Oregon	Workers' Compensation Division 350 Winter Street NE Salem, OR 97310	(503) 947-7810
Pennsylvania	Bureau of Workers' Compensation Department of Labor and Industry 1171 So. Cameron Street, Rm. 324 Harrisburg, PA 17104-2501	(717) 783-5421
Puerto Rico	Industrial Commission G.P.O. Box 364466 San Juan, PR 00936-4466	(787) 781-0545

STATE	ADDRESS	TELEPHONE
Rhode Island	Division of Workers' Compensation Department of Labor and Training P.O. Box 20190 Cranston, RI 02920-0942	(401) 462-8100
South Carolina	Workers' Compensation Commission 1612 Marion Street P. O. Box 1715 Columbia, SC 29202-1715	(803) 737-5700
South Dakota	Division of Labor & Management 700 Governors Drive, Kneip Building Pierre, SD 57501-2291	(605) 773-3681
Tennessee	Division of Workers' Compensation Andrew Johnson Tower, 2nd Floor 710 James Robertson Parkway Nashville, TN 37243-0661	(615) 741-2395
Texas	Workers' Compensation Commission Southfield Building, MS-4C 4000 South IH-35 Austin, TX 78704-7491	(512) 804-4000
Utah	Industrial Accident Division Labor Commission 160 East 300 South, 3rd Floor P. O. Box 146610, Salt Lake City, UT 84114-6610	(800) 530-6988
Vermont	Department of Labor and Industry National Life Building, Drawer 20 Montpelier, VT 05620-3401	(802) 828-2286
Virginia	Worker's Compensation Commission 1000 DMV Drive Richmond, VA 23220	(804) 367-8600
Washington	Department of Labor and Industries 7273 Linderson Way SW Tumwater, WA 98501-4850	(360) 902-4213
West Virginia	Worker's Compensation Division 4700 MacCorkle Ave. SE Charleston, WV 25304	(304) 926-5048
Wisconsin	Worker's Compensation Division Department of Workforce Development 201 E. Washington Ave. P.O. Box 79-1 Madison, WI 53707	(608) 266-1340

STATE	ADDRESS	TELEPHONE
Wyoming	Workers' Safety & Compensation Division 122 West 25th Street, 2nd Floor Herschler Building, East Wing Cheyenne, WY 82002-0700	(307) 777-7159

APPENDIX 6:
TYPE OF INSURANCE REQUIRED UNDER
STATE WORKERS' COMPENSATION LAWS

STATE	TYPE OF LAW	STATE FUND	PRIVATE CARRIER	SELF-INSURANCE
Alabama	Compulsory	No	Yes	Yes
Alaska	Compulsory	No	Yes	Yes
Arizona	Compulsory	Competitive	Yes	Yes
Arkansas	Compulsory	No	Yes	Yes
California	Compulsory	Competitive	Yes	Yes
Colorado	Compulsory	Competitive	Yes	Yes
Connecticut	Compulsory	No	Yes	Yes
Delaware	Compulsory	No	Yes	Yes
District of Columbia	Compulsory	No	Yes	Yes
Florida	Compulsory	No	Yes	Yes
Georgia	Compulsory	No	Yes	Yes
Hawaii	Compulsory	Competitive	Yes	Yes
Idaho	Compulsory	Competitive	Yes	Yes
Illinois	Compulsory	No	Yes	Yes
Indiana	Compulsory	No	Yes	Yes
Iowa	Compulsory	No	Yes	Yes
Kansas	Compulsory	No	Yes	Yes
Kentucky	Compulsory	Competitive	Yes	Yes

STATE	TYPE OF LAW	STATE FUND	PRIVATE CARRIER	SELF-INSURANCE
Louisiana	Compulsory	Competitive	Yes	Yes
Maine	Compulsory	Competitive	Yes	Yes
Maryland	Compulsory	Competitive	Yes	Yes
Massachusetts	Compulsory	No	Yes	Yes
Michigan	Compulsory	No	Yes	Yes
Minnesota	Compulsory	Competitive	Yes	Yes
Mississippi	Compulsory	No	Yes	Yes
Missouri	Compulsory	No	Yes	Yes
Montana	Compulsory	Competitive	Yes	Yes
Nebraska	Compulsory	No	Yes	Yes
Nevada	Compulsory	No	Yes	Yes
New Hampshire	Compulsory	No	Yes	Yes
New Jersey	Elective	No	Yes	Yes
New Mexico	Compulsory	Competitive	Yes	Yes
New York	Compulsory	Competitive	Yes	Yes
North Carolina	Compulsory	No	Yes	Yes
North Dakota	Compulsory	Exclusive	No	No
Ohio	Compulsory	Exclusive	No	Yes
Oklahoma	Compulsory	Competitive	Yes	Yes
Oregon	Compulsory	Competitive	Yes	Yes
Pennsylvania	Compulsory	Competitive	Yes	Yes
Rhode Island	Compulsory	Competitive	Yes	Yes
South Carolina	Compulsory	No	Yes	Yes
South Dakota	Compulsory	No	Yes	Yes
Tennessee	Compulsory	No	Yes	Yes
Texas	Elective	Competitive	Yes	Yes
Utah	Compulsory	Competitive	Yes	Yes
Vermont	Compulsory	No	Yes	Yes
Virginia	Compulsory	No	Yes	Yes

STATE	TYPE OF LAW	STATE FUND	PRIVATE CARRIER	SELF-INSURANCE
Washington	Compulsory	Exclusive	No	Yes
West Virginia	Compulsory	Exclusive	No	Yes
Wisconsin	Compulsory	No	Yes	Yes
Wyoming	Compulsory	Exclusive	No	No
United States-FECA	Compulsory	Exclusive	No	Yes
United States-LHWCA	Compulsory	No	Yes	Yes

Source: United States Department of Labor

APPENDIX 7:
WORKERS' COMPENSATION COVERAGE REQUIREMENTS FOR AGRICULTURAL AND DOMESTIC WORKERS

STATE	AGRICULTURAL WORKERS	DOMESTIC WORKERS
Alabama	Voluntary	Voluntary
Alaska	Compulsory	Compulsory
Arizona	Compulsory	Voluntary
Arkansas	Voluntary	Voluntary
California	Compulsory	Compulsory
Colorado	Compulsory	Compulsory
Connecticut	Compulsory	Compulsory
Delaware	Elective	Compulsory
District of Columbia	Compulsory	Compulsory
Florida	Compulsory	Voluntary
Georgia	Elective	Voluntary
Hawaii	Compulsory	Compulsory
Idaho	Compulsory	Voluntary
Illinois	Compulsory	Compulsory
Indiana	Voluntary	Voluntary
Iowa	Compulsory	Compulsory
Kansas	Voluntary	Compulsory

STATE	AGRICULTURAL WORKERS	DOMESTIC WORKERS
Kentucky	Voluntary	Compulsory
Louisiana	Compulsory	Excluded
Maine	Compulsory	Voluntary
Maryland	Compulsory	Compulsory
Massachusetts	Compulsory	Compulsory
Michigan	Compulsory	Compulsory
Minnesota	Compulsory	Compulsory
Mississippi	Voluntary	Voluntary
Missouri	Elective	Excluded
Montana	Compulsory	Voluntary
Nebraska	Elective	Voluntary
Nevada	Voluntary	Excluded
New Hampshire	Compulsory	Compulsory
New Jersey	Elective	Compulsory
New Mexico	Voluntary	Voluntary
New York	Compulsory	Compulsory
North Carolina	Compulsory	Compulsory
North Dakota	Voluntary	Voluntary
Ohio	Compulsory	Compulsory
Oklahoma	Compulsory	Compulsory
Oregon	Compulsory	Voluntary
Pennsylvania	Compulsory	Voluntary
Rhode Island	Compulsory	Voluntary
South Carolina	Voluntary	Compulsory
South Dakota	Voluntary	Compulsory
Tennessee	Voluntary	Voluntary
Texas	Elective	Voluntary
Utah	Compulsory	Compulsory
Vermont	Compulsory	Voluntary

STATE	AGRICULTURAL WORKERS	DOMESTIC WORKERS
Virginia	Compulsory	Excluded
Washington	Compulsory	Compulsory
West Virginia	Compulsory	Voluntary
Wisconsin	Compulsory	Voluntary
Wyoming	Elective	Excluded

Source: United States Department of Labor

APPENDIX 8:
DIRECTORY OF OCCUPATIONAL SAFETY AND HEALTH ADMINISTRATION (OSHA) OFFICES

STATE	ADDRESS	TELEPHONE	FAX
Alabama	432 Martha Parham West P.O. Box 870388 Tuscaloosa, AL 35487	205-348-7138	205-348-3049
Alaska	3301 Eagle Street P.O. Box 107022 Anchorage, AL 99510	907-269-4954	907-269-4950
Arizona	800 West Washington Phoenix, AZ 85007	602-542-5795	602-542-1614
Arkansas	10421 West Markham Little Rock, AR 72205	501-682-4522	501-682-4532
California	455 Golden Gate Avenue, Room 5246 San Francisco, CA 94102	415-703-4441	415-972-8513
Colorado	110 Veterinary Science Building Fort Collins, CO 80523	303-491-6151	303-491-7778
Connecticut	200 Folly Brook Boulevard Wethersfield, CT 06109	203-566-4550	203-566-6916
Delaware	4425 Market Street Wilmington, DE 19802	302-761-8219	302-761-6601
District of Columbia	950 Upshur Street NW Washington, DC 20011	202-576-6339	202-576-7282
Florida	2002 St. Augustine Road Building E, Suite 45 Tallahassee, FL 32399	904-488-3044	904-922-4538

STATE	ADDRESS	TELEPHONE	FAX
Georgia	Georgia Institute of Technology O'Keefe Building, Room 22 Atlanta, GA 30332	404-894-2646	404-894-8275
Hawaii	830 Punchbowl Street Honolulu, HI 96813	808-586-9100	808-586-9099
Idaho	1910 University Drive Boise, ID 83725	208-385-3283	208-385-4411
Illinois	100 West Randolph Street, Suite 3-400 Chicago, IL 60601	312-814-2337	312-814-7238
Indiana	402 West Washington Indianapolis, IN 46204	317-232-2688	317-2320748
Iowa	1000 East Grand Avenue Des Moines, IA 50319	515-281-5352	515-281-4831
Kansas	512 South West 6th Street Topeka, KS 66603	913-296-7476	913-206-1775
Kentucky	1049 U.S. Highway 127 South Frankfort, KY 40601	502-564-6895	502-564-4769
Louisiana	P.O. Box 94094 Baton Rouge, LA 70804	504-342-9601	504-342-5158
Maine	State House Station #82 Augusta, ME 04333	207-624-6460	207-624-6449
Maryland	501 St. Paul Place, 3rd Floor Baltimore, MD 21202	410-333-4210	410-333-8308
Massachusetts	1001 Watertown Street West Newton, MA 02165	617-969-7177	617-969-4581
Michigan	3423 North Martin Luther King Blvd. Lansing, MI 48909	517-335-8250	517-335-8010
Minnesota	443 Lafayette Road Saint Paul, MN 55155	612-297-2393	612-297-1953
Mississippi	2906 North State Street, Suite 201 Jackson, MS 39216	601-987-3981	601-987-3890
Missouri	3315 West Truman Boulevar-d Jefferson City, MO 65109	573-751-3403	573-751-3721
Montana	P.O. Box 1728 Helena, MT 59624	406-444-6418	406-444-4140

STATE	ADDRESS	TELEPHONE	FAX
Nebraska	State Office Building 301 Centennial Mall South, Lower Level Lincoln, NE 68509	402-471-4717	402-471-5039
Nevada	2500 West Washington Las Vegas, NV 89106	702486-5016	702-486-5331
New Hampshire	6 Hazen Drive Concord, NH 03301	603-271-2024	603-271-2667
New Jersey	Station Plaza 4, CN953 22 South Clinton Avenue Trenton, NJ 08625	609-292-2424	609-292-4409
New Mexico	525 Camino de Los Marquez, Suite 3 P.O. Box 26110 Santa Fe, NM 87502	505-827-4230	505-827-4422
New York	State Office Campus Building 12, Room 457 Albany, NY 12240	518-457-2481	518-457-5545
North Carolina	319 Chapanoke Road, Suite 105 Raleigh, NC 27603	919-662-4644	919-662-4671
North Dakota	1200 Missouri Avenue, Room 304 Bismarck, ND 58506	701-328-5188	701-328-5200
Ohio	145 S. Front Street Columbus, OH 43216	614-644-2246	614-644-3133
Oklahoma	4001 North Lincoln Boulevard Oklahoma City, OK 73105	405-528-1500	405-528-5751
Oregon	350 Winter Street NE, Room 430 Salem, OR 97310	503-378-3272	503-378-5729
Pennsylvania	Indiana University of Pennsylvania 205 Uhler Hall Indiana, PA 15705	412-357-2561	412-357-2385
Rhode Island	3 Capital Hill Providence, RI 02908	401-277-2438	401-277-6953
South Carolina	3600 Forest Drive P.O. Box 11329 Columbia, SC 29211	803-734-9614	803-734-9741

STATE	ADDRESS	TELEPHONE	FAX
South Dakota	South Dakota State University West Hall, Box 510907 Harvey Dunn Street Brookings, SD 57007	605-688-4101	605-688-6290
Tennessee	710 James Robertson Parkway, 3rd Floor Nashville, TN 37243	615-741-7036	615-741-3325
Texas	4000 South I H 35 Austin, TX 78704	512-440-3834	512-440-3831
Utah	160 East 300 South Salt Lake City, UT 84114	801-530-6868	801-530-6992
Vermont	National Life Building, Drawer 20 Montpelier, VT 05602	802-828-2765	802-828-2748
Virginia	13 South 13th Street Richmond, VA 23219	804-786-6539	804-786-8418
Washington	P.O. Box 44643 Olympia, WA 98504	360-902-5638	360-902-5459
West Virginia	Capitol Complex Building #3 1800 East Washington Street, Room 319 Charleston, WV 25305	304-558-7890	304-558-3797
Wisconsin	1414 East Washington Avenue Madison, WI 53703	608-266-8579	608-266-9711
Wyoming	Herschler Building 2 East 122 West 25th Street Cheyenne, WY 82008	307-777-7786	307-777-3646

APPENDIX 9:
JURISDICTIONS PROVIDING
DISFIGUREMENT BENEFITS

STATE	NATURE OF DISFIGUREMENT
Alabama	Serious, materially affecting employability
Alaska	No benefits
Arizona	Permanent, about head or face, including injury to, or loss of teeth
Arkansas	Serious and permanent facial or head
California	Disfigurement of face due to scarring or deformity
Colorado	Serious facial, head, or exposed body parts
Connecticut	Permanent
Delaware	Permanent and serious to exposed parts of the human body
District of Columbia	Serious facial, head, neck or other exposed areas likely to handicap employment
Florida	No benefits
Georgia	No benefits
Hawaii	Scarring and other consequences caused by medical, surgical, and hospital treatment
Idaho	Not specified
Illinois	Serious and permanent to hand, head, face, neck, arm, leg, below knee or chest
Indiana	Permanent, which may impair the future usefulness or opportunities of employee

STATE	NATURE OF DISFIGUREMENT
Iowa	Permanent head or facial, which impairs future usefulness and earnings
Kansas	Amputation or when disfigurement is handicap in obtaining or retaining employment
Kentucky	No benefits
Louisiana	Serious and permanent
Maine	Not available to employees with dates of injury on or after 1/1/1993
Maryland	For mutilations and others not specifically covered in schedule
Massachusetts	Bodily; except disfigurements that are purely scar-based unless on face, neck or hands
Michigan	No benefits
Minnesota	Disfigurement or scarring, not resulting from loss of a member
Mississippi	Serious facial or head
Missouri	Serious and permanent head, neck, hands or arms including loss or loss of use of member
Montana	Serious face, head or neck
Nebraska	No benefits
Nevada	No benefits
New Hampshire	Disfigurement and scarring caused by burns
New Jersey	No benefits
New Mexico	Serious and permanent about the face or head
New York	Serious facial, head, neck or chest
North Carolina	Serious facial or head, and body when no compensation payable under schedule
North Dakota	Not specified
Ohio	Serious facial or head which impairs opportunity to secure or retain employment
Oklahoma	Serious and permanent
Oregon	Not specified
Pennsylvania	Serious and permanent of head, face or neck

STATE	NATURE OF DISFIGUREMENT
Rhode Island	Permanent bodily
South Carolina	Serious and permanent of face, head, neck, or other area normally exposed in employment
South Dakota	Permanent
Tennessee	Serious of the head, face, or hands, so as to materially affect employability
Texas	Any disfigurement is considered
Utah	Areas of the body not specifically covered in schedule
Vermont	Permanent impairment of function
Virginia	Severely marked disfigurement of the body resulting from injury not scheduled
Washington	No benefits
West Virginia	No benefits
Wisconsin	Areas of the body that are exposed in the normal course of employment
Wyoming	Permanent of the face or head that affects earning capacity
United States-FECA	Serious of the face, head, or neck of a character likely to handicap employment
United States-LHWCA	Serious facial, head, or neck or of exposed areas likely to handicap employment

Source: United States Department of Labor

APPENDIX 10:
AVAILABILITY OF BENEFITS FOR
OCCUPATIONAL HEARING LOSS

STATE	COMPENSABLE	TIME LIMIT TO FILE
Alabama	Yes	1 year
Alaska	Yes	Discovery—2 years
Arizona	Yes	1 year
Arkansas	Yes	2 years
California	Yes	Discovery—1 year
Colorado	Yes	2–3 years
Connecticut	Yes	Discovery—3 years
Delaware	Yes	Discovery—1 year
District of Columbia	Yes	1 year
Florida	Yes	Discovery—2 years
Georgia	Yes	1 year
Hawaii	Yes	Discovery—2 years
Idaho	Yes	1 year
Illinois	Yes	3 years
Indiana	Yes, if traumatic injury	2–3 years
Iowa	Yes	2 years
Kansas	Yes	1 year
Kentucky	Yes	Discovery—2 years

STATE	COMPENSABLE	TIME LIMIT TO FILE
Louisiana	Yes	Discovery—4 months
Maine	Yes	2 years
Maryland	Yes	2 years
Massachusetts	Yes	Discovery—4 years
Michigan	No	Discovery—4 months
Minnesota	Yes	Discovery—3 years
Mississippi	Yes	Discovery—2 years
Missouri	Yes	Discovery—1 year
Montana	Yes	1 year
Nebraska	Yes	Discovery—2 years
Nevada	Yes	Discovery—90 days
New Hampshire	Yes	2 years
New Jersey	Yes	Discovery—1 to 2 years
New Mexico	Yes	2 years and 30 days
New York	Yes	Notice within 2 years or 90 days of knowledge that hearing loss is or was due to nature of employment
North Carolina	Yes	Discovery—2 years
North Dakota	Yes	1 year
Ohio	Yes	6 months
Oklahoma	Yes	Discovery—2 years from date of last hazardous exposure
Oregon	Yes	Discovery—180 days to 5 years
Pennsylvania	Yes	3 years
Rhode Island	Yes	Discovery—2 years
South Carolina	Yes	Discovery—2 years
South Dakota	Yes	2 years
Tennessee	Yes	1–3 years
Texas	Yes	1 year from date of injury or 1 year from date knew or should have known disease was related to employment

STATE	COMPENSABLE	TIME LIMIT TO FILE
Utah	Yes	Discovery—1 year
Vermont	Yes	3 years
Virginia	Yes	Discovery—2 years
Washington	Yes	Discovery—1 year
West Virginia	Yes	Discovery—3 years
Wisconsin	Yes	None
Wyoming	Yes	Discovery—1 year

Source: United States Department of Labor

APPENDIX 11:
DEATH BENEFITS FOR SURVIVING SPOUSES AND CHILDREN

STATE	PERCENTAGE (%) OF EMPLOYEE'S WAGE - SPOUSE ONLY	PERCENTAGE (%) OF EMPLOYEE'S WAGE - SPOUSE AND CHILDREN
Alabama	50	66-2/3
Alaska	80% of worker's spendable earnings	100% of worker's spendable earnings
Arizona	66-2/3	66-2/3
Arkansas	35	35 (spouse); 15 (each child)
California	66-2/3	66-2/3
Colorado	66-2/3	66-2/3
Connecticut	75% of worker's spendable earnings	75% of worker's spendable earnings
Delaware	66-2/3	80
District of Columbia	50	66-2/3
Florida	50	66-2/3
Georgia	66-2/3	66-2/3
Hawaii	50	66-2/3
Idaho	45	60
Illinois	66-2/3	66-2/3
Indiana	66-2/3	66-2/3

STATE	PERCENTAGE (%) OF EMPLOYEE'S WAGE - SPOUSE ONLY	PERCENTAGE (%) OF EMPLOYEE'S WAGE - SPOUSE AND CHILDREN
Iowa	80% of worker's spendable earnings	80% of worker's spendable earnings
Kansas	66-2/3	66-2/3
Kentucky	50	75
Louisiana	32-1/2	65
Maine	80% of worker's after tax earnings	80% of worker's after tax earnings
Maryland	66-2/3	66-2/3
Massachusetts	66-2/3	66-2/3
Michigan	80% of worker's spendable earnings	80% of worker's spendable earnings
Minnesota	50	66-2/3
Mississippi	35	66-2/3
Missouri	66-2/3	66-2/3
Montana	66-2/3	66-2/3
Nebraska	66-2/3	75
Nevada	66-2/3	66-2/3
New Hampshire	60	60
New Jersey	70	70
New Mexico	66-2/3	66-2/3
New York	66-2/3	66-2/3
North Carolina	66-2/3	66-2/3
North Dakota	66-2/3	66-2/3
Ohio	66-2/3	66-2/3
Oklahoma	70	Spouse (70); each child (up to 100)
Oregon	66-2/3	Spouse (66-2/3); each child (10%)

STATE	PERCENTAGE (%) OF EMPLOYEE'S WAGE - SPOUSE ONLY	PERCENTAGE (%) OF EMPLOYEE'S WAGE - SPOUSE AND CHILDREN
Pennsylvania	51	66-2/3
Rhode Island	75	80
South Carolina	66-2/3	66-2/3
South Dakota	66-2/3	66-2/3
Tennessee	50	66-2/3
Texas	75	75
Utah	66-2/3	66-2/3
Vermont	66-2/3	66-2/3
Virginia	66-2/3	66-2/3
Washington	60	70
West Virginia	66-2/3	66-2/3
Wisconsin	66-2/3	Child gets 10% of surviving spouse's benefit
Wyoming	Unspecified	Unspecified
United States-FECA	50	75
United States-LHWCA	50	66-2/3

Source: United States Department of Labor

APPENDIX 12:
MAXIMUM BURIAL ALLOWANCES

STATE	MAXIMUM AMOUNT ($)
Alabama	3,000
Alaska	5,000
Arizona	5,000
Arkansas	6,000
California	5,000
Colorado	7,000
Connecticut	4,000
Delaware	3,500
District of Columbia	5,000
Florida	7,500
Georgia	7,500
Hawaii	Mortician expenses not to exceed 10 times maximum weekly benefit rate allowable at time of death; cemetery expenses not to exceed 5 times maximum weekly benefit rate
Idaho	6,000 (Actual expenses of transportation of employee's body to his or her place of residence within the United States or Canada are covered)
Illinois	4,200
Indiana	7,500
Iowa	7,500
Kansas	5,000

STATE	MAXIMUM AMOUNT ($)
Kentucky	If death occurs within four years of injury, a lump-sum payment of $62,002.42 (to be adjusted annually) shall be made to the deceased's estate, from which the cost of burial and cost of transportation of the body to the employee's place of residence shall be paid
Louisiana	7,500
Maine	4,000 (Additional $3,000 will be paid to the employee's estate as incidental compensation)
Maryland	5,000 (Burial expenses in excess of maximum are payable if approved by the Workers' Compensation Commission and there are no dependents)
Massachusetts	4,000
Michigan	6,000
Minnesota	15,000
Mississippi	2,000
Missouri	5,000
Montana	4,000
Nebraska	6,000
Nevada	5,000 (Also, transportation expenses are allowed for the deceased and an accompanying person to a mortuary)
New Hampshire	5,000
New Jersey	3,500
New Mexico	7,500
New York	Funeral expenses are limited to amounts established in fee schedule of charges and costs for funeral services established by Chair of the New York Workers' Compensation Board
North Carolina	3,500
North Dakota	6,500
Ohio	5,500

STATE	MAXIMUM AMOUNT ($)
Oklahoma	Up to $10,000 will be paid for funeral expenses if there are surviving beneficiaries, otherwise up to $8,000
Oregon	Cost of burial of deceased worker cannot exceed 10 times the state's average weekly wage
Pennsylvania	3,000 (Maximum of $750 will be paid directly to the undertaker for burial in cases of death resulting from occupational disease)
Rhode Island	15,000
South Carolina	2,500
South Dakota	5,000 (Costs allowed to cover transportation of decedent's remains to community of burial)
Tennessee	7,500
Texas	6,000 (Plus the cost to transport the body from the employee's place of death back to the employee's place of work)
Utah	8,000 (The employer or the insurance carrier shall pay the burial expenses in ordinary cases as established by rule, to be reviewed every two years)
Vermont	5,500 (Additional amount not to exceed $1,000 will be paid for out-of-state transportation of decedent to place of burial
Virginia	10,000 (Reasonable expenses will be authorized not exceeding $1,000 for transportation of the decedent's remains for burial)
Washington	Maximum burial reimbursement is 200 percent of the State's average monthly wage, depending on date of injury
West Virginia	Funeral expenses will be reimbursed in an amount to be set from time to time by the Insurance Commissioner. The current maximum payable benefit is $5000
Wisconsin	6,500
Wyoming	5,000 (Maximum amount indicated unless other arrangements exist between employer and employee under agreement. Wyoming will pay an additional amount of $5,000 to cover other related expenses)

STATE	MAXIMUM AMOUNT ($)
United States-FECA	800 (Provision is also made for embalming, a hermetically sealed casket, and transportation costs for return of the remains of the deceased employee who has died away from home or home office. An additional $200 is payable to the personal representative of the decedent for terminating the decedent's status as an employee of the United States
United States-LHWCA	3,000

Source: United States Department of Labor

Workers' Compensation Law

APPENDIX 13:
EMPLOYEE'S STATEMENT OF RIGHTS UNDER THE NEW YORK STATE WORKERS' COMPENSATION PROGRAM

STATE OF NEW YORK
Eliot Spitzer, Governor

WORKERS' COMPENSATION BOARD
Donna Ferrara, Chair

STATEMENT OF RIGHTS

TO ALL WORKERS WHO ARE INJURED WHILE WORKING OR WHO SUFFER FROM AN OCCUPATIONAL DISEASE

YOU MAY BE ENTITLED TO WORKERS' COMPENSATION BENEFITS

1. You should file a claim for benefits within two years of the date you are injured, unless your injury is very minor, requiring no medical treatment and causing no lost time from work. If you do not file within two years your right to benefits may be lost. Obtain and file a claim form (Form C-3, or VF-3 for volunteer firefighters, or VAW-3 for volunteer ambulance workers) with the nearest Workers' Compensation Board office (see addresses below).

2. You may be entitled to lost time benefits if your work-related injury keeps you from work for more than seven days, compels you to work at lower wages or results in permanent disability to any part of your body. You may be entitled to rehabilitation services if you need help returning to work. (In volunteer firefighters' and volunteer ambulance workers' cases, compensation for lost time or loss of earning capacity may be payable from date of injury.)

3. You are entitled to obtain any necessary medical treatment related to your injury and you should do so immediately.

4. For the treatment of your work-related injury or illness, you may choose any physician, podiatrist, chiropractor, or psychologist (upon referral from an authorized physician) who is Board authorized and who is accepting workers' compensation patients. If, however, your employer is involved in a certified preferred provider organization (PPO) arrangement, you must obtain initial treatment for any workers' compensation injury or illness from the preferred provider organization. Employers participating in this statutory program are required to provide their employees with written notification describing their employees' rights and obligations under the program.

5. You should inform your doctor to file copies of medical reports concerning your claim with the Workers' Compensation Board and your employer's insurance company, which is indicated at the bottom of this form.

6. You should not pay any medical providers directly for treatment of your work-related injury or illness. They should send their bills to your employer's insurance carrier. If there is a dispute, the provider must wait until the Board makes a decision before it attempts to collect payment from you. If you do not pursue your claim or the Board rules that your injury is not work-related, you may be responsible for the payment of the bills.

7. The employer is liable for the replacement or repair of an employee's prosthesis (e.g., artificial members, false teeth, eyeglasses), which has been lost or damaged in the course of employment, whether or not there was bodily injury to the employee. You are also entitled to be reimbursed for drugs, crutches or any apparatus properly prescribed by your doctor, and transportation and other necessary expenses going to and from your doctor's office or hospital. (You should get receipts for all such expenses.)

8. You are entitled to be represented by an attorney or licensed representative, but it is not required. If you do hire an attorney or licensed representative, you should not pay him/her directly. Any fee will be set by the Board and will be deducted from your award.

9. Lost time and medical benefits are payable directly without a formal direction from the Board, unless your claim is disputed. If your claim is disputed on the grounds that your injury is not work-related or did not arise in the line of volunteer firefighter or ambulance worker duties, then you may qualify for disability benefits for non-work injuries. For more information on entitlement to disability benefits, contact the Workers' Compensation Board office nearest you.

10. You should go back to work as soon as you are able; compensation is never as high as your wage. If you need help returning to work, or with family or financial problems because of your injury, you should contact the nearest Board office and ask for a rehabilitation counselor or social worker.

11. Your employer may not ask you to waive your right to compensation nor may your employer deduct any money from your pay to contribute to the payment of workers' compensation insurance premiums. Further, you cannot be discharged or discriminated against because you filed a claim for workers' compensation benefits.

IF YOU HAVE DIFFICULTY IN OBTAINING A CLAIM FORM OR NEED HELP IN FILLING IT OUT, OR IF YOU HAVE ANY OTHER QUESTIONS OR PROBLEMS ABOUT A JOB-RELATED INJURY OR DISEASE, CONTACT ANY OFFICE OF THE WORKERS' COMPENSATION BOARD.

This information is a simplified presentation of your rights under the Workers' Compensation Law. It is provided, as required by Section 110 of the Workers' Compensation Law, by your employer's insurance carrier:

DONNA FERRARA
CHAIR

| DOWNSTATE CENTRALIZED MAILING (for New York City, Hempstead, Hauppauge & Peekskill Districts) PO Box 5205 Binghamton, NY 13902-5205 NYC (800)877-1373 / Hemp. (866)805-3630 / Haup. (866)681-5354 / Peek. (866)746-0552 | 100 Broadway Menands ALBANY 12241 (866) 750-5157 | State Office Building 44 Hawley Street BINGHAMTON 13901 (866) 802-3604 | Statler Towers 107 Delaware Ave. BUFFALO 14202 (866) 211-0645 | 130 Main Street W. ROCHESTER 14614 (866) 211-0644 | 935 James St. SYRACUSE 13203 (866) 802-3730 |

THE WORKERS' COMPENSATION BOARD EMPLOYS AND SERVES PEOPLE WITH DISABILITIES WITHOUT DISCRIMINATION.

C-430S (1-07)   ESTE RESUMEN ESTÁ ESCRITO EN ESPAÑOL AL DORSO

www.wcb.state.ny.us

APPENDIX 14:
EMPLOYEE'S CLAIM FOR COMPENSATION UNDER NEW YORK STATE WORKERS' COMPENSATION PROGRAM

STATE OF NEW YORK
WORKERS' COMPENSATION BOARD
EMPLOYEE'S CLAIM FOR COMPENSATION

IMPORTANT: Your Social Security Number Must Be Entered:
IMPORTANTE: El Numero de su Seguro Social Debe Ser Indicado:

ANSWER ALL QUESTIONS FULLY - TYPE OR PRINT CLEARLY

WCB Case No. (If known)_____ Carrier Case No.(if known)_____

A.
Injured Person
	1. Name...
	    First Name Middle Name Last Name
	2. Mailing Address..
	    Number and Street (include Apartment No.) City State Zip Code
	3. Residential Address (if different from mailing address) ....
	4. Sex ☐ Male ☐ Female Date of Birth.................Telephone No. ( )...........
	5. Do you speak English? ☐ Yes ☐ No If no, what language do you speak?...........
	6. Name of union and local number, if member......................
	7. State what your regular work/occupation was......................
	8. Wages or average earnings per day, including overtime, board, rent and other allowances......................
	9. Were you paid full wages for the day of injury? ☐ Yes ☐ No
	10. Your work week at time of injury was: ☐ Five day ☐ Six day ☐ Seven day ☐ Other............

B. Employer(s)	1. Employer......................................Telephone No. ( )........... 2. Employer's Address...................................... 3. Were you employed by any other employer or employers at the time of your injury/illness? ☐ Yes ☐ No 4. If yes, did you lose time from work at this other employment as a result of your injury/illness? ☐ Yes ☐ No
C. Place/Time	1. Address where injury occurred......................................County...................... 2. Date of Injury......................at..................o'clock, ☐ AM ☐ PM
D. The Injury	1. How did injury/illness occur?...................................... 2. Did anyone witness the injury? ☐ Yes ☐ No If yes, name(s)...................... 3. Is the injury the result of the use or operation of a motor vehicle? ☐ Yes ☐ No If Yes, ☐ your vehicle ☐ employer's vehicle If your vehicle was involved, give name & address of your motor vehicle (No-Fault) insurance carrier.........................
E. Nature and Extent of Injury/Illness	1. State fully the nature of your injury/illness, including all parts of body injured............ 2. Date you stopped work because of this injury/illness?...................... 3. Have you returned to work? ☐ Yes ☐ No If yes, on what date?...................... 4. Does injury/illness keep you from work? ☐ Yes ☐ No 5. Have you done any work during period of disability? ☐ Yes ☐ No 6. Have you received any wages since your injury/illness? ☐ Yes ☐ No

F.
Medical Benefits
	1. Did you receive or are you now receiving medical care? ☐ Yes ☐ No
	2. Are you now in need of medical care? ☐ Yes ☐ No
	3. Name of attending doctor......................
	   Doctor's address......................
	4. If you were in a hospital, give the dates hospitalized......................
	   Name of hospital......................
	   Hospital's Address......................

G. Comp. Payments	1. Have you received or are you now receiving workers' compensation payments for the injury reported above? ☐ Yes ☐ No 2. Do you claim further workers' compensation payments? ☐ Yes ☐ No
H. Notice	1. Have you given your employer (or supervisor) notice of injury? ☐ Yes ☐ No 2. If yes, notice was given ☐ orally ☐ in writing, on...................... to......................

EMPLOYEE'S CLAIM FOR COMPENSATION

I hereby present my claim to the Chair, Workers' Compensation Board, for compensation for disability resulting from an accidental injury or occupational disease arising out of and in the course of my employment and not occasioned by my willful intention or solely through intoxication, and in support of it I make the foregoing statement of facts.

Signed by... Dated..
(Claimant)

SEE OTHER SIDE FOR IMPORTANT INFORMATION - VEASE AL DORSO PARA INFORMACION DE IMPORTANCIA

THE WORKERS' COMPENSATION BOARD EMPLOYS AND SERVES PEOPLE WITH DISABILITIES WITHOUT DISCRIMINATION.
LA JUNTA DE COMPENSACION OBRERA EMPLEA Y SIRVE A PERSONAS INCAPACITADAS SIN DISCRIMINAR.

C-3 (11-06)   www.wcb.state.ny.us

APPENDIX 15:
ALLOWABLE ATTORNEY FEES UNDER STATE WORKERS' COMPENSATION LAWS

STATE	ALLOWABLE ATTORNEY FEES
Alabama	15%; statute
Alaska	No fee cap; fee awards must be compensatory and reasonable; minimum fee is 25% of first $1,000 of benefits awarded and 10% of balance; one-time consultation fee up to $300; statute
Arizona	25%; statute
Arkansas	25% of indemnity benefits; statute
California	Individual case basis; however an attorney cannot collect a fee for representation
Colorado	20%; statute
Connecticut	Individual case basis
Delaware	30% of award or 10 times the state average weekly wages, whichever is less; statute
District of Columbia	20%; statute
Florida	20%—first $5,000; 15%—second $5,000; 10% on amount received over first 10 years; 5% on balance; statute
Georgia	25%; statute
Hawaii	Individual case basis
Idaho	25% non-litigated; 30% litigated
Illinois	20%; statute

STATE	ALLOWABLE ATTORNEY FEES
Indiana	Individual case basis
Iowa	Individual case basis
Kansas	25%; statute
Kentucky	20%—first $25,000; 15%—next $10,000; 5% balance up to a maximum of $12,000; statute
Louisiana	20% of all amounts recovered; 10% on balance; statute
Maine	Individual case basis; settlement cap is $7,500
Maryland	Permanent partial disability—20% of the first 75 weeks of compensation; 15% of compensation due for weeks 76–195; 10% of compensation due for weeks 196+; cap is 20 times state average weekly wages for a year
Massachusetts	If employee prevails before hearing, twice state average weekly wages; otherwise depends on when appellate process, settlement occurs; statute
Michigan	30%; up to time of trial, 15%—first $25,000; 10% balance on redemption settlements; 10% on voluntary payment settlements
Minnesota	25%—first $4,000; 20%—next $60,000; statute
Mississippi	25% before Commission; 33-1/3% before Court; statute
Missouri	25%; policy
Montana	20%–25%; rule
Nebraska	Reasonable; statute
Nevada	No special provision
New Hampshire	20%; policy
New Jersey	20%; statute
New Mexico	Maximum of $16,500; statute
New York	Individual case basis
North Carolina	Individual case basis
North Dakota	Hourly fees and maximum caps depend on whether injured worker prevails and the level at which the case was resolved. At administrative hearing level, the cap is $4,620 and at the Supreme Court level, the cap is $9,356 with different levels of resolution in between having different maximum caps

STATE	ALLOWABLE ATTORNEY FEES
Ohio	Individual case basis
Oklahoma	10%—total temporary disability; 20%—other types; statute
Oregon	25% of increased compensation not to exceed $4,600 (permanent partial disability; $12,500 (permanent temporary disability; $1,500 (temporary disability); rule
Pennsylvania	20%; statute
Rhode Island	Individual case basis
South Carolina	Individual case basis
South Dakota	25%—settlements; 30%—lower court cases; 35%—State Supreme Court cases; statute
Tennessee	20%; statute
Texas	25%; statute
Utah	20%—first $15,000; 15%—next $15,000; 10%—balance; maximum—$10,850
Vermont	20% up to maximum of $9,000; rule
Virginia	Individual case basis
Washington	30%; statute
West Virginia	Limited to 20% of claimant's or dependent's award; 208 week limit; statute
Wisconsin	20% in disputed cases; statute
Wyoming	Individual case basis

Source: United States Department of Labor

APPENDIX 16:
WAITING PERIOD FOR BENEFITS UNDER STATE WORKERS' COMPENSATION LAWS

STATE	WAITING PERIOD
Alabama	3 days (temporary total disability only)
Alaska	3 days
Arizona	7 days
Arkansas	7 days
California	3 days (temporary total disability only)
Colorado	3 days
Connecticut	3 days
Delaware	3 days (none if amputation or hospitalization of employee)
District of Columbia	3 days
Florida	7 days
Georgia	7 days
Hawaii	3 days (temporary total disability only)
Idaho	5 days
Illinois	3 days (temporary total disability only)
Indiana	7 days (temporary disability only)
Iowa	3 days (temporary total disability)
Kansas	7 days (temporary total/permanent partial disability only)
Kentucky	7 days

STATE	WAITING PERIOD
Louisiana	7 days
Maine	7 days
Maryland	3 days
Massachusetts	5 days
Michigan	7 days
Minnesota	3 days (temporary total disability)
Mississippi	5 days
Missouri	3 days (first 3 days employer is open for business)
Montana	4 days (or 32 hrs. to take into consideration shift work)
Nebraska	7 days
Nevada	5 days (temporary disability only)
New Hampshire	3 days
New Jersey	7 days (compensation of certain volunteers-no waiting period)
New Mexico	7 days
New York	7 days
North Carolina	7 days
North Dakota	4 days
Ohio	7 days
Oklahoma	3 days (temporary total disability only)
Oregon	3 days (temporary total and temporary partial disability)
Pennsylvania	7 days (no waiting period for scheduled injuries)
Rhode Island	3 days
South Carolina	7 days
South Dakota	7 days
Tennessee	7 days
Texas	7 days
Utah	3 days (temporary total disability only)
Vermont	3 days (total disability only)
Virginia	7 days

STATE	WAITING PERIOD
Washington	3 days (temporary total disability)
West Virginia	3 days
Wisconsin	3 days
Wyoming	3 days (temporary total disability only)
United States - FECA	3 days (temporary disability only)
United States - LHWCA	3 days

Source: United States Department of Labor

APPENDIX 17:
RETROACTIVITY OF BENEFITS UNDER
STATE WORKERS' COMPENSATION LAWS

STATE	RETROACTIVITY OF BENEFITS
Alabama	Compensation is retroactive if disability continues for 21 days from date of injury
Alaska	Compensation is retroactive if disability continues for more than 28 days from date of injury
Arizona	Compensation is retroactive if disability continues for 14 days from date of injury
Arkansas	Compensation is retroactive if disability continues for 2 weeks from date of injury
California	Compensation is retroactive if disability continues for 14 days from date of injury
Colorado	Compensation is retroactive if disability continues for 2 weeks from date of injury
Connecticut	Compensation is retroactive if disability continues for 7 days from date of injury
Delaware	Compensation is retroactive if disability continues for 7 days from date of injury
District of Columbia	Compensation is retroactive if disability continues for more than 14 days from date of injury
Florida	Compensation is retroactive if disability continues for 21 days from date of injury
Georgia	Compensation is retroactive if disability continues for 21 days from date of injury
Hawaii	None

STATE	RETROACTIVITY OF BENEFITS
Idaho	Compensation is retroactive if disability continues for more than 2 weeks from date of injury
Illinois	Compensation is retroactive if disability continues for 14 days or more from date of injury
Indiana	Compensation is retroactive if disability continues for 21 days from date of injury
Iowa	Compensation is retroactive if disability continues for more than 14 days from date of injury
Kansas	Compensation is retroactive if disability continues for 3 weeks from date of injury
Kentucky	Compensation is retroactive if disability continues for 2 weeks from date of injury
Louisiana	Compensation is retroactive if disability continues for 6 weeks from date of injury
Maine	Compensation is retroactive if disability continues for 14 days from date of injury
Maryland	Compensation is retroactive if disability continues for more than 14 days from date of injury
Massachusetts	Compensation is retroactive if disability continues for 21 or more days from date of injury
Michigan	Compensation is retroactive if disability continues for 2 weeks from date of injury
Minnesota	Compensation is retroactive if disability continues for 10 days from date of injury
Mississippi	Compensation is retroactive if disability continues for 14 days from date of injury
Missouri	Compensation is retroactive if disability continues for more than 14 days from date of injury
Montana	No provision
Nebraska	Compensation is retroactive if disability continues for 6 weeks from date of injury
Nevada	Compensation is retroactive if disability continues for 5 or more days from date of injury
New Hampshire	Compensation is retroactive if disability continues for 14 days or more from date of injury

STATE	RETROACTIVITY OF BENEFITS
New Jersey	Compensation is retroactive if disability continues for 7 days from date of injury
New Mexico	Compensation is retroactive if disability continues for 4 weeks from date of injury
New York	Compensation is retroactive if disability continues for 14 days from date of injury
North Carolina	Compensation is retroactive if disability continues for 21 days from date of injury
North Dakota	Compensation is retroactive if disability continues for 5 days from date of injury
Ohio	Compensation is retroactive if disability continues for 2 weeks from date of injury
Oklahoma	None
Oregon	Compensation is retroactive if disability continues for 14 days from date of injury
Pennsylvania	Compensation is retroactive if disability continues for 14 days from date of injury
Rhode Island	None, compensation begins on 4th day after injury
South Carolina	Compensation is retroactive if disability continues for 14 days from date of injury
South Dakota	Compensation is retroactive if disability continues for 7 days from date of injury
Tennessee	Compensation is retroactive if disability continues for 14 days from date of injury
Texas	Compensation is retroactive if disability continues for 2 weeks from date of injury
Utah	Compensation is retroactive if disability continues for more than 14 days from date of injury
Vermont	Compensation is retroactive if disability continues for 7 days from date of injury
Virginia	Compensation is retroactive if disability continues for 3 weeks from date of injury
Washington	Compensation is retroactive if disability continues for 14 days from date of injury
West Virginia	Compensation is retroactive if disability continues for more than 7 days from date of injury

STATE	RETROACTIVITY OF BENEFITS
Wisconsin	Compensation is retroactive if disability continues for more than 7 days from date of injury
Wyoming	Compensation is retroactive if disability continues for more than 8 days from date of injury
United States-FECA	Compensation is retroactive if disability continues for more than 14 days from date of injury
United States-LHWCA	Compensation is retroactive if disability continues for more than 14 days from date of injury

Source: United States Department of Labor

APPENDIX 18:
PERCENTAGE OF WAGES PAYABLE FOR TEMPORARY TOTAL DISABILITY UNDER STATE WORKERS' COMPENSATION LAWS

STATE	PERCENTAGE OF WAGES
Alabama	66-2/3%
Alaska	80%
Arizona	66-2/3%
Arkansas	66-2/3%
California	66-2/3%
Colorado	66-2/3%
Connecticut	75%
Delaware	66-2/3%
District of Columbia	66-2/3%
Florida	66-2/3%
Georgia	66-2/3%
Hawaii	66-2/3%
Idaho	67%
Illinois	66-2/3%
Indiana	66-2/3%
Iowa	80%
Kansas	66-2/3%

STATE	PERCENTAGE OF WAGES
Kentucky	66-2/3%
Louisiana	66-2/3%
Maine	80%
Maryland	66-2/3%
Massachusetts	60%
Michigan	80%
Minnesota	66-2/3%
Mississippi	66-2/3%
Missouri	66-2/3%
Montana	66-2/3%
Nebraska	66-2/3%
Nevada	66-2/3%
New Hampshire	60%
New Jersey	70%
New Mexico	66-2/3%
New York	66-2/3%
North Carolina	66-2/3%
North Dakota	66-2/3%
Ohio	72% reduced to 66.67% after 12 weeks
Oklahoma	70%
Oregon	66-2/3%
Pennsylvania	66-2/3%
Rhode Island	75%
South Carolina	66-2/3%
South Dakota	66-2/3%
Tennessee	66-2/3%
Texas	70%
Utah	66-2/3%
Vermont	66-2/3%

STATE	PERCENTAGE OF WAGES
Virginia	66-2/3%
Washington	60–75% depending on marital status
West Virginia	66-2/3%
Wisconsin	66-2/3%
Wyoming	66-2/3%
United States - FECA	66-2/3 - 75%
United States - LHWCA	66-2/3%

Source: United States Department of Labor

APPENDIX 19:
PERCENTAGE OF WAGES PAYABLE FOR PERMANENT TOTAL DISABILITY UNDER STATE WORKERS' COMPENSATION LAWS

STATE	PERCENTAGE OF WAGES
Alabama	66-2/3%
Alaska	80%
Arizona	66-2/3%
Arkansas	66-2/3%
California	66-2/3%
Colorado	66-2/3%
Connecticut	75%
Delaware	66-2/3%
District of Columbia	66-2/3%
Florida	66-2/3%
Georgia	66-2/3%
Hawaii	66-2/3%
Idaho	67%
Illinois	66-2/3%
Indiana	66-2/3%
Iowa	80%
Kansas	66-2/3%

STATE	PERCENTAGE OF WAGES
Kentucky	66-2/3%
Louisiana	66-2/3%
Maine	80%
Maryland	66-2/3%
Massachusetts	66-2/3%
Michigan	80%
Minnesota	66-2/3%
Mississippi	66-2/3%
Missouri	66-2/3%
Montana	66-2/3%
Nebraska	66-2/3%
Nevada	66-2/3%
New Hampshire	60%
New Jersey	70%
New Mexico	66-2/3%
New York	66-2/3%
North Carolina	66-2/3%
North Dakota	66-2/3%
Ohio	66-2/3%
Oklahoma	70%
Oregon	66-2/3%
Pennsylvania	66-2/3%
Rhode Island	75%
South Carolina	66-2/3%
South Dakota	66-2/3%
Tennessee	66-2/3%
Texas	75%
Utah	66-2/3%
Vermont	66-2/3%

STATE	PERCENTAGE OF WAGES
Virginia	66-2/3%
Washington	60-75% depending on marital status
West Virginia	66-2/3%
Wisconsin	66-2/3%
Wyoming	66-2/3%
United States - FECA	66-2/3 - 75%
United States - LHWCA	66-2/3%

Source: United States Department of Labor

APPENDIX 20:
PERCENTAGE OF WAGES PAYABLE FOR PERMANENT PARTIAL DISABILITY UNDER STATE WORKERS' COMPENSATION LAWS

STATE	PERCENTAGE OF WAGES
Alabama	66-2/3%
Alaska	statutory computation
Arizona	55%
Arkansas	66-2/3%
California	66-2/3%
Colorado	statutory computation
Connecticut	75%
Delaware	66-2/3%
District of Columbia	66-2/3%
Florida	statutory computation
Georgia	66-2/3%
Hawaii	66-2/3%
Idaho	N/A
Illinois	60%
Indiana	66-2/3%
Iowa	80%

STATE	PERCENTAGE OF WAGES
Kansas	66-2/3%
Kentucky	66-2/3%
Louisiana	66-2/3%
Maine	80%
Maryland	66-2/3%
Massachusetts	60%
Michigan	80%
Minnesota	66-2/3%
Mississippi	66-2/3%
Missouri	66-2/3%
Montana	66-2/3%
Nebraska	66-2/3%
Nevada	statutory computation
New Hampshire	60%
New Jersey	70%
New Mexico	66-2/3%
New York	66-2/3%
North Carolina	66-2/3%
North Dakota	statutory computation
Ohio	statutory computation
Oklahoma	70%
Oregon	66-2/3%
Pennsylvania	66-2/3%
Rhode Island	75%
South Carolina	66-2/3%
South Dakota	66-2/3%
Tennessee	66-2/3%
Texas	70%
Utah	66-2/3%

STATE	PERCENTAGE OF WAGES
Vermont	66-2/3%
Virginia	66-2/3%
Washington	statutory computation
West Virginia	66-2/3%
Wisconsin	66-2/3%
Wyoming	N/A
United States - FECA	66-2/3- 75%
United States - FECA	66-2/3%

Source: United States Department of Labor

APPENDIX 21:
CHOICE OF PHYSICIAN RULES UNDER
STATE WORKERS' COMPENSATION LAWS

STATE	CHOICE OF PHYSICIAN
Alabama	Employer selects physician
Alaska	Employee makes initial choice of physician; employer may establish preferred provider list but must instruct employees that they may choose any provider without regard to inclusion on employer's list
Arizona	Employee makes initial choice of physician; however, if employer is self-insured, employer may choose physician, except in emergencies
Arkansas	Employer makes initial choice of physician; may be changed by state agency; employee may petition for a one-time change of physician
California	Employer makes initial choice of physician; after specified time, employee has free choice
Colorado	Employer makes initial choice of physician; may be changed by state agency
Connecticut	Employee makes initial choice of physician unless employer does not have a managed care plan established
Delaware	Employee makes initial choice of physician
District of Columbia	Employee makes initial choice of physician
Florida	Employee selects physician from list supplied by carrier or managed care organization when medical care is provided through an authorized managed care arrangement; employee may petition for one-time change of physician; if medical care is provided outside an authorized managed care arrangement, the employer chooses the physician

STATE	CHOICE OF PHYSICIAN
Georgia	Employee selects initial physician from list maintained by employer
Hawaii	Employee makes initial choice of physician
Idaho	Employer makes initial choice of physician; may be changed by state agency
Illinois	Employee makes initial choice of physician
Indiana	Employer selects the physician
Iowa	Employer selects the physician
Kansas	Employer selects the physician
Kentucky	Employee makes initial choice of physician; employee selects from a list supplied by carrier on managed care organization when medical care is provided through an authorized managed care arrangement
Louisiana	Employee makes initial choice of physician
Maine	Employer makes initial choice of physician; after a specified period of time, the employee has free choice
Maryland	Employee makes initial choice of physician
Massachusetts	Employee makes initial choice of physician
Michigan	Employer makes initial choice of physician; after a specified period of time, employee has free choice
Minnesota	Employee makes initial choice of physician; if managed care plan in effect, employee is obligated to see a physician in the plan network unless a relationship has developed with a physician outside plan
Mississippi	Employee makes initial choice of physician
Missouri	Employer selects the physician
Montana	Employee makes initial choice of physician
Nebraska	Employee makes initial choice of physician
Nevada	Employee makes initial choice of physician; in emergency, if employer's workers' compensation insurer has entered into a managed care contract or health care service provider contract, the injured employee must choose the treating physician or chiropractor or health care service provider according to the terms of the contract
New Hampshire	Employee makes initial choice of physician

STATE	CHOICE OF PHYSICIAN
New Jersey	Employer selects the physician
New Mexico	Employer makes initial choice of physician;; after specified period of time, employee has free choice
New York	Employee selects initial physician from a list maintained by the state agency
North Carolina	Employer makes initial selection of physician; may be changed by state agency
North Dakota	Employers may select a designated medical provider; employee may opt out and choose a different provider in writing and prior to injury
Ohio	Employee makes initial choice of physician
Oklahoma	Employer makes initial choice of physician within first three days of actual knowledge of employee injury or per a certified workplace medical plan.
Oregon	Employee makes initial choice of physician
Pennsylvania	Employee selects initial physician from a list maintained by employer; if no list posted by employer, employee can choose any physician
Rhode Island	Employee makes initial choice of physician
South Carolina	Employer selects the physician
South Dakota	Employee makes initial choice of physician
Tennessee	Employee selects initial physician from list maintained by employer
Texas	Non-network: employee chooses physician from division's approved doctor list and is allowed one change of doctor with division approval. Network: employee chooses physician from list of network doctors and is allowed one change without approval; subsequent changes must be approved by network
Utah	Employer makes initial choice of physician;; employee may make one choice of physician after initially seeing the employer's physician
Vermont	Employer makes initial choice of physician; after specified period of time, employee has free choice of treating physician

STATE	CHOICE OF PHYSICIAN
Virginia	Employee selects initial physician from list maintained by employer; employer's list of physicians may also include chiropractors for treatment of employee's injuries
Washington	Employee makes initial choice of physician
West Virginia	Employee makes initial choice of physician
Wisconsin	Employee makes initial choice of physician
Wyoming	Employee makes initial choice of physician

Source: United States Department of Labor

APPENDIX 22:
WORKERS' COMPENSATION/PUBLIC DISABILITY BENEFIT QUESTIONNAIRE (FORM SSA-546)

Social Security Administration

Form Approved
OMB No. 0960-0247

WORKERS' COMPENSATION/PUBLIC DISABILITY BENEFIT QUESTIONNAIRE

NAME OF WORKER	SOCIAL SECURITY NUMBER

PRIVACY ACT/PAPERWORK ACT NOTICE: Your responses to this request is voluntary; however, failure to provide all or part of the requested information could prevent an accurate and timely decision on this claim and could affect your Social Security benefits. The Social Security Administration uses the information you furnish to determine the effect of your worker's compensation or other public disability benefit on your Social Security disability insurance benefits, as provided in section 224 of the Social Security Act (42 U.S.C. 424). The information on this form may be disclosed by the Social Security Administration to another person or agency for the following purposes: (1) to assist the Social Security Administration in establishing the right of a beneficiary to Social Security benefits; (2) to facilitate statistical research and audit activities necessary to assure the integrity and improvement of the Social Security programs; and (3) to comply with laws requiring the exchange of information between the Social Security Administration and another agency.

We may also use the information you give us when we match records by computer. Matching programs compare our records with those of other Federal, State, or local government agencies. Many agencies may use matching programs to find or prove that a person qualifies for benefits paid by the Federal government. The law allows us to do this even if you do not agree to it.

These and other reasons why information about you may be used or given out are explained in the Federal Register. If you want to learn more about this, contact any Social Security Office.

Paperwork Reduction Act Statement - This information collection meets the requirements of 44 U.S.C. § 3507, as amended by Section 2 of the Paperwork Reduction Act of 1995. You do not need to answer these questions unless we display a valid Office of Management and Budget control number. We estimate that it will take about 12.5 minutes to read the instructions, gather the facts, and answer the questions. **SEND OR BRING THE COMPLETED FORM TO YOUR LOCAL SOCIAL SECURITY OFFICE. The office is listed under U. S. Government agencies in your telephone directory or you may call Social Security at 1-800-772-1213 (TTY 1-800-325-0778). You may send comments on our time estimate above to: SSA, 6401 Security Blvd, Baltimore, MD 21235-6401.** Send only comments relating to our time estimate to this address, not the completed form.

1. What type of benefit are you receiving, did you receive or do you expect to receive in connection with your disability?

WORKERS' COMPENSATION:
- [ ] Workers' Compensation - State (including) occupational disease payments)
- [ ] Black Lung Benefits
- [ ] Longshore and Harbor Workers' Compensation
- [ ] Federal Employees' Compensation (FECA-workers' compensation for Federal employees)

PUBLIC DISABILITY BENEFITS:
- [ ] Civil Service Disability or Federal Employees' Retirement System (FERS) Disability Benefits
- [ ] State Temporary Disability Payments
- [ ] Federal, State or Local Government Employee Disability Benefits
- [ ] Other: _____

2. For each benefit checked. above, enter the claim number, employer, insurance carrier and date of injury/illness.3

TYPE OF BENEFIT	CLAIM NUMBER	EMPLOYER	INSURANCE CARRIER	DATE OF INJURY/ILLNESS

3. Indicate the State in which you worked when these benefits began or, if workers' compensation is one of the benefits involved, the State in which the injury occurred.

STATE

4. If you are receiving one of the public disability benefits listed in item 1, were Social Security taxes always paid on your earnings?
- [ ] Yes [ ] No (If "No," explain. For example, you were a federal, State or local government employee whose earnings were not covered or were not always covered by Social Security.)

---

5. Indicate the status of your claim for workers' compensation or other public disability benefits. If you are receiving more than one type of benefit, indicate the status of each claim.

a. ☐   Filed for Benefits, or Intend to File but not yet Entitled

d. ☐   Currently Receiving Benefits

b. ☐   Filed for Benefits, but Claim was Denied

e. ☐   Received Payments in the Past but not Presently Receiving Them

c. ☐   Claim Denied; Appeal Pending (if appeal is pending, give date you expect a decision.)

f. ☐   Other (e.g., lump-sum payment) Explain: _____

Date _____

_____

If a., b., or c. is checked, go on to Item 11 (signature block). If d., e., or f. is checked, complete the remainder of the form.

6. How are (or were) those disability payments made?

☐ Weekly   ☐ Monthly   ☐ Every Two Weeks   ☐ Other (Explain): _____

FORM **SSA**-546 (6-2004) EF (09-2007)

7. a. List the amount(s) and the period(s) of time for which those disability benefits were made. (if only lump-sum payment was made, see item 8.)

TYPE OF BENEFIT	AMOUNT	FROM	TO

b. If those payments have stopped, indicate the reason:

☐ Lump-Sum Settlement Pending   ☐ Appeal Pending

☐ Permanent Rating Pending   ☐ Other (Explain in item 10, "Remarks")

c. Do you expect those payments to begin again? ☐ Yes ☐ No   IF "YES", WHEN (Date)

8. Have you ever received or been awarded a lump-sum settlement (including "compromise and release" or similar type of settlement)?   Yes (If "Yes", ☐ complete item 9) ☐ No

9. Lump-sum payment:

a. Date(s) settlement(s) or award(s) made   b. Gross Amount(s)

$

c. The lump sum represents:

$ _____ per week for _____ weeks beginning _____

d. The amount shown in 9.b. (Gross amount) includes:

(1) MEDICAL EXPENSES OF	(2) ATTORNEY FEES OF	(3) RELATED EXPENSES OF
$	$	$

10. Remarks:

IMPORTANT INFORMATION. PLEASE READ THE FOLLOWING CAREFULLY AND SIGN BELOW

I agree to report if I apply for or begin to receive a workers' compensation (including black lung benefits) or a public disability benefit or the amount that I am receiving changes or stops, or I receive a lump-sum settlement. I understand that such benefits may affect my Social Security payments or result in an overpayment which I may have to pay back. I declare under penalty of perjury that I have examined all the information on this form, and on any accompanying statements or forms, and it is true and correct to the best of my knowledge. I understand that anyone who knowingly gives a false or misleading statement about a material fact in this information, or causes someone else to do so, commits a crime and may be sent to prison, or may face other penalties, or both.

SIGNATURE OF PERSON MAKING STATEMENT	DATE
SIGNATURE (First Name, Middle Initial, Last Name) (Write in Ink) **SIGN HERE** ▶	TELEPHONE NUMBERS(S) at which you may be contacted during the day ( )

MAILING ADDRESS (Number Street, Apt. No., P.O. Box., Rural Route)

CITY AND STATE	ZIP CODE

Witnesses are required ONLY if this form has been signed by mark (X) above. If signed by mark (X), two witnesses to the signing who know the person requesting reconsideration must sign below, giving their full addresses.

(1) SIGNATURE OF WITNESS	(2) SIGNATURE OF WITNESS
ADDRESS (Number and Street, City, State and ZIP Code)	ADDRESS (Number and Street, City, State and ZIP Code)

FORM **SSA-546** (6-2004) EF (09-2007)

APPENDIX 23:
FEDERAL EMPLOYEE'S NOTICE OF
INJURY AND CLAIM FOR COMPENSATION
(FORM CA-1)

Federal Employee's Notice of Traumatic Injury and Claim for Continuation of Pay/Compensation	Reset Print	**U.S. Department of Labor** Employment Standards Administration Office of Workers' Compensation Programs

Employee: Please complete all boxes 1 - 15 below. Do not complete shaded areas.
Witness: Complete bottom section 16.
Employing Agency (Supervisor or Compensation Specialist): Complete shaded boxes a, b, and c.

Employee Data

1. Name of employee (Last, First, Middle)	2. Social Security Number

3. Date of birth Mo. Day Yr.	4. Sex Male Female	5. Home telephone	6. Grade as of date of injury Level Step

7. Employee's home mailing address (Include city, state, and ZIP code)	8. Dependents Wife, Husband Children under 18 years Other

Description of Injury

9. Place where injury occurred (e.g. 2nd floor, Main Post Office Bldg., 12th & Pine)

10. Date injury occurred Mo. Day Yr.	Time a.m. p.m.	11. Date of this notice Mo. Day Yr.	12. Employee's occupation

13. Cause of injury (Describe what happened and why)

	a. Occupation code
14. Nature of injury (Identify both the injury and the part of body, e.g., fracture of left leg)	b. Type code c. Source code
	OWCP Use - NOI Code

Employee Signature

15. I certify, under penalty of law, that the injury described above was sustained in performance of duty as an employee of the United States Government and that it was not caused by my willful misconduct, intent to injure myself or another person, nor by my intoxication. I hereby claim medical treatment, if needed, and the following, as checked below, while disabled for work:

a. Continuation of regular pay (COP) not to exceed 45 days and compensation for wage loss if disability for work continues beyond 45 days. If my claim is denied, I understand that the continuation of my regular pay shall be charged to sick or annual leave, or be deemed an overpayment within the meaning of 5 USC 5584.

b. Sick and/or Annual Leave

I hereby authorize any physician or hospital (or any other person, institution, corporation, or government agency) to furnish any desired information to the U.S. Department of Labor, Office of Workers' Compensation Programs (or to its official representative). This authorization also permits any official representative of the Office to examine and to copy any records concerning me.

Signature of employee or person acting on his/her behalf _____ Date _____

Any person who knowingly makes any false statement, misrepresentation, concealment of fact or any other act of fraud to obtain compensation as provided by the FECA or who knowingly accepts compensation to which that person is not entitled is subject to civil or administrative remedies as well as felony criminal prosecution and may, under appropriate criminal provisions, be punished by a fine or imprisonment or both.

Have your supervisor complete the receipt attached to this form and return it to you for your records.

Witness Statement

16. Statement of witness (Describe what you saw, heard, or know about this injury)

Name of witness	Signature of witness		Date signed
Address	City	State	ZIP Code

Form CA-1
Rev. Apr. 1999

FEDERAL EMPLOYEE'S NOTICE OF INJURY AND CLAIM FOR COMPENSATION (FORM CA-1)

Official Supervisor's Report: Please complete information requested below:

Supervisor's Report

17. Agency name and address of reporting office (include city, state, and zip code)

OWCP Agency Code

OSHA Site Code

ZIP Code

18. Employee's duty station (Street address and ZIP code)

19. Employee's retirement coverage CSRS FERS Other, (identify)

20. Regular work hours From: ___ a.m. / p.m. To: ___ a.m. / p.m.

21. Regular work schedule Sun. Mon. Tues. Wed. Thurs. Fri. Sat.

22. Date of Injury Mo. Day Yr.

23. Date notice received Mo. Day Yr.

24. Date stopped work Mo. Day Yr. Time: ___ a.m. / p.m.

25. Date pay stopped Mo. Day Yr.

26. Date 45 day period began Mo. Day Yr.

27. Date returned to work Mo. Day Yr. Time: ___ a.m. / p.m.

28. Was employee injured in performance of duty? Yes No (If "No," explain)

29. Was injury caused by employee's willful misconduct, intoxication, or intent to injure self or another? Yes (If "Yes," explain) No

30. Was injury caused by third party? Yes No (If "No," go to item 32.)

31. Name and address of third party (Include city, state, and ZIP code)

32. Name and address of physician first providing medical care (Include city, state, ZIP code)

33. First date medical care received Mo. Day Yr.

34. Do medical reports show employee is disabled for work? Yes No

35. Does your knowledge of the facts about this injury agree with statements of the employee and/or witnesses? Yes No (If "No," explain)

36. If the employing agency controverts continuation of pay, state the reason in detail.

37. Pay rate when employee stopped work $ ___ Per ___

Signature of Supervisor and Filing Instructions

38. A supervisor who knowingly certifies to any false statement, misrepresentation, concealment of fact, etc., in respect of this claim may also be subject to appropriate felony criminal prosecution.

I certify that the information given above and that furnished by the employee on the reverse of this form is true to the best of my knowledge with the following exception:

Name of supervisor (Type or print)

Signature of supervisor   Date

Supervisor's Title   Office phone

39. Filing instructions

☐ No lost time and no medical expense: Place this form in employee's medical folder (SF-66-D)
☐ No lost time, medical expense incurred or expected: forward this form to OWCP
☐ Lost time covered by leave, LWOP, or COP: forward this form to OWCP
☐ First Aid Injury

Form CA-1
Rev. Apr. 1999

FEDERAL EMPLOYEE'S NOTICE OF INJURY AND CLAIM FOR COMPENSATION (FORM CA-1)

Instructions for Completing Form CA-1

Complete all items on your section of the form. If additional space is required to explain or clarify any point, attach a supplemental statement to the form. Some of the items on the form which may require further clarification are explained below.

Employee (Or person acting on the employees' behalf)

13) Cause of injury

Describe in detail how and why the injury occurred. Give appropriate details (e.g.: if you fell, how far did you fall and in what position did you land?)

14) Nature of Injury

Give a complete description of the condition(s) resulting from your injury. Specify the right or left side if applicable (e.g., fractured left leg: cut on right index finger).

15) Election of COP/Leave

If you are disabled for work as a result of this injury and filed CA-1 within thirty days of the injury, you may be entitled to receive continuation of pay (COP) from your employing agency. COP is paid for up to 45 calendar days of disability, and is not charged against sick or annual leave. If you elect sick or annual leave you may not claim compensation to repurchase leave used during the 45 days of COP entitlement.

Supervisor

At the time the form is received, complete the receipt of notice of injury and give it to the employee. In addition to completing items 17 through 39, the supervisor is responsible for obtaining the witness statement in Item 16 and for filling in the proper codes in shaded boxes a, b, and c on the front of the form. If medical expense or lost time is incurred or expected, the completed form should be sent to OWCP within 10 working days after it is received.

The supervisor should also submit any other information or evidence pertinent to the merits of this claim.

If the employing agency controverts COP, the employee should be notified and the reason for controversion explained to him or her.

17) Agency name and address of reporting office

The name and address of the office to which correspondence from OWCP should be sent (if applicable, the address of the personnel or compensation office).

18) Duty station street address and zip code

The address and zip code of the establishment where the employee actually works.

19) Employers Retirement Coverage.

Indicate which retirement system the employee is covered under.

30) Was injury caused by third party?

A third party is an individual or organization (other than the injured employee or the Federal government) who is liable for the injury. For instance, the driver of a vehicle causing an accident in which an employee is injured, the owner of a building where unsafe conditions cause an employee to fall, and a manufacturer whose defective product causes an employee's injury, could all be considered third parties to the injury.

32) Name and address of physician first providing medical care

The name and address of the physician who first provided medical care for this injury. If initial care was given by a nurse or other health professional (not a physician) in the employing agency's health unit or clinic, indicate this on a separate sheet of paper.

33) First date medical care received

The date of the first visit to the physician listed in item 31.

36) If the employing agency controverts continuation of pay, state the reason in detail.

COP may be controverted (disputed) for any reason; however, the employing agency may refuse to pay COP only if the controversion is based upon one of the nine reasons given below:

a) The disability was not caused by a traumatic injury.

b) The employee is a volunteer working without pay or for nominal pay, or a member of the office staff of a former President;

c) The employee is not a citizen or a resident of the United States or Canada;

d) The injury occurred off the employing agency's premises and the employee was not involved in official "off premise" duties;

e) The injury was proximately caused by the employee's willful misconduct, intent to bring about injury or death to self or another person, or intoxication;

f) The injury was not reported on Form CA-1 within 30 days following the injury;

g) Work stoppage first occurred 45 days or more following the injury;

h) The employee initially reported the injury after his or her employment was terminated; or

i) The employee is enrolled in the Civil Air Patrol, Peace Corps, Youth Conservation Corps, Work Study Programs, or other similar groups.

Employing Agency - Required Codes

Box a (Occupation Code), Box b (Type Code), Box c (Source Code), OSHA Site Code

The Occupational Safety and Health Administration (OSHA) requires all employing agencies to complete these items when reporting an injury. The proper codes may be found in OSHA Booklet 2014, "Recordkeeping and Reporting Guidelines.

OWCP Agency Code

This is a four-digit (or four digit plus two letter) code used by OWCP to identify the employing agency. The proper code may be obtained from your personnel or compensation office, or by contacting OWCP.

Form CA-1
Rev. Apr. 1999

FEDERAL EMPLOYEE'S NOTICE OF INJURY AND CLAIM FOR COMPENSATION (FORM CA-1)

Benefits for Employees under the Federal Employees' Compensation act (FECA)

The FECA, which is administered by the Office of Workers' Compensation Programs (OWCP), provides the following benefits for job-related traumatic injuries:

(1) Continuation of pay for disability resulting from traumatic, job-related injury, not to exceed 45 calendar days. (To be eligible for continuation of pay, the employee, or someone acting on his/her behalf, must file Form CA-1 within 30 days following the injury and provide medical evidence in support of disability within 10 days of submission of the CA-1. Where the employing agency continue's the employee's pay, the pay must not be interrupted unless one of the provision's outlined in 20 CFR 10.222 apply.

(2) Payment of compensation for wage loss after the expiration of COP, if disability extends beyond such point, or if COP is not payable. If disability continues after COP expires, Form CA-7, with supporting medical evidence, must be filed with OWCP. To avoid interruption of income, the form should be filed on the 40th day of the COP period.

(3) Payment of compensation for permanent impairment of certain organs, members, or functions of the body (such as loss or loss of use of an arm or kidney, loss of vision, etc.), or for serious defringement of the head, face, or neck.

(4) Vocational rehabilitation and related services where directed by OWCP.

(5) All necessary medical care from qualified medical providers. The injured employee may choose the physician who provides initial medical care. Generally, 25 miles from the place of injury, place of employment, or employee's home is a reasonable distance to travel for medical care.

An employee may use sick or annual leave rather than LWOP while disabled. The employee may repurchase leave used for approved periods. Form CA-7b, available from the personnel office, should be studied BEFORE a decision is made to use leave.

For additional information, review the regulations governing the administration of the FECA (Code of Federal Regulations, Chapter 20, Part 10) or pamphlet CA-810.

Privacy Act

In accordance with the Privacy Act of 1974, as amended (5 U.S.C. 552a), you are hereby notified that: (1) The Federal Employees' Compensation Act, as amended and extended (5 U.S.C. 8101, et seq.) (FECA) is administered by the Office of Workers' Compensation Programs of the U.S. Department of Labor, which receives and maintains personal information on claimants and their immediate families. (2) Information which the Office has will be used to determine eligibility for and the amount of benefits payable under the FECA, and may be verified through computer matches or other appropriate means. (3) Information may be given to the Federal agency which employed the claimant at the time of injury in order to verify statements made, answer questions concerning the status of the claim, verify billing, and to consider issues relating to retention, rehire, or other relevant matters. (4) Information may also be given to other Federal agencies, other government entities, and to private-sector agencies and/or employers as part of rehabilitative and other return-to-work programs and services. (5) Information may be disclosed to physicians and other health care providers for use in providing treatment or medical/vocational rehabilitation, making evaluations for the Office, and for other purposes related to the medical management of the claim. (6) Information may be given to Federal, state and local agencies for law enforcement purposes, to obtain information relevant to a decision under the FECA, to determine whether benefits are being paid properly, including whether prohibited dual payments are being made, and, where appropriate, to pursue salary/administrative offset and debt collection actions required or permitted by the FECA and/or the Debt Collection Act. (7) Disclosure of the claimant's social security number (SSN) or tax identifying number (TIN) on this form is mandatory. The SSN and/or TIN, and other information maintained by the Office, may be used for identification, to support debt collection efforts carried on by the Federal government, and for other purposes required or authorized by law. (8) Failure to disclose all requested information may delay the processing of the claim or the payment of benefits, or may result in an unfavorable decision or reduced level of benefits.

Note: This notice applies to all forms requesting information that you might receive from the Office in connection with the processing and adjudication of the claim you filed under the FECA.

Receipt of Notice of Injury

This acknowledges receipt of Notice of Injury sustained by (Name of injured employee)

Which occurred on (Mo., Day, Yr.)

At (Location)

Signature of Official Superior   Title   Date (Mo., Day, Yr.)

*U.S. GPO: 1999-454-845/12704

Form CA-1
Rev. Apr. 1999

APPENDIX 24:

FEDERAL EMPLOYEE'S NOTICE OF OCCUPATIONAL DISEASE AND CLAIM FOR COMPENSATION (FORM CA-2)

Notice of Occupational Disease and Claim for Compensation

| Reset | Print |

U. S. Department of Labor
Employment Standards Administration
Office of Workers' Compensation Programs

Employee: Please complete all boxes 1 - 18 below. Do not complete shaded areas.
Employing Agency (Supervisor or Compensation Specialist): Complete shaded boxes a, b, and c.

Employee Data

1. Name of Employee (Last, First, Middle)

2. Social Security Number

3. Date of birth   Mo.   Day   Yr.

4. Sex   M

5. Home telephone

6. Grade as of date of last exposure   Level   Step

7. Employee's home mailing address (Include city, state, and ZIP code)

8. Dependents
☐ Wife, Husband
☐ Children under 18 years
☐ Other

Claim Information

9. Employee's occupation

a. Occupation code

10. Location (address) where you worked when disease or illness occurred (include City, state, and ZIP code)

11. Date you first became aware of disease or illness   Mo.   Day   Yr.

12. Date you first realized the disease or illness was caused or aggravated by your employment   Mo.   Day   Yr.

13. Explain the relationship to your employment, and why you came to this realization

14. Nature of disease or illness

OWCP Use - NOI Code

b. Type code   c. Source code

15. If this notice and claim was not filed with the employing agency within 30 days after date shown above in item #12, explain the reason for the delay.

16. If the statement requested in item I of the attached instructions is not submitted with this form, explain reason for delay.

17. If the medical reports requested in item 2 of attached instructions are not submitted with this form, explain reason for delay.

FEDERAL EMPLOYEE'S NOTICE OF OCCUPATIONAL DISEASE

18. I certify, under penalty of law, that the disease or illness described above was the result of my employment with the United States Government, and that it was not caused by my willful misconduct, intent to injure myself or another person, nor by my intoxication. I hereby claim medical treatment, if needed, and other benefits provided by the Federal Employees' Compensation Act.

I hereby authorize any physician or hospital (or any other person, institution, corporation, or government, agency) to furnish any desired information to the U.S. Department of Labor, Office of Workers' Compensation Programs (or to its official representative). This authorization also permits any official representative of the Office to examine and to copy any records concerning me.

Signature of employee or person acting on his/her behalf _____ Date _____

Have your supervisor complete the receipt attached to this form and return it to you for your records.

Any person who knowingly makes any false statement, misrepresentation, concealment of fact or any other act of fraud to obtain compensation as provided by the FECA or who knowingly accepts compensation to which that person is not entitled is subject to civil or administrative remedies as well as felony criminal prosecution and may, under appropriate criminal provisions, be punished by a fine or imprisonment or both.

For sale by the Superintendent of Documents, U.S. Government Printing Office Washington, DC 20402

Form CA-2
Rev. Jan. 1997

Official Supervisor's Report of Occupational Disease: Please complete information requested below

Supervisor's Report

19. Agency name and address of reporting office (include city, state, and ZIP Code)

OWCP Agency Code

OSHA Site Code

ZIP Code

20. Employee's duty station (Street address and ZIP Code)

ZIP Code

21. Regular work hours From: ☐ a.m. ☐ p.m. To: ☐ a.m. ☐ p.m.

22. Regular work schedule ☐ Sun. ☐ Mon. ☐ Tues. ☐ Wed. ☐ Thurs. ☐ Fri. ☐ Sat.

23. Name and address of physician first providing medical care (include city, state, ZIP code)

24. First date medical care received — Mo. Day Yr.

25. Do medical reports show employee is disabled for work? ☐ Yes ☐ No

26. Date employee first reported condition to supervisor — Mo. Day Yr.

27. Date and hour employee stopped work — Mo. Day Yr. Time ☐ a.m. ☐ p.m.

28. Date and hour employee's pay stopped — Mo. Day Yr. Time ☐ a.m. ☐ p.m.

29. Date employee was last exposed to conditions alleged to have caused disease or illness — Mo. Day Yr.

30. Date returned to work — Mo. Day Yr. Time ☐ a.m. ☐ p.m.

31. If employee has returned to work and work assignment has changed, describe new duties

32. Employee's Retirement Coverage ☐ CSRS ☐ FERS ☐ Other, (Specify)

33. Was injury caused by third party? ☐ Yes ☐ No If "No," go to Item 34.

34. Name and address of third party (include city, state, and ZIP code)

Signature of Supervisor

35. A supervisor who knowingly certifies to any false statement, misrepresentation, concealment of fact, etc., in respect to this claim may also be subject to appropriate felony criminal prosecution.

I certify that the information given above and that furnished by the employee on the reverse of this form is true to the best of my knowledge with the following exception:

Name of Supervisor (Type or print)

Signature of Supervisor

Date

Supervisor's Title

Office phone

Form CA-2
Rev.Jan.1997

FEDERAL EMPLOYEE'S NOTICE OF OCCUPATIONAL DISEASE

The FECA, which is administered by the Office of Workers' Compensation Programs (OWCP), provides the following general benefits for employment-related occupational disease or illness:

(1) Full medical care from either Federal medical officers and hospitals, or private hospitals or physicians of the employee's choice.

(2) Payment of compensation for total or partial wage loss.

(3) Payment of compensation for permanent impairment of certain organs, members, or functions of the body (such as loss or loss of use of an arm or kidney, loss of vision, etc.), or for serious disfigurement of the head, face, or neck.

(4) Vocational rehabilitation and related services where necessary.

The first three days in a non-pay status are waiting days, and no compensation is paid for these days unless the period of disability exceeds 14 calendar days, or the employee has suffered a permanent disability. Compensation for total disability is generally paid at the rate of 2/3 of an employee's salary if there are no dependents, or 3/4 of salary if there are one or more dependents.

An employee may use sick or annual leave rather than LWOP while disabled. The employee may repurchase leave used for approved periods. Form CA-7b, available from the personnel off ice, should be studied BEFORE a decision is made to use leave.

If an employee is in doubt about compensation benefits, the OWCP District Office servicing the employing agency should be contacted. (Obtain the address from your employing agency.)

For additional information, review the regulations governing the administration of the FECA (Code of Federal Regulations, Title 20, Chapter 1) or Chapter 810 of the Office of Personnel Management's Federal Personnel Manual.

Receipt of Notice of Occupational Disease or Illness

This acknowledges receipt of notice of disease or illness sustained by:
(Name of injured employee)

I was first notified about this condition on (Mo., Day, Yr.)

At (Location)

Signature of Official Superior   Title   Date (Mo., Day, Yr.)

This receipt should be retained by the employee as a record that notice was filed.

Form CA-2

Complete all items on your section of the form. If additional space is required to explain or clarify any point, attach a supplemental statement to the form. In addition to the information requested on the form, both the employee and the supervisor are required to submit additional evidence as described below. If this evidence is not submitted along with the form, the responsible party should explain the reason for the delay and state when the additional evidence will be submitted.

Employee (or person acting on the Employee's behalf)

Complete items 1 through 18 and submit the form to the employee's supervisor along with the statement and medical reports described below. Be sure to obtain the Receipt of Notice of Disease or Illness completed by the supervisor at the time the form is submitted.

1) Employee's statement

In a separate narrative statement attached to the form, the employee must submit the following information:

a) A detailed history of the disease or illness from the date it started.

b) Complete details of the conditions of employment which are believed to be responsible for the disease or illness.

c) A description of specific exposures to substances or stressful conditions causing the disease or illness, including locations where exposure or stress occurred, as well as the number of hours per day and days per week of such exposure or stress.

d) Identification of the part of the body affected. (If disability is due to a heart condition, give complete details of all activities for one week prior to the attack with particular attention to the final 24 hours of such period.)

e) A statement as to whether the employee ever suffered a similar condition. if so, provide full details of onset, history, and medical care received, along with names and addresses of physicians rendering treatment.

2) Medical report

a) Dates of examination or treatment.

b) History given to the physician by the employee.

c) Detailed description of the physician's findings.

d) Results of x-rays, laboratory tests, etc.

e) Diagnosis.

f) Clinical course of treatment.

g) Physician's opinion as to whether the disease or illness was caused or aggravated by the employment, along with an explanation of the basis for this opinion. (Medical reports that do not explain the basis for the physician's opinion are given very little weight in adjudicating the claim.)

3) Wage loss

If you have lost wages or used leave for this illness, Form CA-7 should also be submitted.

Supervisor (Or appropriate official in the employing agency)

At the time the form is received, complete the Receipt of Notice of Disease or Illness and give it to the employee. In addition to completing items 19 through 34, the supervisor is responsible for filling in the proper codes in shaded boxes a, b, and c on the front of the form. If medical expense or lost time is incurred or expected, the completed form must be sent to OWCP within ten working days after it is received. In a separate narrative statement attached to the form, the supervisor must:

a) Describe in detail the work performed by the employee. Identify fumes, chemicals, or other irritants or situations that the employee was exposed to which allegedly caused the condition. State the nature, extent, and duration of the exposure, including hours per days and days per week, requested above.

b) Attach copies of all medical reports (including x-ray reports and laboratory data) on file for the employee.

c) Attach a record of the employee's absence from work caused by any similar disease or illness. Have the employee state the reason for each absence.

d) Attach statements from each co-worker who has first-hand knowledge about the employee's condition and its cause. (The co-workers should state how such knowledge was obtained.)

e) Review and comment on the accuracy of the employee's statement requested above.

The supervisor should also submit any other information or evidence pertinent to the merits of this claim.

Item Explanation: Some of the items on the form which may require further clarification are explained below.

14. Nature of the disease or illness

Give a complete description of the disease or illness. Specify the left or right side if applicable (e.g., rash on left leg; carpal tunnel syndrome, right wrist).

19. Agency name and address of reporting office

The name and address of the off ice to which correspondence from OWCP should be sent (if applicable, the address of the personnel or compensation office).

23. Name and address of physician first providing medical care

The name and address of the physician who first provided medical care for this injury. If initial care was given by a nurse or other health professional (not a physician) in the employing agency's health unit or clinic, indicate this on a separate sheet of paper.

24. First date medical care received

The date of the first visit to the physician listed in item 23.

32. Employee's Retirement Coverage.

Indicate which retirement system the employee is covered under.

33. Was the injury caused by third party?

A third party is an individual or organization (other than the injured employee or the Federal government) who is liable for the disease. For instance, manufacturer of a chemical to which an employee was exposed might be considered a third party if improper instructions were given by the manufacturer for use of the chemical.

Employing Agency - Required Codes

Box a (Occupational Code), Box b. (Type Code), Box c (Source Code), OSHA Site Code

The Occupational Code, Type Code, and Source Code and OSHA Site Code. The Occupational Safety and Health Administration (OSHA) requires all employing agencies to complete these items when reporting an injury. The proper codes may be found in OSHA Booklet 2014, Record Keeping and Reporting Guidelines.

OWCP Agency Code

This is a four digit (or four digit two letter) code used by OWCP to identify the employing agency. The proper code may be obtained from your personnel or compensation office, or by contacting OWCP.

Form CA-2
Rev.Jan.1997

APPENDIX 25:
CLAIM FOR CONTINUANCE OF COMPENSATION UNDER THE FEDERAL EMPLOYEES' COMPENSATION ACT (FORM CA-12)

Claim for Continuance of Compensation Under the Federal Employees' Compensation Act	**U.S. Department of Labor** Employment Standards Administration Office of Workers' Compensation Programs	

INSTRUCTIONS TO BENEFICIARIES	OMB No. 1215-0154 Expires: 06-30-08

1. It is important that you carefully complete the other side of this form and return it to the OWCP within 30 days. Your failure to do so will result in suspension of the compensation you are receiving.

2. Complete Section A by printing the full name of the deceased employee and the OFFICE OF WORKERS' COMPENSATION PROGRAMS file number.

3. Answer all questions in the section or sections that apply to you. If you are receiving compensation as the:

   (A) WIDOW OR WIDOWER Complete Section B.
   (B) WIDOW OR WIDOWER RECEIVING COMPENSATION ON HER OR HIS ACCOUNT AND ON ACCOUNT OF A MINOR CHILD OR CHILDREN - Complete Sections B and C.
   (C) GUARDIAN OR CUSTODIAN OF A MINOR CHILD OR GRANDCHILD OR A PERSON INCAPABLE OF SELF-SUPPORT - Complete Section C.
   (D) PARENT, GRANDPARENT, OR A PERSON WHO IS PHYSICALLY INCAPABLE OF SELF-SUPPORT - Complete Section D.
   (E) Complete Block C if dependent is receiving educational benefits.

4. Carefully read and comply with directions in Section E.

5. Complete and sign the certificate in Section F.

6. Please return the completed form, in an envelope, to the address shown below.

The information on this form will be used to determine your eligibility for continuing benefits. Your response to this information is required to retain your compensation benefits. (20 CFR 10.126)

RETURN TO: U.S. DEPARTMENT OF LABOR, DFEC
CENTRAL MAILROOM
P.O. BOX 8300
LONDON, KY 40742-8300

CLAIM FOR CONTINUANCE OF COMPENSATION (FORM CA-12)

Privacy Act

Note: Persons are not required to respond to this collection of information unless it displays a currently valid OMB number.

Public Burden Statement

CLAIM FOR CONTINUANCE OF COMPENSATION (FORM CA-12)

IMPORTANT: READ CAREFULLY THE INSTRUCTIONS ON THE OTHER SIDE OF THIS FORM BEFORE ANSWERING THE QUESTIONS BELOW

I HEREBY APPLY FOR CONTINUANCE OF COMPENSATION BENEFITS AWARDED TO ME (OR TO THE CLAIMANT ON WHOSE BEHALF I AM NOW ACTING) BY THE OFFICE OF WORKERS' COMPENSATION (OWCP) ON ACCOUNT OF THE DEATH OF:

A. Name of Deceased Employee	Employee's Federal Retirement Plan			OWCP File No.
	☐ CSRS	☐ FERS	☐ Other	

THIS BLOCK TO BE COMPLETED BY WIDOW/WIDOWER RECEIVING COMPENSATION

B. 1. Have You Married since the Death of Above Named Employee? ☐ Yes ☐ No (If "Yes" complete 10)

2. Do You Receive a Pension or Allowance from any other Federal Agency such as the Veterans' Administration, Social Security Administration or the Civil Service Commission on Account of the Death of this Employee? ☐ Yes ☐ No (If "Yes" complete 11)

THIS BLOCK TO BE COMPLETED BY ANY PERSON RECEIVING COMPENSATION ON BEHALF OF CHILD GRANDCHILD, OR DEPENDENT INCAPABLE OF SELF-SUPPORT

C. 3. Have any Dependents You Claim Compensation for Married Since the Death of the Above Named Employee? ☐ Yes ☐ No (If "Yes" complete 10)

4. Do Any Dependents You Claim Compensation for Receive a Pension or Allowance from Any Other Federal Agency Such as the Veterans' Administration, Social Security Administration, or the Civil Service Commission on Account of the Death of this Employee? ☐ Yes ☐ No (If "Yes" complete 11)

5. Give the Following Information for Each Person You Receive Compensation For:

NAME	AGE	IS PERSON IN YOUR CUSTODY? (Yes or No)	NAME, ADDRESS, AND RELATIONSHIP OF PERSON(S) HAVING CUSTODY IF NOT IN YOUR CUSTODY

THIS BLOCK IS TO BE COMPLETED BY PARENT, GRANDPARENT, OR DEPENDENT PHYSICALLY INCAPABLE OF SELF-SUPPORT

D. 6. Have You Married Since the Death of the Above Named Employee'? ☐ Yes ☐ No (If "Yes" complete 10)

7. Do You Receive a Pension or Allowance from any other Federal Agency such as the Veterans' Administration or the Civil Service Commission on Account of the Death of this Employee? ☐ Yes ☐ No (If "Yes" complete 11)

8. Are You Capable of Self-Support? ☐ Yes ☐ No

9. Have You Been Employed Since Filing Your Last Claim Form? ☐ Yes ☐ No (If "Yes" complete 12)

ADDITIONAL INFORMATION: THIS BLOCK TO BE COMPLETED ONLY WHEN AN ANSWER TO 1, 2, 3, 4, 5, 6, 7, or 9 IS "YES."

E. 10. When and Where was the Marriage Performed and What was the Change in Name, If Any?

11. What Agency is Paying the Benefits and For What Reason Are They Being Paid?

(Space for Answers to questions 10, 11, and 12)

12. State the Name of Your Employer, Nature of Employment, Dates Employed, and Amount Earned.

CLAIMANT'S CERTIFICATION - TO BE COMPLETED IN ALL INSTANCES

F. I DECLARE UNDER THE PENALTIES OF PERJURY THAT THE INFORMATION CONTAINED ON THIS FORM IS TRUE AND CORRECT: AND THAT I WILL IMMEDIATELY NOTIFY THE OFFICE OF WORKERS' COMPENSATION PROGRAMS OF ANY CHANGES IN STATUS.

Signature of Claimant (or guardian)

Date (month, day, year)

Address of Claimant (or guardian)

Telephone Where You Can Be Reached

Signature of Witness and Date Witnessed if Claimant Signs by Mark (X)

Form CA-12

APPENDIX 26:
NOTICE OF EMPLOYEE'S INJURY OR DEATH UNDER THE LONGSHORE AND HARBOR WORKERS' COMPENSATION ACT (FORM LS-201)

Notice of Employee's Injury or Death
Longshore and Harbor Workers' Compensation Act,
As Extended (See instructions on reverse)

U.S. Department of Labor
Employment Standards Administration
Office of Workers' Compensation Programs

This form should be furnished by the employer to any employee covered by the Longshore and Harbor Workers' Compensation Act or a related law who reports an occupational injury or illness to his/her employer. This form is used to provide written notice of an injury or death. Notice is required to obtain a benefit (20 CFR 702.212). The information will be used to determine entitlement to benefits. Persons are not required to respond to this collection of information unless it displays a currently valid OMB control number.

OMB No. 1215-0160

| Print | Reset |

1. Employee's Name (Last, first, middle)
Last Name   First Name   M.I.

2. Home Mailing Address (Number, street, city, state, ZIP code)
line 1:   city:
line 2:   st: zip:
country:

3. Date of Birth (Month, day, year)

4. Sex
☐ Male
☐ Female

5. Social Security Number (Required by Law)

6. Home Telephone
Area Code + Number

7. Name and Address of Employer (Number, street, city, state, ZIP code)
name:
line 1:   city:
line 2:   st: zip:
country:

8. Employee's Job Title

9. Date of Injury (Month, day, year)

10. Hour of Injury

11. Place Where Injury Occurred

12. Name of Supervisor at Time of Injury

13. Did Employee Stop Work Due to Injury?
☐ Yes   ☐ No

14. If Yes, Date Stopped

15. Cause of Injury (Explain in what way the injury or occupational illness was caused by employment)

16. Effects of Injury (Indicate parts of body affected or if death occurred)

► NOTE: **If reporting injury, employee signs Item 17; if reporting death, claimant or representative signs Item 18** ◄

17. I am requesting the employer named in item 7 to provide me appropriate compensation and medical care for my injury, and I hereby make claim for all benefits to which I may be entitled under the Longshore and Harbor Workers' Compensation Act, or a related law.

Signature of Employee
Print Name

Date

18. Request is hereby made to the employer named in Item 7 to provide appropriate death benefits to the survivors of the employee named in Item 1, and a claim is hereby made for those death benefits to which these survivors may be entitled under the Longshore and Harbor Workers' Compensation Act, or a related law.

Signature of Compensation Claimant or Representative of Claimant   Date

Print Name

19. This notice is being personally delivered, or mailed, to the employer named in Item 7 (or his/her representative) and a copy is being sent to the District Director of the Office of Workers' Compensation Programs by the party named in either Item 17 or 18 on this date.

Date

IMPORTANT NOTICE

Section 31 (a)(1) of the Longshore and Harbor Workers' Compensation Act , 33 U.S.C. 931 (a)(1), provides as follows: Any claimant or representative of a claimant who knowingly and willfully makes a false statement or representation for the purpose of obtaining a benefit or payment under this Act shall be guilty of a felony, and on conviction thereof shall be punished by a fine not to exceed $10,000, by imprisonment not to exceed five years, or by both.

Form LS-201
Rev. Jan 1999

INSTRUCTIONS TO EMPLOYEE

IT IS IMPORTANT THAT WRITTEN NOTICE OF EMPLOYMENT-CAUSED INJURY OR ILLNESS BE GIVEN PROMPTLY TO THE EMPLOYER AND THE DISTRICT DIRECTOR IN THE LOCAL OFFICE OF THE OFFICE OF WORKERS' COMPENSATION PROGRAMS, U.S. DEPARTMENT OF LABOR.

Written notice needs to be given so that the District Director may see that an employee in case of injury, or his or her survivors in case of death, receive all the benefits to which they may be entitled. No benefit need be paid under the appropriate law unless a notice of injury or death is filed. [33 U.S.C. 912(a)]

WHO FILES

Injured employees or survivors of employees whose deaths were due to employment covered by the Longshore and Harbor Workers' Compensation Act, or its extensions.

Those Acts which extend the provisions of the Longshore and Harbor Workers' Compensation Act are:

Defense Base Act
Nonappropriated Fund Instrumentalities Act
Outer Continental Shelf Lands Act

WHEN TO FILE

As soon as possible or within 30 days after the date of injury or death, or

Within 30 days after the employee or survivor first became aware, or in the exercise of reasonable diligence or by reason of medical advice should have been aware, of a relationship between the injury or death and the employment, or

in the case of an occupational disease which does not immediately result in a disability or death, within one year after the employee or claimant becomes aware, or in the exercise of reasonable diligence or by reason of medical advice should have been aware, of the relationship between the employment, the disease, and the death or disability, or

In the case of hearing loss, within 30 days after receipt by an employee of an audiogram, with the accompanying report thereon, indicating that the employee has suffered a loss of hearing.

WHY FILE

The employer needs to have notice so that it or its insurance carrier may see that medical care is given promptly and compensation payments for loss of income may be provided without delay.

WHERE TO FILE

Give original copy to employer and send one copy to the District Director at the following address:

**District Director
U.S. Department of Labor
Office of Workers' Compensation Programs (ESA)**

 FAILURE TO GIVE WRITTEN NOTICE MAY RESULT IN SOME LOSS OF BENEFITS.

PRIVACY ACT OF 1974 NOTICE

In accordance with the Privacy Act of 1974 (Public Law No. 93-579, 5 U.S.C. 522a), you are hereby notified that: (1) The Longshore and Harbor Workers' Compensation Act, as amended and extended (33 U.S.C. 901 et seq.) is administered by the Office of Workers' Compensation Programs of the U.S. Department of Labor. In accordance with this responsibility, the Office receives and maintains personal information on claimants and their immediate families. (2) The information will be used to determine eligibility for the amount of benefits payable under the Act. (3) The information may be used by other agencies or persons in handling matters relating, directly or indirectly, to the subject matter of the claim, so long as such agencies or persons have received the consent of the individual claimant, or have complied with the provisions of 20 CFR 702. (4) Furnishing all requested information will facilitate the claims adjudication process; and the effects of not providing all or any part of the requested information may delay the process, or result in an unfavorable decision or a reduced level of benefits.

IMPORTANT NOTICE

Section 31 (a)(1) of the Longshore and Harbor Workers' Compensation Act, 33 U.S.C. 931(a)(1), provides as follows: Any claimant or representative of a claimant who knowingly and willfully makes a false statement or representation for the purpose of obtaining a benefit or payment under this Act shall be guilty of a felony, and on conviction thereof shall be punished by a fine not to exceed $10,000, by imprisonment not to exceed five years, or by both.

Public Burden Statement

We estimate that it will take an average of 15 minutes to complete this collection of information, including time for reviewing instructions, searching existing data sources, gathering and maintaining the data needed, and completing and reviewing the collection of information. If you have any comments regarding this burden estimate or any other aspect of this collection of information, including suggestions for reducing this burden, send them to the U.S. Department of Labor, Division of Longshore and Harbor Workers' Compensation, Room C4315, 200 Constitution Avenue, N.W., Washington, D.C. 20210. **DO NOT SEND THE COMPLETED FORM TO THIS OFFICE**

APPENDIX 27:
DIRECTORY OF BLACK LUNG DISTRICT OFFICES AND JURISDICTIONS SERVED

DISTRICT OFFICE ADDRESS	TELEPHONE	JURISDICTIONS SERVED
U.S. Department of Labor 105 N. Main Street Suite 100 Wilkes Barre, PA 18701	800-347-3755	Eastern Pennsylvania, the northeastern states and the District of Columbia
U.S. Department of Labo 1160 Dublin Road Suite 300 Columbus, OH 43215	800-347-3771	Illinois, Indiana, Michigan, Minnesota, Ohio, and Wisconsin
U.S. Department of Labor 319 Washington Street 2nd Floor Johnstown, PA 15901	800-347-3754	Central Pennsylvania and Virginia
U.S. Department of Labor 1999 Broadway Suite 690 Denver, CO 80201-6550	800-366-4612	all states west of the Mississippi River
U.S. Department of Labor 1225 S. Main Street Suite 405 Greensburg, PA 15601	800-347-3753	Western Pennsylvania and Maryland
U.S. Department of Labor, Charleston Federal Center, Suite 110, 500 Quarrier Street, Charleston, WV 25301	800-347-3749	Southeastern West Virginia
U.S. Department of Labor 425 Juliana Avenue Suite 3116 Parkersburg, WV 26101	800-347-3751	Remainder of West Virginia

Source: United States Department of Labor

APPENDIX 28:
DIRECTORY OF ENERGY EMPLOYEES OCCUPATIONAL ILLNESS COMPENSATION PROGRAM (EEOICP) DISTRICT OFFICES

DISTRICT OFFICE	AREAS COVERED	ADDRESS	TELEPHONE	FAX
DISTRICT OFFICE 1— JACKSONVILLE, FL	Alabama, Florida, Georgia, Kentucky, Mississippi, North Carolina, South Carolina and Tennessee	214 North Hogan Street Suite 810 Jacksonville, FL 32202	904-357-4705	904-357-4704
DISTRICT OFFICE 2— CLEVELAND, OH	Connecticut, Delaware, District of Columbia, Illinois, Indiana, Maine, Maryland, Massachusetts, Michigan, Minnesota, New Hampshire, New Jersey, New York, Ohio, Pennsylvania, Puerto Rico, Rhode Island, Vermont, Virgin Islands, Virginia, West Virginia and Wisconsin	1001 Lakeside Avenue Suite 350 Cleveland, OH 44114	216-802-1300	216-802-1308

DISTRICT OFFICE	AREAS COVERED	ADDRESS	TELEPHONE	FAX
DISTRICT OFFICE 3— DENVER, CO	Arkansas, Colorado, Iowa, Kansas, Louisiana, Missouri, Montana, Nebraska, New Mexico, North Dakota, Oklahoma, South Dakota, Texas, Utah, Wyoming, and RECA Section 5 Awardees	1999 Broadway Suite 1120 P.O. Box 46550 Denver, CO 80201-6550	720-264-3060	720-264-3099
DISTRICT OFFICE 4— SEATTLE, WA	Alaska, Arizona, California, Idaho, Hawaii, Marshall Islands, Nevada, Oregon and Washington	719 2nd Avenue Suite 601 Seattle, WA 98104	206-373-6750	206-373-6798

Source: United States Department of Labor

APPENDIX 29:
DIRECTORY OF ENERGY EMPLOYEES OCCUPATIONAL ILLNESS COMPENSATION PROGRAM (EEOICP) RESOURCE CENTERS

RESOURCE CENTER	ADDRESS	TELEPHONE	FAX	E-MAIL ADDRESS
ANCHORAGE	2501 Commercial Drive Anchorage, AK 99501	907-258-4070	907-258-4240	doecomp@ acsalaska.net
CALIFORNIA	2600 Kitty Hawk Road Suite 101 Livermore, CA 94551	925-606-6302	925-606-6303	California. center@rrohio. com
ESPANOLA	412 Paseo De Onate Suite D Espanola, NM 87532	505-747-6766	505-747-6765	espanola. center@rrohio. com
HANFORD	303 Bradley Boulevard Suite 104 Richland, WA 99352	509-946-3333	509-946-2009	Hanford. center@rrohio. com

RESOURCE CENTER	ADDRESS	TELEPHONE	FAX	E-MAIL ADDRESS
IDAHO FALLS	1820 East 17th Street Suite 375 Idaho Falls, ID 83404	208-523-0158	208-557-0551	idaho.center@ rrohio.com
LAS VEGAS	1050 East Flamingo Road Suite W-156 Las Vegas, NV 89119	702-697-0841	702-697-0843	vegas.center@ rrohio.com
OAK RIDGE	800 Oak Ridge Turnpike Suite C-103 Oak Ridge, TN 37830	865-481-0411	865-481-8832	Or.center@ rrohio.com
PADUCAH	125 Memorial Drive Paducah, KY 42001	270-534-0599	270-534-8723	paducah. center@rrohio. com
PORTSMOUTH	1200 Gay Street Portsmouth, OH 45662	740-353-6993	740-353-4707	portsmouth. center@rrhio. com
ROCKY FLATS	8758 Wolff Court Suite 101 Westminster, CO 80031	720-540-4977	720-540-4976	denver. center@rrhio. com
SAVANNAH RIVER	1708 Bunting Drive North Augusta, SC 29841	803-279-2728	803-279-0146	srs.center@ rrohio.com

Source: United States Department of Labor

APPENDIX 30:
CLAIM FOR BENEFITS UNDER THE ENERGY EMPLOYEES' OCCUPATIONAL ILLNESS COMPENSATION ACT (FORM EE-1)

Claim for Benefits Under the Energy Employees Occupational Illness Compensation Program Act	U.S. Department of Labor Employment Standards Administration Office of Workers' Compensation Programs

Note: Provide all information requested below. Do not write in the shaded areas.

OMB Number: 1215-0197
Expiration Date: 08/31/2010

Employee Information (Please Print Clearly) | Submit | Reset | Print

1. Name (Last, First, Middle Initial)

2. Social Security Number

3. Date of Birth Month Day Year

4. Sex ☐ Male ☐ Female

5. Dependents ☐ Spouse ☐ Children ☐ Other:

6. Address (Street, Apt. #, P.O. Box)

(City, State, ZIP Code)

7. Telephone Number(s)
a. Home: ( ) -
b. Other: ( ) -

8. Identify the Diagnosed Condition(s) Being Claimed as Work-Related (check box and list specific diagnosis)

	9. Date of Diagnosis		
	Month	Day	Year
☐ **Cancer** (List Specific Diagnosis Below)			
a.			
b.			
c.			
☐ **Beryllium Sensitivity**			
☐ **Chronic Beryllium Disease** (CBD)			
☐ **Chronic Silicosis**			
☐ **Other Work-Related Condition(s) due to exposure to toxic substances or radiation** (List Specific Diagnosis Below)			
a.			
b.			
c.			

Awards and Other Information

10. Did you work at a location designated as a Special Exposure Cohort (SEC)?	☐ YES	☐ NO
11. Have you filed a lawsuit seeking either money or medical coverage for the above claimed condition(s)?	☐ YES	☐ NO
12. Have you filed any workers' compensation claims in connection with the above claimed condition(s)	☐ YES	☐ NO
13. Have you or another person received a settlement or other award in connection with a lawsuit or workers' compensation claim for the above claimed condition(s)?	☐ YES	☐ NO
14. Have you either pled guilty or been convicted of any charges connected with an application for or receipt of federal or state workers' compensation?	☐ YES	☐ NO
15. Have you applied for an award under Section 5 of the Radiation Exposure Compensation Act (RECA)?	☐ YES	☐ NO
If yes, provide RECA Claim #:		
16. Have you applied for an award under Section 4 of the Radiation Exposure Compensation Act (RECA)?	☐ YES	☐ NO

Employee Declaration

	Resource Center Date Stamp
Any person who knowingly makes any false statement, misrepresentation, concealment of fact, or any other act of fraud to obtain compensation as provided under EEOICPA or who knowingly accepts compensation to which that person is not entitled is subject to civil or administrative remedies as well as felony criminal prosecution and may, under appropriate criminal provisions, be punished by a fine or imprisonment or both. Any change to the information provided on this form once it is submitted must be reported immediately to the district office responsible for the administration of the claim. I hereby make a claim for benefits under EEOICPA and affirm that the information I have provided on this form is true. If applicable, I authorize the Department of Justice to release any requested information, including information related to my RECA claim, to the U.S. Department of Labor, Office of Workers' Compensation Programs (OWCP). Furthermore, I authorize any physician or hospital (or any other person, institution, corporation, or government agency, including the Social Security Administration) to furnish any desired information to the U.S. Department of Labor, Office of Workers' Compensation Programs.	

Employee Signature	Date

Form EE-1
April 2005

Next Page

Instructions for Completing Form EE-1

Complete all items on the form. If additional space is required to explain or clarify any point, attach a supplemental statement to the form. If the requested information is not submitted, the responsible party should explain the reason(s) for the delay and indicate when the information will be forthcoming. Submit the completed claim form and all other pertinent documentation to the appropriate district office administering the EEOICPA in the region where your most recent Energy employer is/was located.

Illness(es) Being Claimed

Item #8 – Identify the specific physician-diagnosed condition(s) that you claim are work related. Do not list the symptoms (e.g. aches, pains, cough, wheezing, breathing problems, etc.) associated with the diagnosed condition(s). If you require additional space, attach a signed supplemental statement to this form.

Item #9 – List the date a qualified physician first diagnosed the claimed condition(s).

Awards and Other Information

Item #10 – The EEOICPA allows for employees who have met particular criteria and have been employed at certain facilities to be designated as members of the Special Exposure Cohort (SEC). Indicate whether or not you worked at a location designated as an SEC.

Item #11- Indicate whether you have filed a civil lawsuit in regard to your claimed condition(s). If you mark YES, provide copies of all court documentation.

Item #12 - Indicate whether you have filed any workers' compensation claims in connection with the claimed condition(s). If you mark YES, provide copies of all workers' compensation documentation.

Item #13 – Indicate whether you or another person received a settlement or other type award from a workers' compensation claim or a lawsuit in connection with the claimed condition(s)? If YES, provide copies of all pertinent documentation.

Item #14 - Mark the appropriate box indicating whether or not you have ever pled guilty or been convicted of any charges connected to an application for or receipt of federal or state workers' compensation.

Item #15 - Indicate whether you have filed for an award under Section 5 of the Radiation Exposure Compensation Act. If you mark "yes," provide the claim number associated with that RECA claim.

Item #16 - Indicate whether you have filed for an award under Section 4 of the Radiation Exposure Compensation Act.

Privacy Act

In accordance with the Privacy Act of 1974, as amended (5 U.S.C. 552a), you are hereby notified that: (1) The Energy Employees Occupational Illness Compensation Program Act (42 U.S.C. 7384 *et seq.*) (EEOICPA) is administered by the Office of Workers' Compensation Programs of the U.S. Department of Labor, which receives and maintains personal information on claimants and their immediate families. (2) Information which the Office has received will be used to determine eligibility for, and the amount of, benefits payable under EEOICPA, and may be verified through computer matches or other appropriate means. (3) Information may be given to the Federal agencies or private entities that employed the claimant at the time of injury in order to verify statements made, answer questions concerning the status of the claim, verify billing, and to consider other relevant matters. (4) Information may be disclosed to physicians and other health care providers for use in providing treatment or medical rehabilitation, making evaluations for the Office of Workers' Compensation Programs and for other purposes related to the medical management of the claim. (5) Information may be given to Federal, state, and local agencies for law enforcement purposes, to obtain information relevant to a decision under the EEOICPA, to determine whether benefits are being paid properly, including whether prohibited payments have been made, and, where appropriate, to pursue salary/administrative offset and debt collection actions required or permitted by the Debt Collection Act. (6) Disclosure of the claimant's social security number (SSN) or tax identification number (TIN) is mandatory. The SSN or TIN, and other information maintained by the Office, may be used for identification, to support debt collection efforts carried on by the Federal government, and for other purposes required or authorized by law. (7) Failure to disclose all requested information may delay the processing of the claim or the payment of benefits, or may result in an unfavorable decision.

Public Burden Statement

Public reporting burden for this collection of information is estimated to average 17 minutes per response, including time for reviewing instructions, searching existing data sources, gathering the data needed, and completing and reviewing the collection of information. If you have any comments regarding the burden estimate or any other aspect of this collection of information, including suggestions for reducing this burden, send them to the Office of Workers' Compensation Programs, U.S. Department of Labor, Room S3524, 200 Constitution Avenue, N.W., Washington, D.C. 20210. **Do not submit the completed claim form to this address.** Completed claims are to be submitted to the appropriate district office of the Office of Workers' Compensation Programs. Persons are not required to respond to the information collections on this form unless it displays a currently valid OMB number.

Form EE-1
April 2005

GLOSSARY

Accrue—To occur or come into existence.

Action at Law—A judicial proceeding whereby one party prosecutes another for a wrong done.

Actionable—Giving rise to a cause of action.

Actionable Negligence—The breach or nonperformance of a legal duty through neglect or carelessness, resulting in damage or injury to another.

Activities of Daily Living—Impairments are generally defined as conditions which interfere with a person's "activities of daily living," including: (1) self-care and personal hygiene; (2) communication; (3) physical activity; (4) sensory function; (5) hand functions; (6) travel; (7) sexual function; (8) sleep; (9) social and recreational activities.

Actual Damages—Actual damages are those damages directly referable to the breach or tortious act, and which can be readily proven to have been sustained, and for which the injured party should be compensated as a matter of right.

ADA—The Americans With Disabilities Act (42 USC 12101 et seq.).

Ad Damnum Clause—The clause in a complaint that sets forth the amount of damages demanded.

Adjudication—The determination of a controversy and pronouncement of judgment.

Admissible Evidence—Evidence that may be received by a trial court to assist the trier of fact, either the judge or jury, in deciding a dispute.

Adversary—Opponent or litigant in a legal controversy or litigation.

Affirmative Defense—In a pleading, a matter constituting a defense.

Agency—The relationship between a principal and an agent who is employed by the principal, to perform certain acts dealing with third parties.

Agent—One who represents another known as the principal.

Aggravation—A worsening of a preexisting medical condition caused by a work-related injury or illness.

Air Quality Criteria—The levels of pollution and lengths of exposure above which adverse health and welfare effects may occur.

Allegation—Statement of the issue that the contributing party is prepared to prove.

Ancillary Care—Care such as physical or occupational therapy provided by a medical service provider other than the attending physician.

Answer—In a civil proceeding, the principal pleading on the part of the defendant in response to the plaintiff's complaint.

Appeal Rights—The right of the parties to a decision to seek review at a higher level.

Appearance—To come into court, personally or through an attorney, after being summoned.

Argument—A discourse set forth for the purpose of establishing one's position in a controversy.

Assumption of Risk—The legal doctrine that a plaintiff may not recover for an injury to which he assents.

Attending Physician—A physician primarily responsible for the treatment of an injured worker.

Attorney In Fact—An attorney-in-fact is an agent or representative of another given authority to act in that person's name and place pursuant to a document called a "power of attorney."

Beneficiary—The spouse, child, or dependent of an injured worker entitled to receive payments under workers' compensation law.

Benefits—An award of compensation paid under a claim, such as lost wages, medical and rehabilitation expenses, etc.

Bona Fide Dispute—A disagreement between the worker and the insurer about the compensability of a claim, which may be resolved by a disputed claim settlement rather than a hearing.

Breach of Duty—In a general sense, any violation or omission of a legal or moral duty.

Bureau of Labor Statistics—A division of the U.S. Department of Labor that compiles statistics related to employment.

Causation—A factor that contributed to the occurrence of an injury or illness.

Cause of Action—The factual basis for bringing a lawsuit.

Circumstantial Evidence—Indirect evidence by which a principal fact may be inferred.

Claim—An application for workers' compensation benefits brought by an employee alleging that he or she suffered a work-related injury or illness. A claim may also be brought by a deceased employee's surviving dependents.

Claimant—A person who files a claim for occupational disease or injury benefits under workers' compensation law.

Claim Closure—The process of closing a claim when an injured worker is found to be medically stationary.

Claims Examiner—Insurer representative who processes a claim filed by an injured worker.

Clinical Evaluation—The assessment of the health status of an individual and implementation of a course of treatment undertaken by a health care provider.

Closing Evaluation—A medical examination to measure impairment, which occurs when the worker is medically stationary.

Combined Condition—A preexisting condition that, combined with a compensable condition, causes disability or prolongs treatment.

Compensable Injury—An accidental injury arising out of and in the course of employment that requires medical services or results in disability or death.

Compensation—Refers to the benefits payable to claimants under a workers' compensation claim, such as lost wages, medical expenses, etc.

Compensatory Damages—Compensatory damages are those damages directly referable to a breach or tortious act, and which can be readily proven to have been sustained, and for which the injured party should be compensated as a matter of right.

Complaint—In a civil proceeding, the first pleading of the plaintiff setting out the facts on which the claim for relief is based.

Compromise and Settlement—An arrangement arrived at, either in court or out of court, for settling a dispute upon what appears to the parties to be equitable terms.

Conclusion of Fact—A conclusion reached by natural inference and based solely on the facts presented.

Conclusion of Law—A conclusion reached through the application of rules of law.

Conclusive Evidence—Evidence that is incontrovertible.

Consequential Condition—A condition arising after a compensable injury of which the major contributing cause is the injury or treatment rendered that increases either disability or need for treatment.

Contingency Fee—The fee charged by an attorney, which is dependent upon a successful outcome in the case, and is often agreed to be a percentage of the party's recovery.

Contributory Negligence—The act or omission amounting to want of ordinary care on the part of the complaining party which, concurring with the defendant's negligence, is the proximate cause of his or her injury.

Costs—A sum payable by the losing party to the successful party for his or her expenses in prosecuting or defending a case.

Counterclaims—Counterdemands made by a respondent in his or her favor against a claimant. They are not mere answers or denials of the claimant's allegation.

Cross-claim—Claim litigated by co-defendants or co-plaintiffs, against each other, and not against a party on the opposing side of the litigation.

Court—The branch of government responsible for the resolution of disputes arising under the laws of the government.

Cross-Examination—The questioning of a witness by someone other than the one who called the witness to the stand concerning matters about which the witness testified during direct examination.

Damages—In general, damages refers to monetary compensation which the law awards to one who has been injured by the actions of another, such as in the case of tortious conduct or breach of contractual obligations.

Death Benefit—The amount of money paid to the surviving spouse of a deceased Social Security beneficiary under certain circumstances.

Death Claim—A claim brought by a deceased employee's surviving dependents due to a work-related injury or illness resulting in the employee's death.

Decedent—A deceased person.

Decontamination—Removal of harmful substances such as noxious chemicals, harmful bacteria or other organisms, or radioactive material from exposed individuals, rooms and furnishings in buildings, or the exterior environment.

De Facto Denial—Failure of an insurer to accept or deny within the statutory time frame.

Degree—A unit of measure for permanent partial disability benefits that is used to convert disability percentages to dollar amounts

Dependent—Those individuals who, because of their financial dependency on the employee, are statutorily entitled to compensation on a death claim, such as surviving spouses and dependent children, etc.

Defendant—In a civil proceeding, the party responding to the complaint.

Defense—Opposition to the truth or validity of the plaintiff's claims.

Denied Claim—Written refusal by an insurer to accept compensability or responsibility for a worker's claim of injury.

De Novo Review—A second review of all the evidence.

Deposition—A method of pretrial discovery that consists of a statement of a witness under oath, taken in question and answer form as it would be in court, with opportunity given to the adversary to be present and cross-examine.

Disability—A medical impairment or disability that results in an individual's inability to carry on their usual activities, requires medical treatment, or adversely affects the individual's ability to earn a living.

Disability Payment—Payment for disability resulting from an accident or disease from which a worker is not expected to recover.

Disabling Compensable Injury—An on-the-job injury that entitles the worker to temporary or permanent, partial or total disability compensation or death benefits.

Discovery—Modern pretrial procedure by which one party gains information held by another party.

Disfigurement—An undesirable alteration of a body part usually due to an injury.

Disputed Claim Settlement—Settlement of a claim when there is disagreement about compensability.

Duty—The obligation, to which the law will give recognition and effect, to conform to a particular standard of conduct toward another.

Employability—The ability of an employee to meet the demands of a job and the conditions of employment.

Expert Witness—A witness who has special knowledge about a certain subject, upon which he or she will testify, which knowledge is not normally possessed by the average person.

Eyewitness—A person who can testify about a matter because of his or her own presence at the time of the event.

Fact Finder—In a judicial or administrative proceeding, the person, or group of persons, that has the responsibility of determining the acts relevant to decide a controversy.

Fatality Claim—Claim for benefits made by beneficiaries of a worker whose death resulted from accidental injury or occupational disease.

Federal employer Identification Number (FEIN)—The number assigned to a business by the Internal Revenue Service. This number is the primary identifier for employers in electronic data interchange (EDI) reporting.

Fee schedule—Maximum charges established for medical services under a workers' compensation program.

Finding—Decisions made by the court on issues of fact or law.

FMLA—The Family and Medical Leave Act of 1993, Public Law 103-3 (February 5, 1993), 107 Stat. 6 (29 U.S.C. 2601 et seq.).

Foreseeability—A concept used to limit the liability of a party for the consequences of his acts to consequences that are within the scope of a foreseeable risk.

Frequency Rate—Number of disabling injuries per 1,000,000 hours of work.

General Damages—General damages are those damages directly referable to the breach or tortious act and which can be readily proven to have been sustained, and for which the injured party should be compensated as a matter of right.

HIPAA—A federal law that ensures the privacy and security of protected health information and patients' access to their health-care records.

Immunity—As it relates to workers' compensation law, refers to the protection afforded an employer who is in compliance with workers' compensation statutes from common-law tort actions by employees arising out of the work-related injuries or illness.

Impairment—The loss, or loss of use of, any body part, system, or function.

Impairment Findings—A measurement, by a physician, of loss of use or function of a body part or system.

Independent Contractor—An individual who contracts to perform services for others without qualifying legally as an employee.

Indoor Air Pollution—Chemical, physical, or biological contaminants in indoor air.

Injury—Physical or mental harm or disability arising out of a work-related accident.

Insured employer—An employer who has a workers' compensation insurance policy in place to cover employees.

Insurer—An insurance company, self-insured employer, or self-insured employer group that provides workers' compensation coverage to employers and benefits to injured workers.

Insurer Medical Examination (IME)—A medical examination of an injured worker by a physician other than the worker's attending physician at the request of the insurer.

Interim Compensation—Payment of time-loss benefits during the period between filing a claim and acceptance or denial.

Jones Act—The federal statute permitting a seaman, or a representative, the right to sue for personal injuries suffered in the course of the seaman's employment.

Judgment—A judgment is a final determination by a court of law concerning the rights of the parties to a lawsuit.

Jurisdiction—The power to hear and determine a case.

Jury—A group of individuals summoned to decide the facts in issue in a lawsuit.

Jury Trial—A trial during which the evidence is presented to a jury so that they can determine the issues of fact, and render a verdict based upon the law as it applies to their findings of fact.

Loss of Earning Capacity—The impairment of ability to earn a living attributable to a work-related injury or illness.

Lump Sum—Payment of all or any part of permanent partial disability award in one payment.

Major Contributing Cause (MCC)—A cause deemed to have contributed at least 51 percent to an injured worker's disability or need for treatment.

Managed Care Organization (MCO)—An organization that may contract with an insurer to provide medical services to injured workers.

Maximum Medical Improvement—The point at which an employee has reached maximum recovery after every method of treatment has been employed and a reasonable period of time has elapsed.

Mediation—The act of a third person in intermediating between two contending parties with a view to persuading them to adjust or settle their dispute but without the authority to make a binding decision.

Medical Arbiter—A physician selected by the director to perform an impartial examination for impairment findings.

Medical Only—A workers' compensation claim for an injury or illness that doesn't involve time loss or permanent disability but that requires medical treatment.

Medical Provider—A hospital, medical clinic, or other vendor of medical services.

Medical Service Provider—A person duly licensed to practice one or more of the healing arts.

Medically Stationary—The point at which the attending physician states no further significant improvement can reasonably be expected from medical treatment or the passage of time

Negligence—The failure to exercise the degree of care that a reasonable person would exercise given the same circumstances.

Negligence Per Se—Conduct, whether of action or omission, which may be declared and treated as negligence without any argument or proof as to the particular surrounding circumstances, because it is contrary to the law.

Noncomplying Employer—An employer who fails to provide workers' compensation coverage for its employees.

Non-disabling Claim—A workers' compensation claim for an injury or illness that doesn't involve time loss or permanent disability but that requires medical treatment.

Non-disabling Injury—Any injury that requires medical services only and does not result in an inability to work or permanent disability.

Notice of Closure—A document sent by the insurer to the injured worker that closes the claim, ends time-loss benefits, and states the extent of disability.

Notice of Compliance—A notice from DCBS required to be posted in an employer's place of business notifying employees that the employer has workers' compensation insurance coverage.

Objection—The process by which it is asserted that a particular question, or piece of evidence, is improper, and it is requested that the court rule upon the objectionable matter.

Objective Findings—Indications of an injury or disease that are measurable, observable, or reproducible; used to establish compensability and determine permanent impairment.

Occupational Disease—A disease or infection arising out of and occurring in the course and scope of employment, that is caused by substances or activities to which an employee is not ordinarily subjected or exposed other than during employment, and requires medical services or results in disability or death.

Occupational Safety and Health Administration (OSHA)—The federal agency that oversees workplace safety and health in federal offices and in states without state OSHA programs.

Opinion and Order—A formal decision issued by an administrative law judge at the Workers' Compensation Board to resolve a dispute.

Pain and Suffering—Refers to damages recoverable against a wrongdoer which include physical or mental suffering.

Palliative Care—Medical services rendered to reduce or temporarily moderate the intensity of an otherwise stable condition to enable the worker to continue employment or training.

Parens Patriae—Latin for "parent of his country." Refers to the role of the state as guardian of legally disabled individuals.

Parties—The disputants.

Penalties—Monetary sanctions that can be assessed against employers, insurers, or medical providers for violations of workers' compensation laws or rules; workers may be penalized by means of suspended benefits.

Permanent Impairment—The loss of use or function of a body part due to a compensable injury.

Permanent Partial Disability—A medical impairment, usually statutorily defined as a scheduled loss award that, although it is of indefinite duration, does not prevent the employee from returning to gainful employment.

Permanent Total Disability—A medical impairment that is unlikely to change in spite of further medical or surgical therapy, and which renders the employee unable to return to gainful employment.

Physical Capacity Evaluation—Measurement of a worker's ability to perform a variety of physical tasks.

Plaintiff—In a civil proceeding, the one who initially brings the lawsuit.

Pleadings—Refers to plaintiff's complaint that sets forth the facts of the cause of action, and defendant's answer that sets forth the responses and defenses to the allegations contained in the complaint.

Power of Attorney—A legal document authorizing another to act on one's behalf.

Preexisting Condition—A condition that existed before the compensable injury or disease.

Premium—The amount an employer pays an insurance company for a workers' compensation policy.

Pro Se—A party that participates in a formal or informal dispute process without an attorney.

Prima Facie Case—A case which is sufficient on its face, being supported by at least the requisite minimum of evidence, and being free from palpable defects.

Proximate Cause—That which, in a natural and continuous sequence, unbroken by any efficient intervening cause, produces injury, and without which the result would not have occurred.

Punitive Damages—Compensation in excess of compensatory damages that serves as a form of punishment to the wrongdoer who has exhibited malicious and willful misconduct.

Question of Fact—The fact in dispute that is the province of the trier of fact, i.e. the judge or jury, to decide.

Question of Law—The question of law that is the province of the judge to decide.

Reciprocity agreement—An agreement between states regarding jurisdiction in workers' compensation claims.

Release—A document signed by one party, releasing claims he or she may have against another party, usually as part of a settlement agreement.

Relief—The remedies afforded a complainant by the court.

Res Ipsa Loquitur—Literally, "the thing speaks for itself." Refers to an evidentiary rule which provides that negligence may be inferred from the fact that an accident occurred when such an occurrence would not ordinarily have happened in the absence of negligence, the cause of the occurrence was within the exclusive control of the defendant, and the plaintiff was in no way at fault.

Retainer Agreement—A contract between an attorney and the client stating the nature of the services to be rendered and the cost of the litigation.

Sanctions—Monetary sanctions that can be assessed against employers, insurers, or medical providers for violations of workers' compensation laws or rules; workers may be penalized by means of suspended benefits.

Scheduled Disability—The permanent complete or partial loss of use or function of an arm, hand, leg, foot, or other extremity of the body, or the loss of visual or hearing ability.

Scheduled Loss Award—Compensation for the loss of, or loss of use of, certain body parts or functions, as defined by a statutory schedule, e.g., loss of vision, loss of a finger, etc.

Scope of Employment—Those activities performed while carrying out the business of one's employer.

Self-Insured Employer—An employer that has been authorized by the appropriate agency to administer and pay directly on employee compensation claims.

Service of Process—The delivery of legal court documents, such as a complaint, to the defendant.

Settlement—An agreement by the parties to a dispute on a resolution of the claims, usually requiring some mutual action, such as payment of money in consideration of a release of claims.

State—Any State of the United States or the District of Columbia or any Territory or possession of the United States.

State Insurance Fund—An insurance fund administered by the state instead of, or in addition to, private insurance.

Stipulation—A negotiated agreement between parties to a claim.

Summons—A mandate requiring the appearance of the defendant in an action under penalty of having judgment entered against him for failure to do so.

Supplemental Disability Payment—Wage-replacement benefits to workers who held more than one job at the time of injury.

Supplemental Security Income (SSI)—The government program awarding cash benefits to the needy, aged, blind or otherwise qualifying disabled.

Survival Statute—A statute that preserves for a decedent's estate a cause of action for infliction of pain and suffering and related damages suffered up to the moment of death.

Suspension of benefits—An interruption of payment of benefits to an injured worker.

Temporary Partial Disability—A medical impairment that is expected to be of limited duration and which does not prevent the employee from returning to gainful employment.

Temporary Partial Disability Benefits—Payment for wages lost based on a worker's ability to perform temporary modified or part-time work due to a compensable injury.

Temporary Total Disability—A medical impairment that is expected to be of limited duration, but which prevents the employee from returning to gainful employment.

Temporary Total Disability Benefits—Payment for wages lost based on a worker's temporary inability to work due to a compensable injury

Testimony—The sworn statement make by a witness in a judicial proceeding.

Third-party administrator—A company contracted by self-insured employer or insurer to administer its workers' compensation claims.

Time-loss payments—Compensation paid to an injured worker who loses time or wages as a result of compensable injury.

Tort—A private or civil wrong or injury, other than breach of contract, for which the court will provide a remedy in the form of an action for damages.

Tortfeasor—A wrongdoer.

Tortious Conduct—Wrongful conduct, whether of act or omission, of such a character as to subject the actor to liability under the law of torts.

Trial—The judicial procedure whereby disputes are determined based on the presentation of issues of law and fact. The trier of fact, either the judge or jury, decides issues of fact and the judge decides issues of law.

Trial Court—The court of original jurisdiction over a particular matter.

Unscheduled Disability—The permanent loss of earning capacity as a result of physical limitations; modified by factors of age, education, and ability to return to work at injury.

Venue—The proper place for trial of a lawsuit.

Verdict—The definitive answer given by the jury to the court concerning the matters of fact committed to the jury for their deliberation and determination.

Verification—The confirmation of the authenticity of a document, such as an affidavit.

Vicarious Liability—In tort law, refers to the liability assessed against one party due to the actions of another party.

Vocational Assistance—Services, goods, and allowances used to help injured workers return to work as soon as possible and as nearly as possible to a condition of self-support and maintenance.

Waiting Period—Statutory period of time, e.g., three days, from the date of work-related injury or illness, during which the employee is ineligible for workers' compensation payments, unless disability continues for a specified duration, e.g., two weeks.

Waiver—An intentional and voluntary surrender of a right.

Whistleblower—An employee who reports on violations of the law that occur in the workplace.

Worker—Any person who receives payment for work or services under the direction and control of an employer.

Workers' Compensation—Refers to the benefits payable to claimants under a workers' compensation claim, such as lost wages, medical expenses, etc.

Work-related Injury or Illness—An injury or illness that is causally related to one's employment.

Wrongful Death Statute—A statute that creates a cause of action for any wrongful act, neglect, or default that causes death.

Zone of Employment—The physical area in which injuries to an employee are covered by worker compensation laws.

BIBLIOGRAPHY AND ADDITIONAL READING

Black's Law Dictionary, Fifth Edition. St. Paul, MN: West Publishing Company, 1979.

Insurance Information Institute (Date Visited: October 2007) http://www.iii.org/.

The National Institute for Occupational Safety and Health (Date Visited: October 2007) http://www.cdc.gov/niosh/.

The United States Department of Labor (Date Visited: October 2007) http://www.dol.gov/.

The United States Department of Labor, Bureau of Labor Statistics (Date Visited: October 2007) http://www.bls.gov/.

The United States Department of Labor, Occupational Safety & Health Administration (Date Visited: October 2007) http://www.osha.gov/.

The United States Department of Labor, Office of Workers Compensation (Date Visited: October 2007) http://owcp.gov/.

The United States Equal Employment Opportunity Commission (Date Visited: October 2007) http://www.eeoc.gov/.

The United States Department of Veterans Affairs (Date Visited: October 2007) http://www.va.gov/.